European Marketing

European Marketing

A Strategic Guide to the New Opportunities

Richard Lynch

IRWIN
Professional Publishing
Burr Ridge, Illinois
New York, New York

Editor:	Carol Rogala
Project editor:	Lynne Basler
Assistant production manager:	Jon Christopher
Cover designer:	Tim Kaage
Art manager:	Kim Meriwether
Compositor:	Eastern Composition, Inc.
Typeface:	10/12 Times Roman
Printer:	Arcata Graphics/Kingsport

Library of Congress Cataloging-in-Publication Data

Lynch, Richard L.
    European marketing : a strategic guide to the new opportunities /
Richard Lynch.—North American ed.
      p.   cm.
    Includes bibliographical references and index.
    ISBN 1-55623-757-X
    1. Export marketing—Handbooks, manuals, etc. 2. Europe—
Commerce—Handbooks, manuals, etc. 3. Imports—Europe—Handbooks,
manuals, etc. 4. Europe, 1992—Handbooks, manuals, etc. I. Title.
HF1416.L96   1994
658.8'48—dc20   93–25794

Printed in the United States of America
1 2 3 4 5 6 7 8 9 0 AGK 0 9 8 7 6 5 4 3

For Joseph, Marianne, and Stephen;
for Magnus, Christian, and Jeremy;
for Owen and Aileen
and the whole generation of new Europeans

Acknowledgments

In Autumn 1990, Professors Martin Christopher and Malcolm McDonald of the Cranfield School of Management asked me to contribute to their staff seminar on marketing in Europe. This book is one outcome of that event. While Cranfield has had no involvement in the pages that follow, I appreciated the invitation and lively discussion that started the process. In addition, I am grateful to Professor Christopher for permission subsequently to adapt a chart from *Effective Marketing Management* (see Reference 6 in Chapter 4).

Beyond this, the book would simply not have been possible without the extensive use of data and material from the European Community and, specifically, the European Commision. I record my thanks.

Equally, I would like to thank the Organization for Economic Cooperation and Development for permission to quote from 1991 and 1992 editions of *Economic Outlook*, the World Bank for data from *World Development Report 1991*, and the United Nations for useful international trade statistics.

My thanks are also due to the following: Bill Ramsey of Templeton College, Oxford, both for quotations from his ESOMAR (European Society for Opinion and Marketing Research) paper and for drawing my attention to several other research papers; Professor M J Thomas of Strathclyde University, for material from his 1991 Marketing Education Group (MEG) paper on Poland; Dr C Millar of Thames Polytechnic for quotes from her MEG paper on East Germany; McKinsey and Company, Inc for material from the *McKinsey Quarterly*; Epson (UK) Ltd for data from its 1990 EC survey; the National Westminster Bank plc for material on the Common Agricultural Policy; Goran Grabacic of Inex Interexport, Belgrade, for reworking my pricing calculations; Dr C Haslam of the University of East London for prompting me to look at various research sources; Christopher Jackson, MEP for East Kent, for clarifying matters on the EC and European Union; Jo O'Driscoll of Kogan Page, London, for reorganizing my references.

This book ultimately benefits from the responses of managers and students to the concepts and material. Hence, my thanks are due to the following: Dragan Nestorovich and managers of Inex Interexport, Belgrade; Dr K Newman and MBA students at Middlesex University Business School; staff and students at the Mediterranean Institute of Management, Cyprus; and final year BABS students at the University of East London.

Finally, my thanks are due to my parents, and to my brother and sister, Mike and Gerry Lynch and Anne Dobbing, for their help and encouragement.

PREFACE TO THE NORTH AMERICAN EDITION

Europe has continued to evolve rapidly since the book was first published in Europe in summer 1992. I have updated the text where appropriate. More important, I have recast the material to examine the area from a North American perspective.

Richard Lynch

Contents

CHAPTER 1   INTRODUCTION   1

Definition of Europe, 2

European Marketing: How The Book Is Structured, 5

Developing the Organization's European Mission and Objectives, 7

European Involvement in North American and Global Markets, 9

Implications of Redrawing the Map of Europe, 9

Notes, 10

CHAPTER 2   EUROPEAN MARKETS AND CULTURES   12

Europe in Global Markets, 12

North American Involvement in Europe, 16

EC Common Agricultural Policy and the GATT, 19

European Monetary Union, 23

Western European Markets, 27

Eastern European Markets, 31

Western European Markets: Wealth and Consumption, 32

Sociocultural Issues: Education, Religion, and Law, 34

   Education, 34

   Religion, 37

   Legal Issues, 38

Technical and Environmental Issues, 40

   European Technical Development Projects, 40

   Telecommunications Potential, 42

   European Environmental and Ecological Concerns, 42

Conclusion, 43

Notes, 43

CHAPTER 3   THE EUROPEAN BUSINESS AND POLITICAL BACKGROUND   46

Origins and Decision-Making Processes of the EC, 47

The Single Europe Act and Its Supposed Marketing Potential, 54

The European Economic Area Treaty and Its Impact on EC and EFTA Markets, 58

The EC's Moves to Integration and Their Marketing Implications, 59

Economic and Fiscal Activities, 60

Political and Defense Decision Making, 60

Marketing Implications, 62

Influencing the EC's Political and Business Decision-Making Process, 63

Eastern European Issues, 64

Notes, 69

CHAPTER 4   EUROPEAN CUSTOMERS AND MARKET DEFINITION   71

A Crucial Strategic Question: What Geographical Market Are Our Customers in? 71

Exploring European Customers, 74

Differences from Other Customers around the World, 76

Substantial Differences across Europe Itself, 76

Factors Drawing Europe Together, 77

Pan-European Marketing Segmentation, 80

European Industrial Markets, 80

European Consumer Markets, 81

Eastern European Customer Issues, 84

Conclusions, 87

Notes, 88

CHAPTER 5   EUROPEAN MARKETING RESEARCH   91

European Marketing Research: Some Key Issues, 92

EC Current Research Activity, 94

Special Issues in European Marketing Research, 96

European Data Comparisons, 97

Consumer, Industrial, and Services Research, 98

Questionnaire Design and Responses, 99

Availability of Professional Researchers, 100

Data Sources for Europe, 100

Organization and Decision Making for European Marketing Research, 101

Marketing Research Cost-Effectiveness: Conclusions, 103

Notes, 103

CHAPTER 6   DEVELOPING THE OPTIONS FOR EUROPEAN
             MARKETING STRATEGY   105
             The European Marketing Strategy Development Process, 105
             Identification of European Critical Success Factors, 108
             Sustainable Competitive Advantage in Europe, 109
             Developing the Options, 113
               Strategy Questions, 113
               The Ansoff Matrix, 114
               The Four C's, 114
             Special Strategies for the EC and the European Economic Area, 119
               Exploiting the Single Europe, 119
               Defending the Home Market, 121
               *Seeking Lower Costs from Single European Market Economies of
               Scale*, 123
               *Tackling Overcapacity Arising from Removal of Barriers in the
               EC*, 124
             Special Strategies for Eastern Europe, 124
               Size and Phasing of the Opportunity, 125
               Government Company Privatization Opportunities, 125
               Structural Investment Needed, 126
               Risk and Reward Assessment, 126
             Notes, 127

CHAPTER 7   SELECTING THE BEST OPTION   129
             Selecting the Best Option: The Basic Steps, 129
               Preliminary Study, 130
               European SWOT Analysis, 130
               Scenario Building, 131
               Estimated Financial and Human Consequences and Risks, 131
             European Marketing Strategy Guidelines, 132
               *The PIMS Evidence on Quality, Market Share, Marketing
               Expenditure, and Capital Investment*, 132
               *The Distinction between Market Leaders and Market
               Followers*, 134
               The Concept of Product Life Cycle, 135
               *The Reduction of Barriers to Entry as The Single Market Becomes
               a Reality*, 135
               European Marketing Strategy Guidelines, 135

Options Selection in Global Markets, 137

Implications of Pan-European Markets for Marketing Strategy Selection, 140

Start with Markets, Not Industry Structures, 141

Seek Emerging Pan-European Segments, 141

Concentrate the Product Range, 142

Innovate, 142

Explore Strategy Evolution, 144

Marketing Strategies for Eastern Europe, 144

Planning for Uncertainty, 145

Careful Distinction between the States and within the States of Eastern Europe, 146

Levels of Exposure in Early Market Initiatives, 146

Infrastructure Problems, 148

Notes, 148

CHAPTER 8   EUROPEAN MARKET ENTRY AND COUNTRY
SELECTION   151

European Market Entry Strategy, 151

Basic Options for Entry, 151

Choice among Options, 154

European Country Selection, 156

Pan-European versus Country-by-Country Approach, 156

Concentrating Effort on Certain Countries or Spreading it across Most of Europe, 158

Country Choice, 158

Competitive Reaction to European Entry, 161

Conclusions and Action, 163

Notes, 165

CHAPTER 9   EUROPEAN PRODUCT DECISIONS   167

EC Basics: The Trading and Legal Framework for the Single Europe, 168

Overcoming Barriers to Trade, 169

Compliance with EC Standards and Legislation, 170

Increased Standardization for Multinational Companies, 172

EC Progress on Standardization, 173

European Brand Name, Trademark, and Patent Protection, 173

Defining the European Product Benefit, 174

Developing Benefits for Existing Product to Beat European Competitors, 176

Customization versus Standardization, 177

Positioning Products in Europe, 178

European Branding Opportunities, 179

Private-Label and Original Equipment Manufacture Opportunities in Europe, 182

Service Development across Europe, 183

European Service Quality, 185

New Product Development in The Single Europe, 186

New Product Development Process in a European Context, 186

EC Funding of Research and Development Initiatives, 187

Objectives and Organization of New-Product Opportunities, 188

Test-Marketing and Sales Estimating, 190

Product Marketing Decisions for Eastern Europe, 191

Acquisition and Joint Venture, 192

Investment to Improve Productivity, Infrastructure, and the Environment, 192

Long Time Scales, 194

Simple and Low-Key Product Launches, 194

Professional Services Activity, 194

Difficulty in Repatriating Earnings to the Home Country, 195

Notes, 195

CHAPTER 10   EUROPEAN PRICING DECISIONS   198

European Pricing: The Influence of the EC, 199

EC Pricing Policy, 199

EC Tax Policy, 201

EC Hidden Subsidies, 202

European Credit and Export Pricing Considerations, 203

European Pricing and Currency Issues, 205

Single Europe Pricing Decisions, 208

Basics: The Balance between Costs and Competition, 208

Pricing Strategies for Specific National Markets, 210

Transfer Pricing for Multinational Companies, 212

Eastern European Pricing Decisions, 213

Uncertainty because of Political Developments, 213

High Rates of Inflation, 214

Currency Stability and Convertibility, 214

Notes, 215

CHAPTER 11 EUROPEAN PROMOTION DECISIONS 217

European Promotions: Basic Regulations, 218

European Advertising Legislation and Regulation, 219

EC Media Regulation and Development, 220

EC Direct-Mail Regulation, 221

EC Sales Promotion Regulation, 221

Conclusions, 222

Current EC Advertising and Promotional Activity, 222

European Promotional Objectives and The Promotional Mix, 226

European Promotional Objectives, 226

European Sales Force Activity, 227

European Advertising, 229

European Sponsorship, 231

European Sales Promotions, 231

European Exhibitions and Seminars, 232

European Direct Marketing, 232

Western European Promotional Decision Making, 233

Overall Levels of European Promotional Expenditure, 233

Balance between European Promotional Activities, 234

Eastern European Promotional Decision Making, 235

Purchase of Existing Brands, 236

Few Promotional Controls, 237

Early European Opportunities, 237

Notes, 237

CHAPTER 12 EUROPEAN PLACE DECISIONS 240

EC Place Decisions: Basic Background Issues, 240

EC Cross-Border Restrictions, 242

EC Transport Regulations, 243

EC Retail and Planning Laws, 243

EC Contract Law, 244

EC Company and Tax Law Plus Investment Incentives, 244

EC Distribution Structures, 245

EC Distribution Infrastructure, 245

European Export Agents, Distributors, and Wholesalers, 246

European Retailing, 247

Pan-European Logistics and Distribution Companies, 248

EC Place Decisions: Channels and Logistics, 249

EC Channel Decisions, 249

EC Logistics Decisions, 250

EC Channel Management, 251

European Channels and Logistics: Conclusions, 252

Eastern European Place Decisions, 253

Old System: Highly Centralized, 253

New System: Fragmented and Duplicated, 253

Hungarian Experience, 253

Eastern European Distribution in the Future, 254

Notes, 254

**CHAPTER 13   EUROPEAN HUMAN RESOURCES AND
ORGANIZATION DECISIONS   257**

EC Basics: European Social Policy, 258

European Human Resources Development in Marketing, 259

European Marketing Organization, 261

Basic European Marketing Organizational Structure, 262

The Role of the European Product Manager, 262

Marketing and Selling Organizations in Europe, 263

Some Other Types of European Marketing Organization, 265

Conclusions on European Marketing Organization, 266

Notes, 268

CHAPTER 14   MARKETING PLANNING AND CONTROL FOR EUROPE 269

European Marketing Planning, 269

European Monitoring and Control Systems, 270

Motivation and European Planning, 271

Notes, 272

**CHAPTER 15   FUTURE EUROPEAN DEVELOPMENTS AND THEIR
POTENTIAL FOR NORTH AMERICAN COMPANIES   273**

Marketing Implications for the New Western Europe, 274

World Trade Wars, 274

Strains in the Exchange Rate Mechanism, 274

German Reunification, 274

Economic Growth in Western Europe, 275

Maastricht Treaty, 275

Marketing Scope for Eastern European Developments, 276

A "United States of Europe"? 277

Can a North American Marketing Mix Be Imported into the New Europe? 279

European Competition Against North American Rivals in Global Markets, 281

Innovation and Patents, 282

Company Size, 282

Labor Costs and Export Prices, 283

Global Market Sectors, 285

North American Company Success in European Marketing, 286

Europe's Challenging Future, 286

Consumer Issues, 286

Environmental Issues, 287

Political Uncertainty in Southern and Eastern Europe, 287

European Community Enlargement, 287

The Challenge of Europe, 287

Notes, 288

APPENDIX I   THE CONSTITUTION OF THE EUROPEAN COMMUNITY   290

APPENDIX II   THE ECU   291

APPENDIX III   SUMMARY OF RULES ON CROSS-BORDER MERGERS AND ACQUISITIONS   292

Background, 292

Objective of the Rules, 293

Structure of the New Regulations, 293

How the Regulations Operate, 293

Criteria for Assessment of Concentration, 294

The Future, 295

Notes, 295

| Figures

1–1   Europe: population by nation (1989) 3
1–2   European marketing: decision-making process 6
2–1   Share of world exports—1989 13
2–2   Major European exporters, 1989 (destination of exports) 15
2–3   Major European importers, 1989 (source of imports) 16
2–4   European balance of exports (% share of merchandise exports, 1989) 17
2–5   Exports from the United States and Canada 18
2–6   Imports into the United States and Canada 19
2–7   U.S. Direct investment in EC, by industry (stock to end of 1989) 20
2–8   U.S. Direct investment in EC, by country (stock to end of 1989) 21
2–9   Eastern Europe: a rough balance sheet—assets 32
2–10 Eastern Europe: a rough balance sheet—liabilities 33
2–11 European wealth (GDP per head of population, 1989) 34
3–1   Decision making in the European Community 54
3–2   Wealth predictions for Eastern Europe (wealth per person in U.S. dollars, 1989) 65
4–1   Where "European" customers fit 73
4–2   Europe's major industries (by source of sales in 1988) 75
4–3   Ranking of major EC sectors by output (1989) 79
4–4   Eastern European living standards: ownership (comparison per 1,000 people) 85
4–5   Eastern European living standards: health statistics (comparison per 1,000 people) 86
6–1   European marketing: decision-making process (enlarged section on strategy development) 107
6–2   European options: Ansoff matrix 115
7–1   European competitive strategy options 136
7–2   The European portfolio—annual volume growth of the triad's production 1987–1993 (%) 138
7–3   Portfolio adjustments by a U.S. food manufacturer 143
8–1   Evolution of European market entry 153

8–2 Country selection and evaluation for large companies 160
9–1 European product decisions 169
9–2 European product benefit definition 175
9–3 Product benefit options in Europe 177
9–4 Comprehensive route to European new-product development 188
10–1 Single Europe pricing decisions 199
10–2 Pricing strategy: basic issues 209
11–1 European promotional decisions 218
11–2 European advertising and promotions expenditures in (US$ billions) for 1989 223
11–3 EC advertising media (% share by medium) 225
12–1 European place decisions 241
13–1 Pan-European marketing organization in manufacturing 263
13–2 Pan-European sales organization in manufacturing 264
15–1 Global Company Size: number of companies in global top 500 283

| Tables

1–1 Rates of economic growth 4
2–1 The importance of international trade as percentage of GDP (1989) 14
2–2 EC prices as percentage of world prices (1979–1980) 22
2–3 Specialization indicators for EC industry in 1987 29
2–4 Country ranking of consumption of households per head by purpose (1988) 35
2–5 Percentage of age group enrolled in tertiary education in selected countries (1988) 36
3–1 Some key dates in EC history 48
3–2 General EC budget: 1989 51
3–3 The Cecchini Report and the cost of non-Europe 57
4–1 The 16 European socio-styles 82
4–2 Ranking of Europe's 20 most popular brands 84
5–1 Possible tasks of European marketing research 95
5–2 Sources of revenue for EC market research organizations in 1989 96
5–3 National versus European headquarters—level market research 102
6–1 Examples of critical success factors in European industry 109
8–1 Advantages and disadvantages of routes into Europe 155
9–1 European standardization versus customization 178
9–2 Selected acquisitions and joint ventures in Eastern Europe 1990–1991 193
10–1 The penalty of exporting 204
10–2 Profitability of some of Europe's top companies: 1987 207
11–1 Promotional expenditure, 1989 224
11–2 Advertising expenditure, 1989 224
11–3 European advertising by main media, 1989 225
11–4 European agency selection: national or pan-European? 229
11–5 Approximate EC promotional expenditure by industry, 1989 235
12–1 Concentration of European grocery buying, 1986 248
15–1 Similarities and differences between the United States and the EC 278
15–2 McDonald's Marketing Mix Survey 281
15–3 Patent applications, 1985–1988 (as percent of total worldwide) 282
15–4 Country Competitive Positions (1987 = 100) 284

1

Introduction

The beginning of the 1990s has seen some astonishing changes in the Western world: the reunification of Germany, freedom for the former Eastern European countries, and then revolution in the USSR. At the same time, the European Community (EC) has moved to complete the single market and to join with its rival trading body, the European Free Trade Association (EFTA), to form the European Economic Area, with a total population larger than the United States.

Depending on your viewpoint, the new Europe will represent either a challenging opportunity for North American companies or a competitive threat in global markets and possibly even in U.S. and Canadian home markets.

For North American marketers, new Eastern European markets are opening up, bringing a variety of opportunities and uncertainties. Western European markets are also likely to enlarge over time, renewing the economic growth seen in the 1970s and 1980s. But greater European wealth may also bring more effective European competition in both home and global markets.

European marketing thus raises some real challenges for North American companies. The objective of this book is both to describe the new horizons and to provide the structure for North American marketers to analyze and respond to the new situation. Its role is to act both as a structured sourcebook for those already engaged in marketing to Europe or assessing its potential, and as a textbook for students in this subject area. There cannot be a better time for both these groups to explore such significant new developments. The subjects covered in this chapter are:

- Definition of Europe.
- European marketing: how this book is structured.
- Development of an organization's European mission and objectives.

1

- European involvement in North American and global markets.
- Implications of redrawing the map of Europe.

DEFINITION OF EUROPE

The simplest way to define Europe is to say it is composed of all those countries between the Atlantic in the west and the Ural Mountains, running down the middle of the Russian republic, in the east. There are some 720 million people in this geographical area: if it were ever brought together into one customs union, only China and India would be larger.

There are some anomalies in this definition: Turkey is included as a European country, but some of the southern USSR republics are excluded. In addition, Cyprus and Malta are not included in these boundaries. But this only shows that all definitions have limited usefulness: they are relevant here so long as they provide a working basis for marketing analysis.

To make sense of this vast area from a North American marketing viewpoint, it is useful to split the area into three economic blocks based on their history. These are the EC, EFTA, and COMECON (Council for Mutual Economic Assistance), as shown in Figure 1–1. The republics that formerly made up the USSR were all grouped together at the time the map was drawn; they are now pursuing individual paths. For reasons of clarity, Turkey, Iceland, Malta, Cyprus, and Liechtenstein are not shown on the map.

Since World War II, the countries of Western Europe have grouped themselves into two trade blocks: the EC, with a population of 325 million in 1989, and EFTA, with 32 million people in 1989.[1] Rates of economic growth for these two areas are shown in Table 1–1: EFTA grew faster than the EC and the United States, but not as fast as Japan and Canada.

It is important to understand that growth in wealth across an economic area may well hide significant differences between countries. For example, in the EC, the highest growth, 3.0 percent per annum, occurred in Italy while the lowest growth, 1.8 percent per annum, occurred in Denmark and the Netherlands.[2]

Over the same time period from the end of World War II, the countries of Eastern Europe followed socialist or communist economic policies. Essentially, they were under the dominance of the USSR and traded

FIGURE 1–1
Europe: Population by Nation (1989)

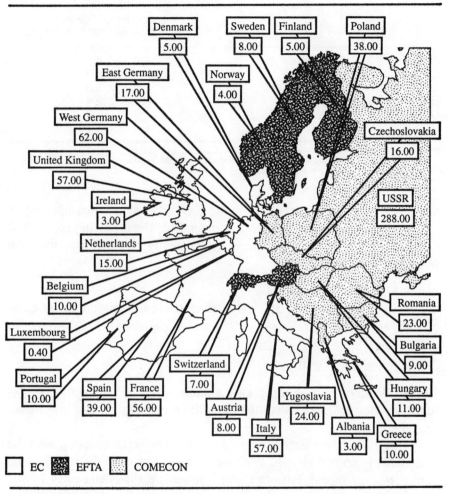

Denmark 5.00	Sweden 8.00	Finland 5.00	Poland 38.00
East Germany 17.00	Norway 4.00
West Germany 62.00	Czechoslovakia 16.00
United Kingdom 57.00	USSR 288.00
Ireland 3.00
Netherlands 15.00
Belgium 10.00	Romania 23.00
Luxembourg 0.40	Bulgaria 9.00
Portugal 10.00	Spain 39.00	France 56.00	Switzerland 7.00	Yugoslavia 24.00	Hungary 11.00
	Austria 8.00	Italy 57.00	Albania 3.00	Greece 10.00

☐ EC   ▓ EFTA   ▒ COMECON

in the COMECON block. None of these countries contributed any data to global statistics on the creation of wealth, as indicated in Table 1–1. Although various vague reasons have been given by their governments for this, the truth is beginning to emerge in the 1990s. Their growth rates were probably much lower than those in the West. The result is that wealth per head in the East is now far below that in the West.[3]

Essentially, Western European economic progress over the last 50

TABLE 1–1
Rates of Economic Growth

	Average Annual Growth in GDP per Head, 1965–1989 (%)
Japan	4.9
Canada	4.0
EFTA	3.2
European Community	2.4
United States	1.6
Eastern Europe	Not available

Source: Aldersgate Consultancy derived from World Bank, *World Development Report 1991*, Table 1, (New York: Oxford University Press, NY, 1991), pp. 204–5.

years has been much faster than in the East. This means that not only is the West more wealthy, but also that in terms of the following concepts it differs greatly from Eastern Europe, only recently liberated from the yoke of one-party dictatorship:[4]

- Ownership of wealth.
- Repatriation of profits from businesses to the foreign parent company.
- Legal status of companies.
- Economic stability.

Hence, Western Europe represents a more developed marketing opportunity for North American companies, with more stability and lower risk, than the East.

Neverthless, the East is moving toward the Western model, with the occasional lurch and hiccup. With the popular demise of the socialist and communist regimes in Eastern Europe in the late 1980s and early 1990s, COMECON no longer exists. EFTA is also changing radically: it has already agreed to formal economic links with the EC, and three of its members—Finland, Sweden, and Austria—have applied for membership in the EC while others are considering application. The EC itself is probably moving toward ever-closer union politically and economically. We will look at the marketing implications of all of this in Chapters 2 and 3. At the same time, many of the countries of Eastern Europe are seeking associations with the new community.

In the late 1980s, our look at European marketing would have concentrated primarily on the EC, with some additional reference to EFTA and a couple of chapters on the special case of Eastern Europe. Now this no longer makes sense. We need to look at the whole of Europe, from the Atlantic to the Urals, with all its opportunities and risks.

EUROPEAN MARKETING: HOW THE BOOK IS STRUCTURED

I assume that the main objective for North American companies exploring material of this kind is to end up with a marketing plan for some aspect of European development. Thus, the flow process for developing a European marketing plan shown in Fig 1–2 has been used to structure the book. It sets each aspect in context and provides overall direction for the development of the text.

With so many recent developments unique to Europe—for example, the EC's Single Europe Act of 1986 and the recent political freedom of Poland and Hungary—opportunity has been taken to insert into this flow process some areas of specific relevance to Europe and to North American marketers. In addition, although this is unusual for marketing books, specific coverage is given to political events because so much will stand or fall on what these events bring.[5,6]

Each chapter covers an area of the flow diagram in Figure 1–2. The flow itself is partly conventional and will be recognized by most of those involved in international marketing.[7] However, I have borrowed some concepts from modern business strategy and have fleshed out European marketing strategy development as a result. This book offers a more structured approach to marketing strategy than is often the case. It is based on the "four C's": Customers, Competition, Company, and Channels. These issues, plus the subject of European market entry, are covered in Chapters 6 to 8 . After this area has been developed, the usual areas of the four P's—Product, Price, Promotion, and Place—are considered along with the people issues that are vital in international marketing. Chapters 9 to 14 cover these areas.

Naturally, the book is packed with examples of North American activity in Europe. Perhaps not surprisingly, examples are easier to obtain and develop for Western Europe than for the East. Because marketing needs such material to bring its lessons alive, I have not hesitated to draw on a variety of sources to present the process.

FIGURE 1–2
European Marketing: Decision-making Process

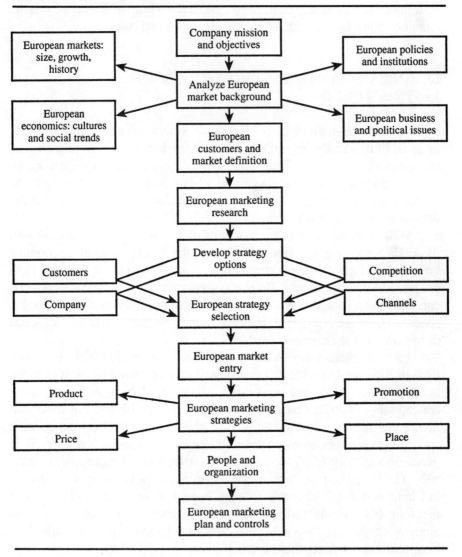

DEVELOPING THE ORGANIZATION'S EUROPEAN MISSION AND OBJECTIVES

In a major study of North American company involvement in European markets,[8] the EC estimated that the United States alone had some $150 billion invested in EC countries by the end of 1989. This is the largest direct investment by the United States in any foreign trade area, roughly three times larger than Japanese investment in the EC. More detail is given in Chapter 2.

For reasons of history and geography, Canada is primarily linked in investment terms with its major trading partner, the United States. Yet for individual Canadian companies, such as Thomson Corporation (publishing and tourism) and Northern Telecom (telecommunications equipment), the EC has also represented an important source of investment and trade over the last 20 years.

More recently, North American companies have been investing in Eastern Europe. We shall examine this in Chapter 9.

The basic reason for all this investment is that North American companies have identified real profit opportunities in Europe. But any business development needs to be set in the context of a company's long-term objectives. The starting point for the successful development of European markets by North American companies must therefore be to set such activity against the organization's mission and objectives and to be informed of relevant EC trends.

In a survey of 352 executives published in August 1990,[9] one in five businesspeople in the United Kingdom (UK) could not name the capital of West Germany, only two-fifths knew what CAP (Common Agriculture Policy) stands for, and fewer than half knew who Jacques Delors (the EC Commission's president) is. In spite of this, 44 percent believed they were equipped to meet the European challenge. This ignorance suggests that many European businesses have not fully considered the implications of a single Europe for their organizations, either in terms of the costs or in terms of the impact on organizational objectives.

A similar lack of knowledge may well apply to some North American companies. In researching this book, I telephoned the commercial affairs sections of the U.S. embassies in London and Brussels and was astonished to discover that all inquiries are treated on an individual European country basis. There was little U.S. government information on the EC as such: there was no EC-wide publication available for U.S. companies, nor was there any data on pan-European EC contracts. There was only material available on individual countries.

For many North American companies, the move into Europe will involve a heavier financial burden compared with working in the home market. For example, these companies will incur extra freight costs to Europe, higher transnational insurance costs, and currency exchange costs. Such increased charges need to be assessed against the organization's objectives and the new European opportunities. Some North American companies, such as IBM and Ford Motor Company, have already organized themselves to take advantage of the EC's economies of scale as well as its high sales potential. We will explore these areas later in the book.

For the present, we need to realize that it is essential for any organization examining the potential of Europe to consider the extra resources required to achieve organizational objectives. Two areas are fundamental to this process:

1. What will Europe deliver to the organization and at what cost?
2. How will this affect the organization's objectives? Are the required resources consistent with the organization's long-term objectives?

Top management commitment is also necessary for successful European entry. Most senior North American company executives draw up their corporate objectives from a consideration of their owners, their employees, and their social responsibilities. What concerns us here is that, for a variety of reasons, such companies will now be considering the decision to add Europe to their overall objectives. Europe will principally affect a company in two ways:

- A new market with new opportunities and threats.
- A new range of laws and regulations.

European marketing objectives will revolve mainly around exploiting these new areas while protecting the company from new competition.[10] Within this, there may be a hierarchy of European marketing objectives concerning, for example, more detailed product or promotional activity. We will tackle these areas as we reach them in the book.

EUROPEAN INVOLVEMENT IN NORTH AMERICAN AND GLOBAL MARKETS

As I have pointed out elsewhere,[11] the single Europe has not necessarily been the focus of company growth strategies for North American and European companies. Nor should it necessarily be.

For the large global company Philip Morris (U.S.), the acquisition in 1990 of the Jacobs Suchard company (Switzerland), with its extensive EC coffee and confectionery brands, for $2.2 billion was part of a global strategy in coffee products. When Unilever (UK and Netherlands) bought Calvin Klein, Fabergé, and other cosmetics and fragrance companies for over $1.5 billion in 1990, this had nothing to do with Europe as such; it was part of a global strategy. We will return to this issue in Chapter 4.

Because the United States and Canada are large and stable markets, it is quite possible that European companies will seek to establish themselves in these countries. For example, Thomson (France) extended its European consumer electronics interests into the United States by acquiring General Electric's RCA and GE consumer electronics businesses in 1988, and Grand Metropolitan (UK) bought Pillsbury in 1989.

The economies of scale provided by the single European market may provide the opportunity for European companies either to acquire U.S. and Canadian companies or to export goods at competitive prices to North America. In theory, European companies should become more competitive in the United States and Canada. In practice, we shall see in Chapters 3 and 9 that the single European market still has some way to go. Moreover, many North American companies are more than capable of competing in their home markets, so a possible future European threat in the United States and Canada will not be a major focus of this book.[12]

IMPLICATIONS OF REDRAWING THE MAP OF EUROPE

Any respectable marketing book must tackle the issues of market size, growth, and competition. But with so much happening in the early 1990s, the whole area is something of a moving target. Specifically, it remains unclear just what are the likely implications of some developments of this period:

- Will there ever be a "United States of Europe" that can match the cohesive power of the United States of America?
- Will Poland, Hungary, and the Czech and Slovak republics gain special access to EC markets to assist their economies? If so, under what terms?
- How will the former Yugoslavia develop? Will we ever have a lasting peace? And in what circumstances? (The first chapter of this book was written in Montenegro in Yugoslavia, with the civil war raging only 40 miles away before the UN sanctions began.)
- How will the economies of Eastern Europe cope with democracy? Will there be evolution to a market-based system, or will the population tire of the sacrifices required and seek to put the clock back?
- Will the EC's Exchange Rate Mechanism survive the attacks by the world's money market speculators?

While the crucial outline of the Maastricht Treaty, which will bring ever-closer European political and monetary union, has been agreed to, it still remains to be ratified by all EC countries, and their economies need to converge. Without this, the process of ever-closer union will grind to a halt.

Some of the uncertainties surrounding the political and monetary developments of the European Community have been resolved, but many remain. What will this mean for North American marketers? Truly a single currency? When? And how will European customers take to the new regime as it is introduced? If they do not like it, then all the talk of pan-European developments may meet the brick wall of democratic resistance.

While these are uncertain times, they are nonetheless exciting. Business cannot wait for the politicians to pick their way toward compromise before companies start to trade. European marketing must go on. It is in this spirit that this book aims to make a contribution.

NOTES

1. World Bank, *World Development Report 1991* (New York: Oxford University Press, 1991), Table 1, pp. 204–5.
2. Ibid.

3. "Survey of Business in Eastern Europe," *The Economist*, September 21, 1990, p. 5.

4. J. Dempsey, "Time to Sort Out Who Owns What," *Financial Times*, April 16, 1991.

5. P. Kotler, *Marketing Management: Analysis, Planning, Implementation and Control*, 6th ed. (Englewood Cliffs, NJ: Prentice Hall, 1988), chapter 5.

6. G. S. Day, *Strategic Market Planning* (St. Paul, MN: West Publishing, 1984), chapter 3.

7. V. Terpstra and R. Sarathy. *International Marketing*, 5th ed. (Orlando, FL: Dryden Press, 1991), chapter 5.

8. S. Thomsen, "Inward Investment in the European Community." Chapter in *Panorama of EC Industry 1991/92* (Luxembourg: OPOCE, 1991), pp. 39–64.

9. Paragon Communications, *How European Are We?* Survey sponsored by Epson (UK) Ltd., England, 1990.

10. M. McDonald, *Marketing Plans: How to Prepare and Use Them*, 2nd ed. (London: Heinemann, 1990), chapter 6.

11. R. Lynch, *European Business Strategies: An Analysis of Europe's Top Companies* (London: Kogan Page, 1990), chapter 1.

12. A. Kupfer, "How American Industry Stands Up," *Fortune*, March 9, 1992, p. 18.

2

European markets and cultures

For North American companies examining the potential for European expansion and the threat from new European competition, it is essential to undertake a background assessment of the new markets. They are not only larger but also politically and culturally more complex than the home market. In this chapter, we consider many of these important issues. We shall leave to Chapter 3 the particularly difficult issues of EC politics and the single Europe.

Subjects covered in this chapter are:

- Europe in global markets.
- North American involvement in Europe.
- EC Common Agricultural Policy and the GATT.
- European Monetary Union.
- Western European markets.
- Eastern European markets.
- Western European markets: wealth and consumption.
- Sociocultural issues: education, religion, and law.
- Technical and environmental issues.

EUROPE IN GLOBAL MARKETS

European countries account for 50 percent of world trade, as can be seen from Figure 2–1. The biggest single area within this is, not surprisingly, the EC, with Eastern Europe a long way behind. Though Europe and, within it, the EC are major regions, a substantial share of the trade takes place *within* the region itself.[1] Intra-EC trade represents 58 percent of the

FIGURE 2–1
Share of World Exports—1989

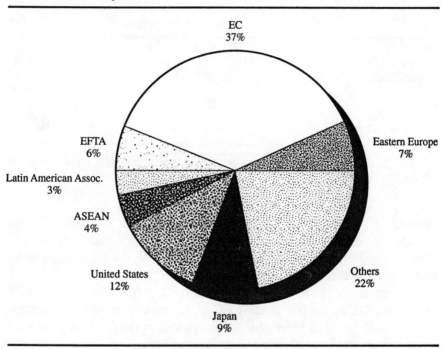

Source: United Nations Conference on Trade and Development, *Handbook of International Trade and Development Statistics 1990* (New York: United Nations, 1991). Table 1.1

total trade of member states. Thus, care must be taken in considering the EC as one single market competing against outside global markets.

Similarly, much of the trade in Eastern Europe has been *between* members of the Eastern European trade bloc COMECON, particularly the USSR. Rather less has been with the EC: around 20 percent of exports from Eastern Europe were to the EC in 1988.[2] Again, it is important to analyze the data with caution.

For the EC, EFTA, and Canada, international trade is a vital contributor to the wealth of the countries involved. The United States and Japan do not need world trade nearly as much. This is shown in Table 2–1.

The EC's main export customers are the United States and EFTA, which together accounted for 46 percent of exports in 1989.[3] Developing countries accounted for 31 percent of exports, while Eastern Europe ac-

TABLE 2–1

The Importance of International Trade as Percentage of GDP (1989)

	Imports	Exports
EC	24.4	23.7
EFTA*	27.3	26.3
United States	9.2	7.1
Japan	7.5	9.8
Canada	20.9	21.2

*Excludes Iceland.

Source: European Commission, *Eurostats: Basic Statistics of the EC*, 28th ed. (Luxembourg: OPOCE, 1991), p. 259.

counted for only 6 percent of exports. Hence, until the late 1980s, Eastern Europe was actually not very significant in terms of trade, for the EC. Canadian trade was mainly with the United States; the EC accounted for only 8 percent of Canada's exports in 1989.

There is not much variation in the overall pattern for individual EC countries. Taking the five leading EC exporting and importing countries, Figures 2–2 and 2–3 show that these countries principally rely on each other to generate trade. Japan and the United States come further down in the order. However, this does not mean that it is always better for EC companies first to seek marketing opportunities with fellow EC members. They may provide better sales leads where the prime method of developing sales is through developing *export* opportunities from a home base. But where the objective is to achieve *global* market share, other member states in the EC represent, at best, simply a stepping-stone to this end. In particular, the sheer size and political stability of the United States would represent a more attractive opportunity. Similarly, as we shall see later, culture and language may be more powerful pointers than trade source for some products and services.

Turning to the type of world trade undertaken, EC export data are shown in Figure 2–4. The chart shows only the *balance* of exports undertaken and takes no account of the *absolute level* of exports, the latter making quite a difference: for example, in 1989 exports from West Germany were US$340 billion, while they were only US$5 billion from Greece.[4] Within this context, it can be seen that Italy, Portugal, and Greece are strong in textiles, while Ireland, Denmark, and the Nether-

FIGURE 2–2
Major European Exporters, 1989 (Destination of Exports)

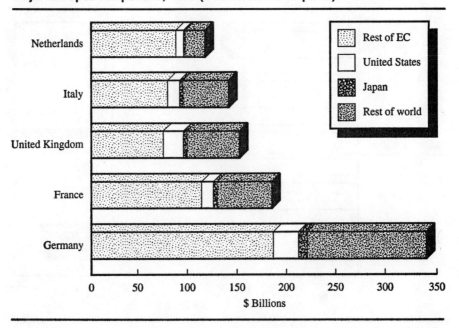

Source: European Commission, *Eurostats: Basic Statistics of the EC*, 28th ed. (Luxembourg: OPOCE, 1991).

lands have major agriculture exports. Germany, the UK, and Italy all export over 75 percent of their goods as manufactured products.

Coupled with import data, such information is important in assessing countries for their sales potential. For example, selling textile goods to Greece may be a more difficult task simply because that country already has a well-developed industry in that sector.

There is a lack of evidence on the differences between the EC and Eastern Europe in the type of world trade undertaken: many of the former communist countries have been remarkably coy about revealing trade statistics to outsiders. This is a real problem for North American companies attempting to research basic data on Eastern European countries. Data from the World Bank and the UN suggest that primary exports such as fuels and agriculture accounted for 25 percent of the EC's total exports in 1989 and 24 percent of Polish/Yugoslav/Czech/Hungarian exports.[5] While there is little difference between the EC and these countries, this

FIGURE 2–3
Major European Importers, 1989 (Source of Imports)

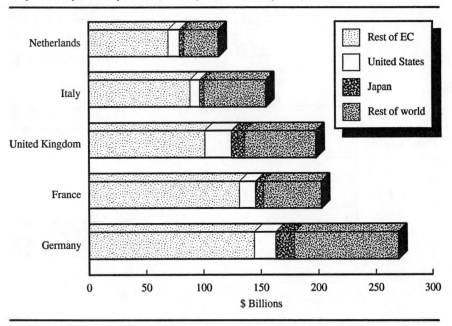

Source: European Commission, *Eurostats: Basic Statistics of the EC,* 28th ed. (Luxembourg: OPOCE, 1991).

takes no account of the USSR/Bulgarian/Romanian exports, which were not published at all. Moreover, it says nothing of the *quality* of the social-ist countries' exports, which are very poor in manufactured goods, ac-cording to anecdotal evidence.[6] Indeed, the Czech and East German car makers, Skoda and Trabant, respectively, have been the raw material of many EC jokes over the last 20 years: "How do you increase the value of a Skoda? Fill up the petrol tank." They will be sadly missed as quality improves during the 1990s.

NORTH AMERICAN INVOLVEMENT IN EUROPE

The United States exports more products to the European Community than to any other destination: in 1989 this accounted for 23.6 percent of total U.S. exports. In addition, the United States sent 2.9 percent of its exports to EFTA countries and 1.5 percent to Eastern Europe. Figure 2–5 shows the overall importance of the EC as an export destination.

FIGURE 2–4
European Balance of Exports (% Share of Merchandise Exports, 1989)

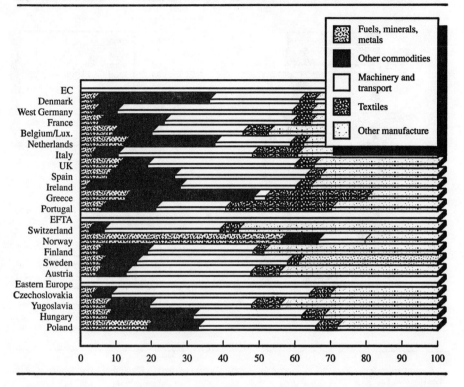

Source: Aldersgate Consultancy derived from World Bank, *World Development Report 1991*, (New York: Oxford University Press, NY), Table 16, pp. 234–5.

By contrast, Canada's biggest export destination was the United States, which took 74.2 percent of Canadian exports in 1989. The EC accounted for 8.5 percent, EFTA 1.3 percent, and Eastern Europe 0.7 percent.

As for imports, the United States took 18.1 percent of its imports from the EC, 2.9 percent from EFTA, and 0.5 percent from Eastern Europe in 1989. Japan was the largest source of imports into the United States, with 19.8 percent of the total, as can be seen in Figure 2–6.

Canadian imports were dominated by the United States, with 65.4 percent coming from this source in 1989. Another 11.1 percent came from the EC, 2.3 percent from EFTA, and 0.4 percent from Eastern Europe.

But import and export activities are not the only way in which North America is involved with Europe: direct investment from the United

FIGURE 2–5
Exports from the United States and Canada

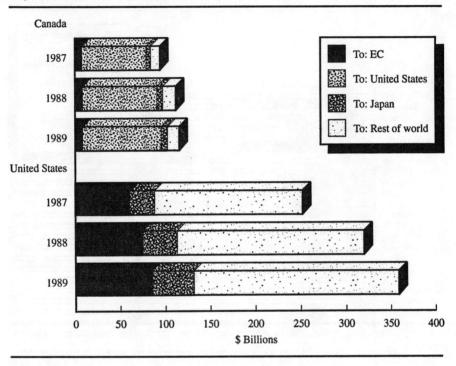

Source: European Commission, *Eurostats: Basic Statistics of the EC*, 28th ed. (Luxembourg: OPOCE, 1991).

States into the EC has also taken place over many years. Figures 2–7 and 2–8 show that much of this has been in manufacturing activity and directed at the United Kingdom. Similar data have not been published on Canadian direct investment.

Overall, the United States now has three times the level of Japanese investment in the EC and has invested more in this area than in any other part of the world. With international trade and direct investment taken together, the United States in particular is heavily involved in the European Community.

For both U.S. and Canadian companies, therefore, European marketing may represent two opportunities:

- A major export destination.
- An important investment area for acquisitions, joint ventures, and other trading partnerships.

FIGURE 2–6
Imports into the United States and Canada

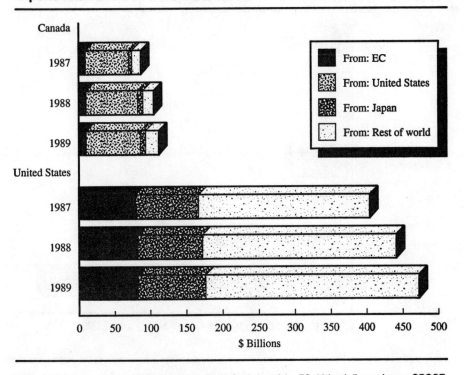

Source: European Commission, *Eurostats: Basic Statistics of the EC*, 28th ed. (Luxembourg: OPOCE, 1991).

EC COMMON AGRICULTURAL POLICY AND THE GATT

To some extent the EC has built a "trade wall" around itself since its foundation in 1957. According to the EC,[7] one of the reasons it was set up was to develop trade between member countries. The EC has had considerable success in this area. While exports to nonmember countries showed a nominal 16-fold increase in terms of U.S. dollars between 1958 and 1986, trade between member states went up by a factor of 36.[7] The EC's agricultural trade barriers to the outside world have been an important contributor to this process, much to the concern of North American farmers.

These barriers are regulated through the Common Agriculture Policy (CAP) of the EC. They take some 60 percent of the EC's total expenditure[7] and cost US$41 billion in 1991.[8] They were one of the main reasons

FIGURE 2–7
U.S. Direct Investment in the EC, by Industry (Stock to End of 1989)

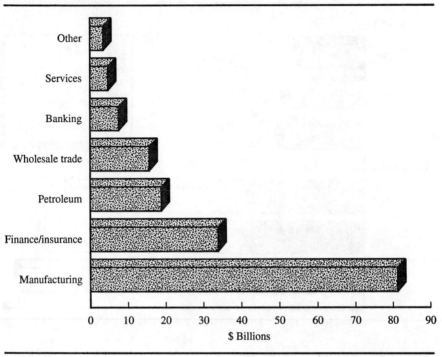

Source: European Commission, *Panorama of EC Industry 1991/92* (Luxembourg: OPOCE, 1991), pp. 50–51.

for the lack of success in the world tariff negotiations in 1990.[9] From a marketing viewpoint, the EC's agriculture policies are thus a cause of friction with the rest of the world and an example of how the EC can operate as a trade bloc. It is therefore useful to examine briefly CAP as a distorted market mechanism.

Until late 1992, CAP operated by guaranteeing farmers a high support price for their produce, the main subsidy coming from EC central funds collected from the European citizen (i.e., the customer). Prices were maintained by blocking lower-priced imports by "variable levies." When farmers produced more than customers desired, an intervention system bought up and stored surplus production. Originally, this was intended as a safety net to help farmers in short-term difficulty. But it proved so useful to farmers, whose vote is highly influential in some EC countries, that it became one of the major areas of EC policy. This situa-

FIGURE 2–8
U.S. Direct Investment in the EC, by Country (Stock to End of 1989)

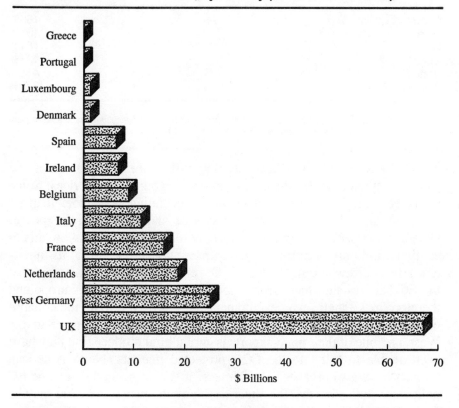

Source: European Commission, *Panorama of EC Industry 1991/92* (Luxembourg: OPOCE, 1991), pp. 50–51.

tion was exacerbated by modern production methods, which allowed EC farm production to outstrip supply significantly: between 1973 and 1988, EC food production rose 2 percent annually while consumption grew by 0.5 percent[8]—hence the massive surpluses that were sold off cheaply to Eastern European countries during the 1980s.

One additional result of CAP was that EC food prices were much higher than world prices, as shown in Table 2–2. What this meant was that not only were European customers paying directly to subsidize EC farmers via CAP, but they were also paying much higher food prices than might otherwise apply. The CAP reform package agreed to in May 1992 reduced EC food prices by only 2 percent. More important for North American interests, it started the process of bringing EC prices down to

TABLE 2–2
EC Prices as a Percentage of World Prices (1979–1980)

Common wheat	163%
Rice	131%
Barley	161%
Sugar	131%
Butter	411%
Skimmed milk	379%

Source: M. J. Roarty, "The Impact of the Common Agricultural Policy on Agricultural Trade and Development," *National Westminster Bank Quarterly Review*, February 1987 (quoted with permission).

world prices. But the CAP subsidy will still be there; it will simply be paid through another mechanism instead of high guarantee prices. Some marketeers might at this point be idly speculating why more markets could not be subject to the same easy ride at the taxpayers' expense. Others, more seriously, will wonder how long the EC will allow this to continue, not only because of the expense but also because of its important effects elsewhere in the world. Developing countries complain that the EC barriers stop them from exporting their products to Europe and therefore make their own development more difficult. With the collapse of communism, Eastern European countries want to sell more to the West, and one of their main exports is agricultural produce, but they have been unable to sell into the EC's protected markets. North American farmers have also protested. In fairness, it should be said that some EC politicians recognize that the situation is unfathomable, but there may be few votes to be gained from shifting this logjam.

From an international marketing viewpoint, the chief impact of any CAP reform is likely to be in its implications for a reduction in overall tariff barriers around the world. The main forum for this process over the last 20 years has been the negotiations surrounding the General Agreement on Trade and Tariffs (GATT). After a number of negotiating rounds since the first in 1946, there have been significant reductions in world tariffs and consequent increases in world trade.[10] The latest Uruguay round of tariff negotiations stalled in December 1992, partly (and some would argue, principally) as a result of the EC's insistence on far lower reductions in its tariff wall on agriculture than were wanted by outside countries.[9]

If the EC agriculture barriers were to be reduced, as has been proposed, over a number of years, then EC European food marketing would change radically within a short time. In addition, there would be a knock-on effect on many other industrial products, with the reduction of tariffs in other areas in compensation. The profound impact on market prices will need careful study once the negotiations have been successfully concluded.

EUROPEAN MONETARY UNION

At present, there are 12 different currencies in the EC. They would disappear if the Community adopted European monetary union (EMU) and used one currency, like the dollar in the United States.

Writing of the EC in 1991, the Commission's president said, "Economic and Monetary Union would be the step which would do more to affect ordinary people's lives than anything else on the menu in Brussels."[11] Thus, if EMU were to happen, it might profoundly affect marketing throughout the EC. This would be felt not only at the pan-European level but also by European national markets. It is therefore essential in developing European marketing to consider the potential impact of EMU.

European monetary union has not yet happened. However, according to the agreement reached at Maastricht in December 1991, it should happen by 1999 at the latest, and possibly by 1997. Both the UK and Denmark have been given the option not to take part, and a Danish national referendum in June 1992 cast further doubt on this accord; see Appendix I for details. All other EC countries will participate if their economies meet the following criteria:

- Inflation within 1.5 to 2 percent of the three best-performing states.
- No excessive budget deficits.
- Stable exchange rate within the Exchange Rate Mechanism over the two previous years.

The European Currency Unit (ECU) already exists. This is a composite artificial currency formed from the main EC currencies by taking proportions of the currencies and putting them into an imaginary "basket." The ECU thus changes as the values of the individual currencies change on international currency markets. This was confirmed at the EC Madrid Summit in 1989. The Maastricht agreement will take this process further if it is implemented.

In stage 1 of EMU all EC currencies were limited to a fluctuation of 2.25 percent against their target or "central" rate against each other and the ECU. Spain (and the UK and Portugal when they entered later) was allowed 6 percent fluctuation. Greece had not yet joined by mid-1992 because its economy still presented significant structural problems (e.g., high inflation). This linking of currencies is called the Exchange Rate Mechanism (ERM). The ERM pressure actually started in 1978 with six EC countries. After severe currency pressure in September 1992, the UK and Italy left the ERM but said they would rejoin sometime in the future.

Stage 2 is scheduled to begin on 1 January 1994 with the formation of the European Monetary Institute. It will take over the gold and foreign currency reserves now pooled as part of the ERM. It will also be able to raise and manage other funds, effectively being a European central bank in waiting. This is important because it will take over the role currently performed by the Bundesbank and adjust EC interest rates with the explicit objective of holding down the rate of inflation among members of EMU.

Stage 3 would then start on 1 January 1997 if at least seven EC member states fulfill the necessary criteria and so decide by majority vote at the Council of Ministers at that time. It will encompass the irrevocable locking of exchange rates without any fluctuation and with an independent central bank and currency. In any event, even if 1977 is not agreed upon or if insufficient member states have not reached the criteria at that time, stage 3 will commence from 1 January 1999 *without* any quorum on the minimum number of states, assuming the Maastricht treaty is ratified.

The costs and benefits of EMU have been studied in detail by the European Commission.[12] This material is summarized in a more readable form by Emerson and Huhne,[11] who also give an extensive bibliography on EMU research. They conclude:

> Overall, EMU is a particularly difficult change to assess. There are no obvious historical precedents for a monetary union of so many different nationalities. Moreover, it is not the sort of small step which economists like to try to assess . . . but EMU represents an enormous change in the whole system of economic management, affecting monetary policy, a new and independent European central bank, rules for national budgets and the international system itself.

In summary, it has been argued[11] that the chief advantages of EMU are the following:

1. Its sheer size, which would allow individual countries to adjust balance of payments deficits gradually and without a major shock to their economies. In the words of the Spanish Finance Minister, Carlos Solchaga, the Spanish balance of payments "will have as much relevance as the balance between Andalucía and the Basque country"[13] (or, he might just as well have said, the balance between Texas and New York state).

2. Elimination of the costs of currency dealing across the EC.

3. Lower capital costs for companies because there will be no risk of currency fluctuations in the EC.

4. Reduced inflation resulting from fixing all interest rates to the ECU and from the European central bank's freedom from government interference, coupled with its main objective of low inflation.

Broadly speaking, the U.S. dollar and Federal Reserve Bank already operate under such a system.

In practice, all rates in the ERM were effectively pegged to the EC's strongest currency, the deutsche mark, from the commencement of stage 1. In turn, these national currencies are supported by the independent status of the German national bank, the Bundesbank, which is by law dedicated to promoting low inflation rates.

However, there have also been strong arguments against EMU, which can be summarized as follows:

1. The transfer of decision making on fiscal policy from national governments to Brussels will result in a loss of sovereignty for national parliaments. In practice, as Brittan has argued,[13] it may not be necessary to do anything more than have a binding agreement to prevent member countries from running excessive budget deficits. Discretion could still rest with national parliaments on many tax issues.

2. There is no conclusive evidence that substantial gains will be made by EMU beyond those already obtained by the control regime put in place for stage 1 of the ERM.

3. The transition process for the weaker economies joining the ERM will be unnecessarily painful for those countries and not necessarily successful. Indeed, Walters has argued that the restrictive regime needed by national economies attempting to bring their

inflation rates down so that they could join the ERM will lead to periods of boom and bust: a "roller-coaster economy."[14] In addition, he has said that the ERM is "half-baked" and that the pound sterling should either be allowed to float or join a full EMU.

4. There will be little room for maneuver for governments needing to manage their economies when they cannot use the exchange rate weapon. It is argued that this will make it difficult for countries such as the UK and Spain to obtain real improvements in competitiveness, as compared with the leading EC countries.

Some North American commentators have also argued against EMU. For example, Barro has argued that it has all the disadvantages of a centrally planned economy.[15] However, the ERM's similarity to the U.S. system seems to have been largely ignored.

Overall, when EMU is fully implemented, the balance of payments for individual countries will assume lower importance. In addition, at a minimum, there will be some loss of national sovereignty, but this might be restricted to an agreement on limits for budget deficits. Although some real decisions will need to move to the center, both U.S. and Canadian experience suggests that this need not be all bad: there are still real price differences across these countries in housing, labor, fuels, and other basic areas.

Thus, from a *marketing viewpoint*, EMU could have some profound effects, both positive and negative:

- The introduction of a common currency may mean that there is increased identification by customers of a common pan-European identity, particularly by the young. Whether this is positive or negative will depend on the product or service.
- Common prices have been predicted across the EC on some products.[11] This would enable vigorous price comparisons to be made. However, if the United States is any guide, the vast distances across the EC will always allow excuses for local variations.
- The commitment to low inflation and stable economies will lead to better predictability in the marketing environment.
- There will be lower transaction costs for some types of international business where individual currencies are now involved.
- The transitional phase will undoubtedly be difficult for the UK, Italy, Spain, Portugal, and Greece. This will lead to depressed

markets, making it difficult for marketeers to operate in the early 1990s.

- The shift of decision making to Brussels will produce its own uncertainties in the political climate and will introduce another tier of government that will need to be influenced on key decisions.
- There may be some customer reaction against the pan-European nature of EMU: the local, regional, and national tastes, languages, and traditions will need to find a new balance across Europe. This will be both an opportunity and a problem for marketing.

More generally, the interaction of EMU with some specific *national* economies may also have a profound effect on the marketing task. Even before its reunification, Germany dominated EC trading. Indeed, most of the largest EC countries have in recent years had a trade deficit with German manufactured products. Commentators such as Cutler et al. have argued that this means that only Germany has really gained so far from the EC, while other states have become weaker in consequence.[16] On this argument, EMU will only underline this dominance, as it will in effect be pegged to the German deutsche mark. However, Germany does not have significantly more companies in the "European Top 500" largest company list by turnover than other European countries.[17] Thus, the evidence is not, perhaps, conclusive. (We shall look at companies in more depth in Chapter 4.)

Nevertheless, during and after the EMU transitional phase, it will be difficult for the poorer EC countries to catch up. Arguably, this will have a direct effect on companies and competition in those countries, and thus on marketing. With their lesser supply of resources for new product development, lower discretionary incomes, lower levels of education and training, and all the other effects of the catching-up process, EMU will make the marketing task markedly different across the EC. Perhaps the main contrast will be between the richer countries of Germany, France, the Netherlands, Denmark, Belgium, and Luxembourg, and the poorer countries of Italy, the UK, Spain, Portugal, Greece, and Ireland. North American companies will no doubt wish to assess this carefully.

WESTERN EUROPEAN MARKETS

In his researches on global competition between nations, Porter[17] has produced evidence that the basic skills, resources, and structures of a country have profound effects on company strategy and market development. His research suggests that those countries that are strongest internationally have vigorous competition within the nation to develop competitive advantage. Eventually, the whole national economy is stimulated by such activity, and this generates spin-offs into related markets. Thus, in the competitive country the national economy reinforces itself. Japan and Germany have been cited as prime examples of this type of development.

In considering the background issues affecting European marketing, it is therefore necessary to examine the relative strengths of countries in both Western and Eastern Europe. However, a word of caution is also necessary. We are examining *broad* evidence, at the macroeconomic level: there will be many exceptions for individual markets and companies. We should not, therefore, treat the data that follow as giving anything other than a general indication of market strengths and weaknesses. We shall look at Western Europe, principally the EC, in this section and Eastern Europe in the next.

The European Commission regularly sponsors data collection and research into the economies of the 12 nations of the EC. One macroeconomic comparison made is the degree of *specialization* of the different member states in the main sectors of the EC economy. For example, states such as Germany are highly industrialized, and some such as Greece rely heavily on agricultural production. Detailed economic statistics are collected on areas of the economy for each country, and a special factor called the "specialization rate" is derived for each sector of each nation.[18] This rate is defined as the difference between the share of each sector in the total value added of the country considered, minus the share of the sector in value added in the EC as a whole. The analysis of specialization coefficients by country makes it possible to analyze certain characteristic traits of the industrial structure of the different member states.

From a marketing strategy viewpoint, it is thus useful to be aware of the relative strengths of the countries of the EC. These are given in detail in EC publications[18] and summarized in Table 2–3.

- *Belgium* has a manufacturing sector below the European average, but no particular area is responsible for this. The share of market services (e.g., repair and transport services) is higher than average, reflecting the country's geographical position.
- *West Germany* (only) has a strong manufacturing sector, especially in electrical equipment, industrial machinery, and agricul-

TABLE 2–3
Specialization Indicators for EC Industry in 1987

	B	DK	GER	GR	SP	F	IRL	I	L	NL	P	UK
Agriculture	-1.1	1.3	-1.5	11.0	2.4	0.5	4.9	1.1	-0.6	1.0	4.2	-1.9
Fuel and power	-0.8	-3.9	-1.0	-1.8	2.6	-0.7	N/A	-0.7	-3.5	3.7	-2.1	2.1
Manufacturing	-3.1	-6.7	5.8	-7.3	0.2	-3.5	N/A	-0.3	4.7	-5.3	3.6	-0.8
Building and construction	-0.4	-0.1	-0.2	0.3	1.5	-0.2	0.0	0.2	0.3	-0.1	0.0	0.0
Market services	4.0	-5.8	-2.3	-10.9	3.3	-0.3	-11.4	3.0	14.7	1.7	-2.8	0.2
Nonmarket services	0.0	4.4	-0.9	-0.5	-3.1	2.6	2.1	-1.6	-1.1	-2.1	-2.0	1.1

Source: European Commission, *Panorama of EC Industry 1990* (Luxembourg: OPOCE, 1990).

tural and transport equipment. These areas are ideally placed for international trade. Sectors in which it is lower than average, such as food and beverages, are geared toward domestic trade.

- *Denmark* is a strongly agricultural country. Its problems in balance of payments are reflected in its comparatively low manufacturing base.
- *Spain* has a fast-growing but relatively undeveloped economy. Thus, it still has strengths in agriculture but also in building.
- *France* has a slightly lower share of manufacturing than average with the biggest differences in agricultural and industrial machinery. Its relatively high coefficients in market and nonmarket shares reflect the extended role that the state has in the economy.
- *Greece* is particularly strong in agriculture and weak in manufacturing and the service sectors. This is mirrored in its economic development status within the EC.
- *Italy* has a strong agricultural base and extensive state services. It has some strengths in manufacturing in textiles and metallic products, but these are offset by weaknesses elsewhere.
- *Ireland* is essentially an agricultural community. Detailed data are not available in some other sectors.
- *Luxembourg* has specialized in steel production and financial services. The economy is thus sensitive to international fluctuations in these two sectors.
- *The Netherlands* has strong natural gas activities, as reflected in the high energy coefficient. Its well-developed social services and general service provisions are also evident in the table.
- *Portugal* has manufacturing strengths in textiles, footwear, and clothing, reflecting its low-wage economy and quota protection in these areas before it joined the EC in 1986. It is still relatively poor and has an agriculture-based economy.
- *The UK* has benefited from North Sea oil. Its below-average coefficient on manufacturing is a combination of strengths in foods, agricultural machinery, and printing and paper, coupled with weaknesses in electrical equipment, transport equipment, and office equipment. The more recent Japanese car and electrical goods company investment in transport and electrical equipment will alter this picture.

Overall, this brief summary of country economies in the EC is clearly no more than indicative of the type of data that are available. North American marketers will no doubt make good use of this material in researching markets and opportunities. In particular, it should be noted that some data are available on *regions* within each EC country, making more accurate assessments possible. Unfortunately, similar information is not currently available for EFTA countries.

EASTERN EUROPEAN MARKETS

The countries of Eastern Europe are beginning to emerge into the world democracy of nations. But all have had chronic underinvestment over the last 50 years, primarily from the lack of any market mechanism to direct activity. The main activity undertaken appears to have been directed toward defense (in the USSR), agriculture, and energy to keep the wheels of the state turning. Thus, these economies still rely on raw material production, including metal ores, coal, oil and gas, and agriculture to provide the main means of growth in the post-communist era of the 1990s.

It is possible to draw up a rough balance sheet of assets and liabilities for Eastern European countries (Figures 2–9 and 2–10). While it should be treated as an *indicator* only of the opportunities and problems, such a balance sheet does highlight some major issues. These countries are not Third World countries with low literacy rates, largely reliant on the agriculture and some specialist raw material production. They all have trained work forces with sophisticated state support services in such areas as medicine and transport.

But there will be real problems in turning them into thriving and prosperous economies. In a paper delivered at a UK marketing conference in 1991, Thomas commented on Eastern European economies:[19]

> For all of the last 40 years macro demand has never been satisfied by the macro supply system. . . . It is my view that only rapid expansion of the private sector will eliminate shortages that are characteristic of the communist controlled system. Privatisation itself requires a structure for the valuation of enterprises, for the purchase of shares. This will take time.

He pointed out that the West has had plenty of experience moving from the primitive capitalism of the early 20th century to the mixed economies

FIGURE 2–9
Eastern Europe: A Rough Balance Sheet—Assets

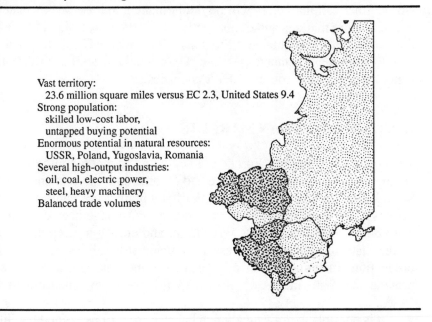

Vast territory:
  23.6 million square miles versus EC 2.3, United States 9.4
Strong population:
  skilled low-cost labor,
  untapped buying potential
Enormous potential in natural resources:
  USSR, Poland, Yugoslavia, Romania
Several high-output industries:
  oil, coal, electric power,
  steel, heavy machinery
Balanced trade volumes

Source: P. Kraljik, "The Economic Gap Separating East and West," *McKinsey Quarterly*, Spring 1990, p. 4.

that now prevail. But there is little experience in moving from pure socialism to a Western mixed economy. As Lech Walesa observed in a powerful metaphor, it is quite easy to make fish soup if you stand next to a well-stocked aquarium, but it is extremely difficult to produce a well-stocked aquarium out of fish soup! The structural problems of Eastern European markets are immense. They will take time and resources to change.

Finally, it should be noted that the communist Eastern European governments of the last 40 years have produced little useful market data. Unfortunately, their production statistics about "record harvests" and "new target achievements in mineral production" are scarcely believable.

WESTERN EUROPEAN MARKETS: WEALTH AND CONSUMPTION

As can be seen in Figure 2–11, the Danes and West Germans have the greatest wealth per head of population within the EC. Moreover, there

FIGURE 2–10
Eastern Europe: A Rough Balance Sheet—Liabilities

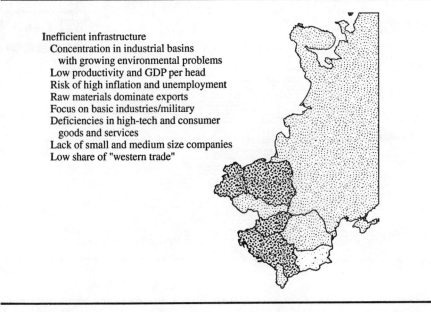

Inefficient infrastructure
Concentration in industrial basins
   with growing environmental problems
Low productivity and GDP per head
Risk of high inflation and unemployment
Raw materials dominate exports
Focus on basic industries/military
Deficiencies in high-tech and consumer
   goods and services
Lack of small and medium size companies
Low share of "western trade"

Source: P. Kraljik, "The Economic Gap Separating East and West," *McKinsey Quarterly*, Spring 1990, p. 4.

has been no fundamental change in the relative positions of the main EC countries over the last few years. The UK has been overtaken marginally by Italy, and the poorer countries of the EC have gained proportionately. The United States and Canada are ahead of EC countries but behind many EFTA countries.

Significantly, the EFTA countries have higher wealth per head than many members of the EC. When these countries join the EC over the next 10 years, this may have a profound effect on the *balance* of purchasing power within the Community. At present, some of these countries provide only limited access to the EC in order to protect home industries. Thus, a new range of wealthy markets and opportunities will then be fully opened up to all EC members.

Within the present EC, overall wealth does not necessarily mean that expenditure is equally high in all market areas. Full data are available in *Eurostats*;[20] Table 2–4 summarizes the ranking of household consumption by country.

Naturally, Table 2–4 will be too general for most European market-

FIGURE 2–11
European Wealth (GDP per Head of Population, 1989)

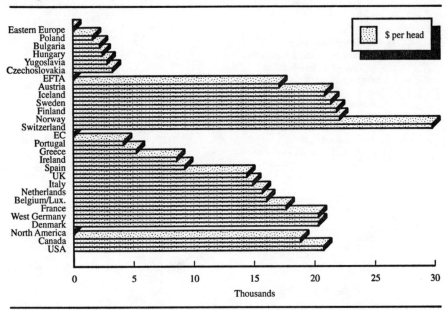

Source: Aldersgate Consultancy derived from World Bank, *World Development Report 1991* (New York: Oxford University Press), Table 1, pp. 204–5.

ing purposes. However, it does provide some clues for research that can be followed up in more detail. It also confirms a few prejudices—for example, that the British do not place as high a value on food and drink consumption as many other European nationalities!

SOCIOCULTURAL ISSUES: EDUCATION, RELIGION, AND LAW

Within the complex area of sociocultural concerns, it is possible only to indicate some of the main factors.

Education

In terms of international growth and competitiveness, there is little doubt that national investment in education is vital to Europe's future develop-

TABLE 2–4
Country Ranking of Final Consumption of Households per Head by Purpose (1988)

	Food, Beverages, and Tobacco	Clothing and Footwear	Rent, Fuel, and Power	Furniture and Household	Medical Care and Health	Transport and Communications	Recreation and Education
Highest	DK	GER	DK	L	GER	L	DK
	L	–	GER	B	NL	F	GER
	IRL	B	L	GER	B	DK	NL
	–	F	F	F	F	GER	UK
	F	L	UK	DK	L	UK	–
	GER	DK	NL	–	–	B	F
	B	NL	B	NL	DK	–	B
	NL	UK	–	UK	SP	NL	IRL
	UK	SP	SP	IRL	IRL	SP	L
	GR	GR	IRL	SP	GR	IRL	SP
	SP	IRL	GR	GR	UK	GR	GR
Lowest	P	P	P	P	P	P	P

Notes:

1. The table shows only the *ranking* and not the *absolute level* of consumption. For example, Denmark consumed 2,071 ECU per head in food, beverages, and tobacco in 1988, while Greece only 1,217 ECU per head.

2. The table gives 1987 data for Ireland and Spain and 1986 data for Portugal.

Source: Aldersgate Consultancy, derived from *Eurostats*.

ment; this has been confirmed in studies by the World Bank[21] and Porter,[17] among others. Broadly, all the countries of Western and Eastern Europe claim to have highly developed primary (ages 6–11) and secondary (ages 12–17) education systems. Nevertheless, there are some differences in the type of education undertaken (e.g., vocational or basic subjects) and the investment made in educational institutions. Moreover, although children can read in most urban areas of Europe, there are remote country areas where the level of educational attainment is basic.

What is also varied is the extent of provision for tertiary education (ages 20–24), as shown in Table 2–5. In the context of the table, it should be noted that further data from the same source indicate that there is no significant difference in the percentages of males and females enrolled in both secondary and tertiary education in European countries. North American training levels are clearly much higher.

From a marketing viewpoint, the level of education achieved affects not only consumer tastes but also the target group's understanding of marketing issues. Marketing employees need to be able to work with advanced concepts and research. Thus, the following are typical areas that will benefit from those who have undertaken tertiary education:

TABLE 2–5
Percentage of Age Group Enrolled in Tertiary Education in Selected Countries (1988)

Canada	62%
United States	60%
Finland	40%
Norway	35%
France	35%
Belgium	33%
Spain	32%
Germany	32%
Denmark	31%
Italy	26%
Switzerland	25%
United Kingdom	23%
Czechoslovakia	18%
Hungary	18%
Yugoslavia	18%

Source: United Nations Conference on Trade and Development, *Handbook of International Trade and Development Statistics 1990*, (New York: United Nations), Table 6.10B.

- *Market research questions*: Will they even understand the questions?

- *Promotional campaigns*: What is the relevance of quoting technical data when the target's educational level is insufficient for comprehension of the material?

- *Relevance of research and new product development*: High technical competence is needed to turn ideas into reality.

- *Computer-driven marketing information systems*: Without technical training, it will be difficult to use the new systems that will become essential to managing marketing in the new Europe.

The evidence on tertiary education provision suggests a wide variation across the continent that will affect an organization's ability to recruit at a standard high enough to achieve its marketing objectives. Moreover, what is not shown in Table 2–5 is the level of *language* proficiency; a high level will be essential for some aspects of pan-European marketing management in the 21st century. It is likely that some European countries, notably the EFTA countries, Germany, and the Benelux countries, are ahead of others, such as the UK. Beyond working in the UK for English speakers, Spain for Hispanics, and France for Quebecois, the language issue will need to be tackled by many North American marketers.

Religion

Europe's history, cultures, and values are intimately entwined with religion. Marketing has to understand such values if it is to make an assessment of customer needs. Religion provides useful insights into this difficult and complex area: as Terpstra has pointed out, it is helpful for international managers, primarily interested in *how* potential customers will behave, to understand also *why* they behave as they do.[22] Nominally, at least, much of Europe follows the Christian faith. Certainly, much of its history can be interpreted by the ebb and flow of the various churches within the Christian religion working out their contacts with each other and with other, non-Christian faiths. Some will no doubt argue that the majority in Europe no longer allow their daily lives to be guided by religious beliefs, Christian or otherwise. They would point to the evidence of poor church attendance, increased crime, and lack of respect for human values in much of European society, where church attendance is lower than in North America.

But religion is still a powerful force in Europe. For example, the persecution of some religious sects in Eastern Europe continued until the late 1980s, and the conflict in Northern Ireland has a religious background. In the Netherlands, both Protestant and Catholic groups have political representation and newspapers. Moreover, immigration from other parts of the world has brought a rich variety of new religions to Europe—the Muslim, Hindu, and Buddhist faiths, for example. This has produced new tensions in some German, French and UK cities.

Practical consequences of these issues in the daily lives of Europeans include the following:

- Dietary needs: vegetarian, no pork (Jewish and Islamic), or no beef (Hindu).
- The role of women in Islamic society.
- The caste system in Indian society.
- Religious holidays and festivals affecting working patterns.
- How the relationship between Church and State affects legislation and lifestyle—for example, the Church linked to the State in the UK versus total separation in France.

North American marketers need to be aware of these issues as they extend their activity into Europe. They need to be sensitive and respectful of their potential customers. For example, the marketing of a new cosmetic product needs to take into account the wide variation in views on what constitutes moral behavior with regard to nudity across Europe. In the same way, the use of a newborn baby in a Benneton poster advertisement caused widespread offense in several European countries in 1991. Although this was not strictly a religious issue, cultural values and religion are interrelated, and marketing does need to understand and respond to these values across Europe.

Legal Issues

In the course of our study of European marketing we shall be concerned with the law at various points in the text. We have already seen it in operation in the context of international agreements such as the GATT and aspects of the CAP, these being capable of enforcement in courts of law if necessary. Thus, European law is important for marketers in Europe. We shall continue to meet further examples as we progress through the text. Our purpose now is to outline briefly the bases on which the law in Europe may operate.

Within the EC, there are three different legal systems:

- *Common law* operates mainly in the UK. It is decided largely by precedent set by previous decisions in the same legal area as the matter under dispute. Thus, it is necessary to study and understand what the courts have decided in the past and then argue how this applies to the new case.
- *Civil* or *code law* is a fully codified system of laws organized under various subject headings. It is intended to be comprehensive in most circumstances and not to require the same degree of interpretation by the courts as common law. It does not rely on previous court decisions. It is used extensively throughout most of the EC.
- *European law* is concerned with the legally binding Treaty of Rome and its annexes, such as the Single Europe Act of 1986. The various articles of this treaty are codified and *take precedence* over the national laws just cited. All countries in the EC are subject to this law. It is interpreted by the European Court of Justice in Brussels, which is described in Chapter 3.

None of these systems is sufficiently close to U.S. or Canadian practice to enable meaningful lessons to be drawn.

Other Western European countries have their own legal systems, mainly based on codified law. The countries of Eastern Europe have also developed their own legal systems, but these are being modified because they have notable gaps by Western European standards; reference has already been made to some of these areas in Chapter 1. For example, the concept of ownership of property remains to be changed, in some countries, from laws that largely favor the state to those permitting private ownership.

From a marketing viewpoint, European law is an immensely complex area. It is vital to take professional advice and accept its costs, this being preferable to expensive and time-consuming litigation later.

TECHNICAL AND ENVIRONMENTAL ISSUES

It is convenient to split technical and environmental concerns into three separate areas, while recognizing that there may be some interconnections in practice: European technical development projects, telecommunications potential, and European environmental and ecological concerns.

European Technical Development Projects

The EC has sponsored a number of projects over the last few years designed to put Europe at the forefront of new developments, or at least to allow Europe to match Japanese or U.S. leading companies. If such initiatives are at all successful, they will have considerable marketing significance both in the industries directly involved and in their spin-off effects elsewhere.

There has been real concern in countries such as France and Italy that individual European companies do not have the resources individually to match global competitors. In addition, it is believed that once Europe has been left behind in some areas of technology, it will always be reliant on foreign suppliers. The European Commission's own description of this process compared Europe's performance with those of the United States and Japan.[23] It pointed out that in some high-technology industries, such as semiconductors, computers, and computer-integrated manufacturing, Europe is not the market leader, and the outlook is not encouraging. Thus, technological research projects with grants totaling some 5.3 billion ECU (US$5.2 billion) were proposed as part of the Single Europe Act of 1986. They included the following:

- ESPRIT: information technology.
- RACE: advanced telecommunications research.
- BRITE: industrial technology.

It has been reported that these projects were not agreed to without some dispute.[24] The UK held up the resulting five-year plan (1987–1991) on the grounds that the projects were subject to duplication between nations and the program had not been fully approved. As background, there was a more fundamental difference of approach to European business research-based projects. The UK believed that market forces and industry should be the prime movers in any development program; some other member countries held that it was right for European-level sponsorship to take place. (A similar difference in approach can be seen in comparing the Reagan-Bush presidencies with earlier, Democratic incumbents.) It is quite possible that these differences in approach will be reflected in attitudes toward further European initiatives over the next few years.

In addition, over the last few years there have been a number of other European-sponsored initiatives, such as ESPRIT in computer-integrated manufacturing and a high-definition television (HDTV) project to develop new technical standards of television signal broadcasting. There are also projects in other areas, such as energy (e.g., JET) and biological resources (BAP, ECLAIR), which have a Europe-wide dimension though they are not necessarily sponsored by the EC.

They will all have their difficulties. For example, HDTV has run into problems. The European Commission wrote in 1988:[23]

> Japan tends to be the leader in consumer electronics (television sets, HiFi, etc.) worldwide: about 50 per cent of world production comes from Japan and Japanese manufacturers control nearly 70 per cent of the world consumer electronics market if their off-shore production is taken into account. However, the development of high-definition television expected for the 1990s could alter this situation. European manufacturers may be able to make their common MAC standard prevail and present a united front against the Japanese MUSE system.

Unfortunately, since that was written, MAC has had serious problems related more to marketing issues than to technology. The main satellite channel transmitting in the MAC format was called BSB (British Satellite Broadcasting). The channel started in a flurry of publicity about its new technology but has now ceased to use it. After 18 months of heavy expenditure, BSB concluded that there was insufficient customer demand for two technically incompatible channels, so it merged with Rupert Murdoch's SKY channel and moved to the same standard television signal as SKY.

However, this is not the complete story. Because it used standard technology, SKY was able to launch significantly before BSB: SKY realized that customers were concerned more with the quality of the programs than with the signal. Thus, it had a head start over BSB, which could not catch up in any reasonable time frame. It would seem that marketing issues and business logic have forced a delay in MAC development, possibly even its complete abandonment. By early 1993, it had become clear that the EC investment in this area was a complete waste of money. Europe was likely to adopt the U.S. digital HDTV system. So much for European-sponsored initiatives!

This experience suggests that North American marketers should be suspicious of some European technical development projects that are motivated more by a sense of rivalry with other countries than by real market demand. This does not mean that projects should be stopped, but rather that they may need more *marketing* evaluation at an early stage.

Telecommunications Potential

All the major telecommunications companies of the EC and EFTA are now investing in new digital telecommunications technology. In addition, common standards have now been agreed upon for a pan-European mobile telephone network. It will start to operate in 1994. Thus, new telecommunications technology is now making faster, cheaper, and more reliable communications available to all marketing departments across Western Europe. Essentially it is becoming easier and cheaper to transmit information. Technology is shrinking the boundaries of the new Europe.

For Eastern Europe, the story is mixed. The technology is available, but foreign exchange is needed to pay for its installation. And this is in short supply. Some major trunk networks have been arranged and also some contracts to modernize telephone exchanges in the USSR. U.S. companies such as GM's Hughes have been successful here. In addition, the former East Germany is seeing the benefits of German reunification with massive investment in infrastructure over the early 1990s. But it is likely that many Eastern European countries will move at a slower pace than the West.

European Environmental and Ecological Concerns

The EC is becoming increasingly active in the area of the environment. In 1988 there were some 14 EUREKA projects in the field of environmental services. They brought together some 78 participants with a total estimated investment in R&D of US$473 million.[25] However, it is not only research that is being undertaken, but also the development of new market initiatives to meet the concerns of the 1990s.

The EC market for environmental services is large: it was valued at

US$45.9 billion in 1987.[26] However, the same study also reported that it was unevenly distributed across the Community. The West German market was larger than the French and UK markets together, and 50 to 100 times larger than the Greek, Portuguese, and Irish markets; no doubt this partially resulted from the greater industrialization (and thus pollution) in Germany as compared with agricultural economies.

The investment of Western Europe is not at present being matched by the East. The Eastern European countries simply do not have the funds, even if they have the problems. Indeed, there have been reports that pollution is *worse* in these countries, particularly East Germany, the former USSR,[27] and Poland.[28]

All this concern means that European marketeers must be aware of the environmental impact of any major new projects and new product launches throughout the area. There is also a case for the reexamination of the impact of existing products. This is one background marketing issue that will only increase in importance through the 1990s. Although direct comparisons are difficult, it is likely that North American practices are already comparable with those of the European leaders.

CONCLUSION

In this chapter, we have examined the relationships between European markets and the background factors: governments, the European Commission, cultures, the environment, and trade treaties and EC policies. All these will need to be accurately assessed in developing a European marketing plan. We have so far skirted the politics of Europe, but we shall need to tackle this issue if we are to produce a robust plan. We shall therefore do this in the following chapter.

NOTES

1. European Commission, *Panorama of EC Industry 1990* (Luxembourg: OPOCE, 1990), p. 55.
2. European Commission, *Eurostats: Basic Statistics of the EC*, 27th ed. (Luxembourg: OPOCE, 1990), pp. 278–79.
3. United Nations Conference on Trade and Development, *Handbook of International Trade and Development Statistics 1990* (New York: UNCTAD, 1991), p. 60.

4. European Commission, *Eurostats: Basic Statistics of the EC*, 28th ed. (Luxembourg: OPOCE, 1991).

5. World Bank, *World Development Report 1991* (New York: Oxford University Press, NY, 1991), table 16.

6. BBC TV, "Money Programme" on Volkswagen: comment on takeover of Skoda, May 1991.

7. European Commission, *Europe in Figures* (Luxembourg: OPOCE, 1987), section 5.

8. *Independent on Sunday*, July 21, 1991, p. 6; M. du Bois and J. Wolf, "EC Revamps Its Farm Policy on Subsidies: U.S. Remains Skeptical," *The Wall Street Journal*, May 22, 1992, p. A3.

9. *Financial Times*, "Ambitious GATT Round," October 14, 1991, p. 26.

10. World Bank, *World Development Report 1991*, p. 150.

11. M. Emerson and C. Huhne, *The ECU Report* (London: European Commission and Pan Books, 1991), p. 30.

12. "Creation of a European Financial Area," *European Economy*, special issue 36, May 1988.

13. S. Brittan, "EMU—Thatcher Right but Don't Worry," *Financial Times*, October 10, 1991.

14. A. Walters, *Sterling in Danger* (London: Institute of Economic Affairs, 1990).

15. R. J. Barr (1992) "Europe's Road to Serfdom," *The Wall Street Journal*, August 13, 1992, p. A14.

16. T. Cutler, C. Haslam, J. Williams, and K. Williams, *1992—The Struggle for Europe* (Oxford: Berg, 1990).

17. M. Porter. *Competitive Advantage of Nations* (New York: Free Press, 1990).

18. European Commission, *Panorama of EC Industry 1990*, pp. 20–26.

19. M. J. Thomas, "The East European Transition—Marketing in Poland," (Cardiff: Marketing Education Group Conference, 1991), p. 1178.

20. European Commission, *Eurostats*, 27th ed., pp. 44–45.

21. United Nations Conference on Trade and Development, *Handbook of International Trade and Development Statistics 1990*, (New York: United Nations), Table 6.10B.

22. V. Terpstra and R. Sarathy, *International Marketing*. 5th ed. (Orlando, FL: Dryden Press, 1991), p. 110.

23. European Commission, *Panorama of EC Industry 1989* (Luxembourg: OPOCE, 1989), pp. 29–51.

24. R. Owen and M. Dynes, *The Times Guide to 1992* (London: Times Books, 1990), p. 55.

25. European Commission, *Panorama of EC Industry 1990*, p. 142.

26. Ibid., p. 136.

27. USSR supplement, *Financial Times*, March 12, 1990, p. xix.

28. Poland supplement, *Financial Times*, May 2, 1991, p. 13.

3

The European business and political background

Although many marketing books mention politics as a suitable background topic, very few devote a full chapter to this aspect of business marketing. But "Europe" is as inseparable from politics as it is from geography. Moreover, events have moved so fast over the last few years that this special situation poses specific market openings and business risks for North American marketers. Hence, we need to look in detail at this vital topic.

The issues to be covered in this chapter are the following:

- Origins and decision-making processes of the EC.
- The Single Europe Act and its supposed marketing potential.
- The European Economic Area Treaty and its impact on EC and EFTA markets.
- The EC's moves to integration and their marketing implications.
- Influencing the EC's political and business decision-making process.
- Easter European issues.

In the context of political implications, we shall concentrate primarily on the EC because it represents the main political and economic driving force in Western Europe. Moreover it is likely that Sweden, Finland, and Austria will obtain full membership in the EC by 1996, with others to follow.[1] EFTA will therefore have limited *political* significance after that time. Hence, we shall look at EFTA from the viewpoint of the European Economic Area Treaty rather than from any broader political perspective. Eastern Europe has its own special issues and opportunities, so it is handled separately at the end of the chapter.

ORIGINS AND DECISION-MAKING PROCESSES OF THE EC

The EC grew out of World War II and its aftermath in Europe: destruction, poverty, fear of renewed German hegemony, and the conflict between Soviet communism and U.S. capitalism.[2] A group that included the Frenchman Jean Monnet believed that a politically and commercially united Europe might help to provide at least a partial solution to some of these issues, and its members explored the creation of a European nation-state. Inspired by their ideas, the French Foreign Minister Robert Schumann put forward initial proposals in 1951 to create a single market for Europe's iron and steel resources. The European Coal and Steel Community (ECSC), consisting of France, Italy, Germany, Belgium, Luxembourg, and the Netherlands, was formed in 1951.[3] Over the next 20 years, the United States and Canada largely stood back from these developments; their prime focus was on the Atlantic defense alliance against the threat of Soviet communism.

Not for the last time in European development, the UK rejected "full participation" in the ECSC but later became "associated" with the agreement. But it would be too simplistic to regard this attitude as purely a UK problem. In the early days, the Benelux countries were worried about the dominance of Germany and France in the "Six."[3] Later Norway, Sweden, and Finland were equally concerned at various times to maintain a degree of independence.[4] And the great French President, Charles de Gaulle, always had major doubts as to whether there should be a supranational authority in Europe at all.[5]

The significance for marketing assessment is to understand that such judgments have characterized many European nations and do not mean that such a country is "anti-European." In addition, what has subsequently changed the attitudes of the countries concerned is their assessment that the benefits of the single Europe outweigh the problems. "European marketing" may similarly involve a compromise with the national images of the various European nations. North Americans need to recognize the sensitivity of the issue of national identity when dealing with Europe.

The EC of the 1990s is the outcome of these beginnings in the early 1950s: its principal binding agreement, the Treaty of Rome, can be best understood in the context of that history. (Other principal treaties governing the EC are listed in Appendix I.) Although this is perhaps oversimplifying, the treaty involved a balance of two elements: the German industrial strength and German willingness to let competitive forces act without central direction in the marketplace, a laissez-faire approach; and the French desire to protect Europe's agricultural interests and its view that the state should provide some overall guidance as to how the state should direct its resources, a *dirigiste* approach.[6]

Naturally, the six national countries of the original EC, those that had made up the ECSC in 1951, took their time in forming the EC. There were a number of stages; some came before the main treaty and some later. The Treaty of Rome was signed six years after the formation of the ECSC. The Common Agricultural Policy (CAP) was introduced only in 1962, and the full customs union of the Six, which we now take for granted, was not enacted until 1968. Some of the more significant dates over the years since the EC's foundation are shown in Table 3–1. For North American marketing managers attempting to interpret discussions in Brussels in the 1990s, it must be understood that the development of the EC was not a smooth process. It was marked by periods of real decision making followed by years when little apparent progress was made.[7]

TABLE 3–1
Some Key Dates in EC History

Date	Event
1951	Treaty to establish ECSC
1957	EEC treaty signed
1960	European Social Fund
1962	Common Agricultural Policy
1967	VAT introduced
1968	Customs union of the "Six"
1973	Denmark, Ireland, and the UK join
1975	European regional development fund
1979	EMS created
1979	First European Parliament election
1981	Greece joins
1986	Spain and Portugal join
1986	Single Europe Act signed
1989	New public tendering and works directives
1990	European merger directives
1991	Free movement of capital
1991	Maastricht: Monetary Union and Political Treaty agreed to subject to ratification as well as social protocol

Key point: "Frontierless Europe" by 1 January 1993

The sense of unity and purpose of the founding fathers of the United States did not characterize the EC's early history.

In its early period, the EC was referred to as the European *Economic* Community (EEC). However, the treaty envisaged that it would extend beyond an economic grouping to a political and monetary union.[8] Four fundamental freedoms within the Community were enshrined in the Treaty of Rome:

1. *Freedom of capital:* the ability of capital to flow freely between countries within the EC.
2. *Freedom of goods:* the complete absence of barriers to the sale of good anywhere in the Community.
3. *Freedom of labor:* the right of all workers to obtain employment anywhere in the EC.
4. *Freedom of services:* the provision of services throughout the Community without any barriers.

No new countries have joined since 1986. Since that time, the EC has concentrated on achieving these freedoms and creating as a consequence the single market. The Single Europe Act of 1986 was the key move in this regard; its main points are described later in this chapter. Freedom of capital has been largely achieved, while freedom of labor has been achieved at the employee level but not fully at the professional level.[9] Even when the remaining obstructions are removed, the real problem here will be the linguistic ability to practice a profession throughout the EC, rather than the professional qualification itself.

Freedom of goods and services will depend less on the formal steps enshrined in the Single Europe Act than on removal of the hidden barriers to their achievement.[10] For example, the procurement policies of national governments previously tended to favor home-based companies over bidding companies of other nationalities within the EC. An important marketing and sales task remains for the 1990s in this area.

By 1987 the processes to achieve the four freedoms had, for the most part, been initiated. To maintain the momentum, a natural next step was to reconsider earlier discussions on possible moves toward European political union. This also had the merit of countering growing criticism, particularly in the UK, of government by an unelected and largely faceless European Commission in Brussels.[11] Such considerations were complicated by other aspects of the way the EC had grown over its 30-year life—specifically, its finances and its decision-making processes. It is difficult to consider any political union without debating how it will be funded and how it will make its decisions. To make sense of this, we have to understand the Community's status prior to any such proposed changes and this, in turn, is bound up with the EC's development over the last 30 years. Henry Ford may have regarded history as "bunk," but such knowledge is important for any North American marketer wishing to evaluate how European marketing may develop in the 1990s.

Agriculture is a useful starting point. The European nations that had become major exporters of agricultural products over the years (France, Denmark, Ireland, and the Netherlands) would lose substantially if the CAP were reduced in scope. Moreover, European farmers such as those in southern Germany have always been a powerful voting lobby in some nations within the Community: they were not averse to parading animals or dumping manure on the steps of the EC Parliament building to make their points. Both the farmers and their governments have certainly been vocal.

However, other formidable pressure groups such as the UK miners did not understand early enough the need to argue their own case at the EC with the same vigor. Finally, the voting structure in the Council of Ministers allowed two major countries, such as France and Germany, and one minor country, such as Ireland, to block any progress on farming reform. The result has been that the agricultural lobby has been able to obtain and keep measures to protect its interests into the 1990s.[12] This is perhaps not so different from the powerful lobbyists in Washington, D.C.

CAP has therefore been allowed to continue with relatively minor modifications into the 1990s, in the interests of both farmers and some governments. This has affected not only political decision making but also the *finances* of the EC. The Community's budget consists broadly of revenues collected from VAT and excise duties. As shown in Table 3–2, these are spent principally on agriculture. Some funds are also expended on EC regional development (e.g., southern Italy and Northern Ireland).

As mentioned in Chapter 2, CAP was originally intended to provide temporary relief for farmers in times of trouble. Subsequently, it became effectively a means for rebating to some national governments the funds that they had paid to the EC in VAT, for example. It was also a strong contributor to the balance of trade for some countries. The imbalance in EC funding in favor of agricultural nations was the subject of Prime Minister Thatcher's negotiations with the EC in 1984.[13] Once this revised agreement had been achieved, at some emotional cost, there was little incentive for governments to initiate further farming reform until the GATT Uruguay Round. Hence, the strange distortion in EC expenditure produced by the original agreement on the CAP still exists: it dominates EC expenditure, as shown in Table 3–2.

As we examine the EC's budget, it is important to set its total expenditure in context. It is significantly smaller than the budgets of many EC national governments. For example, the UK government's budget in 1989 on the same basis was US$323.84 billion.[14,15] Since 1985 the proportion of total expenditure devoted to agriculture has declined—for example, to 53 percent of the EC 1992 budget of US$84.6 billion. However, even in the 1990s, it remains by far the largest item.

Over the life of the EC, the budget balance between EC funds and European national government funds has remained substantially the same. As new countries have joined (e.g., the UK, Denmark, and Ireland in 1973), there have been some changes. But, broadly speaking, the EC income and expenditure are still substantially smaller than those of national governments. From a marketing viewpoint, this means that money and *therefore power* still rests primarily with national governments. There is nothing like the significant U.S. federal budget. Interestingly, the 1992 Maastricht agreement never really attempted to alter this situation.

TABLE 3–2
General EC Budget: 1989

Income		Expenditure	
Value-added tax	61.6%	Agriculture and fisheries	62.0%
Customs duties	23.4	Regional policy and transport	9.6
Income based on GNP	9.2		
Agricultural levies	3.0	Social policy	7.3
Sugar and isoglucose levies	2.8	Development cooperation	1.2
		Research, energy, and technology	3.5
		Administration costs	4.6
		Other	11.8
Total	100.0%	Total	100.0%
Total 1989 EC budget: US$50.68 billion			

Source: European Community, *Europe in Figures 1989* (Luxembourg: OPOCE, 1989), section 5.

This concept of EC power is also reflected in the decision-making process of the Community. Essentially, there are four main bodies:[16]

- The European Commission.
- The Council of Ministers.
- The European Parliament.
- The European Court of Justice.

The *European Commission* is appointed by national EC governments, not elected. The commissioners come from the EC countries but take an oath of allegiance to the Community. After Maastricht, all EC countries will have one commissioner. Each commissioner is given a specific responsibility area, such as competition or agriculture. The commissioners initiate, debate, and implement proposals. Overall, they have some 15,000 staff members, which is rather fewer than many European or North American metropolitan boroughs. Although they have great power, there is currently no simple democratic process to influence their thinking, nor any open access to their decision-making processes. However, since Maastricht, the European Parliament has the "right to consultation" (whatever that means) and a vote on the appointment of the Commission.

The *European Council of Ministers* represents the governments of the EC nations. It consists of the president of the Commission and the nations' prime ministers (or president, in the case of France) or, in the discussion of specific topics such as agriculture, the national ministers with responsibility for the topic under discussion. The main Council meets twice yearly as an EC summit. It has a six-month, rotating presidency across all EC countries.

The task of the Council of Ministers is to examine draft measures from the Commission and accept, modify, or reject them. Discussions are held in secret (except for the endless leaks and press conferences). Ministers have the right of veto "where any important interests of one or more partners are at stake." (But see the later discussion on how the Single Europe Act has modified this.) This makes the Council the main decision-making body within the Community. It obtains its principal authority as a result of its democratic election by the participating EC countries. But this does mean that the Council's primary source of power derives from the individual nations and not from any supranational European democracy. This is quite different from the U.S. and Canadian systems.

The ministers' work is prepared by COREPER, the Committee of Permanent Representatives, which comprises the ambassadors of the EC member states together with their advisers. It is a key link between the Commission and the member states.

The *European Parliament* still has limited powers. It can discuss most issues but has only restricted ability to initiate areas for debate. As a result of Maastricht, it does have some limited powers of veto. It also exercises joint authority over "nonobligatory" budget expenditure with the Commission. Since obligatory expenditure includes agriculture, Table 3–2 shows that there are significant areas where the Parliament is largely toothless.

The Single Europe Act allowed the Parliament additional control. If Members of the European Parliament (MEPs) propose amendments or reject bills on their second reading, the Council of Ministers must either pass the original version by a unanimous vote or drop the bill. This is called the "second reading" provision and does not appear to have been changed after Maastricht.

The *European Court of Justice* decides matters of EC law. It takes precedence over national laws and has been used increasingly for test cases to explore the provisions of the original Treaty of Rome and the subsequent Single Europe Act. (It should not be confused with the International Court of Justice in the Hague or the European Court of Human Rights in Strasbourg, neither of which has any direct connection with the EC.)

For marketing and sales, the primary time to monitor and influence events is during the formative stages of legislation. A body called the *Economic and Social Committee,* made up of trade unions and consumer and professional bodies, gives opinions on proposals to the Commission and might be a forum for making early representations. In addition, there are now a large number of professional consultancy companies based in Brussels that are capable of advising and representing commercial interests. We shall return to the matter of influencing EC decisions later in this chapter.

The decision-making process of the EC is shown diagrammatically in Figure 3–1.

FIGURE 3–1
Decision Making in the European Community

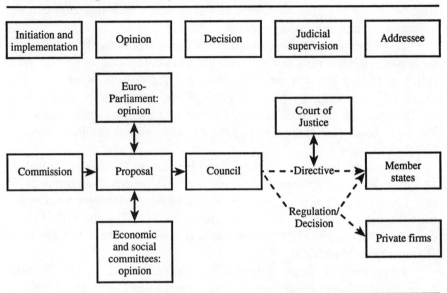

THE SINGLE EUROPE ACT AND ITS SUPPOSED MARKETING POTENTIAL

In late 1985 it was agreed by the Council of Ministers that the EC would form a "frontierless Europe" between its member states by 1 January 1993. The Single Europe Act itself went beyond breaking down the commercial barriers to form one Europe; its main elements are summarized in the following box. But, from a marketing and sales viewpoint, the key provision was the first, concerning the creation of a single European market. The rest of this section therefore concentrates on this area.

The concept of a single European market was based on a white paper prepared by the European Commission on the problems in obtaining free trade throughout the Community.[17] There were said to be three broad types of barrier:[18]

1. Physical barriers, such as intra-EC border stoppages, customs controls, and associated paperwork.
2. Technical barriers, such as meeting divergent national product

---

Single Europe Act, 1986

The eight main provisions were as follows:

1. Internal market to be established by 31 December 1992.
2. Practical steps to reduce administrative and legal constraints on small and medium-sized businesses.
3. Monetary union to be "progressively realized" but not legally binding.
4. Disparities between richer and poorer EC nations to be progressively reduced through structural, regional, and social funds.
5. European Parliament given new "cooperation" procedure to amend legislation.
6. Technological research to be encouraged within agreed-upon framework.
7. EC to take action to improve environment, raise health standards, and use natural resources wisely.
8. European cooperation in the sphere of foreign policy, with subclause encouraging cooperation on defense and security matters.

Key point: European Commission claimed that major quantified increase in EC wealth would result.

---

   standards, technical regulations, and conflicting business laws, and entering nationally protected procurement markets.
3. Fiscal barriers, especially differing rates of VAT and excise duties.

Getting an accurate feel for which barriers are the worst is difficult, but business in the manufacturing sector has supplied its own verdict. A survey specially commissioned for the research involving 11,000 businessmen showed that administrative and customs barriers, coupled with divergent national standards and regulations, top the aggravations list.

   Thus said the Cecchini report. It is a summary in readable language by the European Commission of its own research study[19] (in 16 volumes plus annexes) on the whole matter of the costs to the Community of the barriers to a single market in the EC. The research was initiated by the EC commissioner, Lord Cockfield, and directed by Paolo Cecchini, director of the EC research project on the "Cost of Non-Europe."

It was only after governmental agreement to the Single Europe Act that the European Commission asked a number of distinguished consulting companies to conduct the major study referred to above on the benefits of bringing down barriers to inter-European trade. The resulting aggregate estimate was that the creation of a single European market could lead to gains of 4.25 to 6.50 percent of Community GDP.[20] By any standards, this is a real increase in wealth. However, these estimates are significantly higher than those predicted if the North American Free Trade Association (NAFTA) comes into existence.

As a result, the Commission and the EC member states have conducted a major campaign to encourage business to exploit the benefits of the single Europe. The only difficulty with this highly successful publicity is that it may be based on a shaky analysis of the savings, according to some commentators. This matters because the responsibility for achieving such gains will rest, partly at least, on professional skills in European marketing from both sides of the Atlantic.

Geroski has written that "the 1992 programme has been the subject of an extraordinary amount of PR hype, most of which has involved exaggerating the benefits of 1992 policies and neglecting their costs."[21] Neuberger has also cast doubt on the Cecchini conclusions.[22] Cutler et al. have called the gains "exaggerated and speculative."[23] They conclude that the effect will be a once-and-for-all saving of less than 1 percent of GDP.[24] Certainly, considerable liberties were taken by the Cecchini report in using the data prepared by the consultants, as shown in Table 3–3. Any self-respecting marketing manager would be concerned that the Cecchini analysis pays little attention to such areas as:

- The words of caution from the authors.
- The representative nature of the sample.
- The reliability of some data.
- The grossing of some small sample sizes.

This may well mean that the estimates of net gains need to be treated with considerable caution. However, as Emerson and Huhne have pointed out in their later European Commission report on EMU,[20] it has subsequently emerged that Cecchini may have *underestimated* some areas of saving, so the evidence is not conclusive.

Ultimately, the prospects for the single European market will depend not on the analysis of economists but rather on the ability of marketing

TABLE 3–3
The Cecchini Report and the Cost of Non-Europe

Saving Area Identified in Cecchini Report	Cost of Non-Europe Identified by Cecchini (ECU millions)	Sample Size Used in Study of European Industry	Consultants' Original Comments on Findings
Border controls:			
Administration	7,500	467 com-	
Delays	415–830	panies and	"Treat with
Business forgone	4,500–15,000	85 road	particular
Government spend-ing on customs	500–1,000	haulers	caution"
Government protec-tion in procurement:			
Buying from cheapest	3–8,000	4,000 data-	
Foreign competition	1–3,000	base and	"No reliable
Restructuring	4–8,000	60 cases	data on
		from five	current sit-
		countries	uation"
Industry-specific:			
Financial services	21,700	N/A	"Extreme caution" ex-pressed on quantifica-tion
Telecommunications services	5,750–6,050	Five countries	"Assumed" all savings passed on!
Business services	9,200	100 com-panies and 20 trade as-sociations	
Telecommunications equipment	3–400	N/A	Current mar-ket size unclear
Automobiles	2,600	N/A	
Foodstuffs	500–1,000	20 com-panies	
Building products	2,520	50 products	
Textiles and clothing	None	—	
Pharmaceuticals	160–258	N/A	
Total with all items	216,000		

Sources: The Cecchini report from P. Cecchini, *The European Challenge 1992* (Aldershot, England: Wildwood House 1988); Cost of Non-Europe from European Commission, *Research on the Cost of Non-Europe-Basic Findings,* vol. 1, (Luxembourg, OPOCE, 1988).

and sales managers to exploit the opportunities that have undoubtedly emerged. More generally, the single Europe is certainly going to happen, so marketers, including those from North America, may as well make the most of it. But we should be wary of the claimed market potential and examine each business "opportunity" on its merits.

THE EUROPEAN ECONOMIC AREA TREATY AND ITS IMPACT ON EC AND EFTA MARKETS

In October 1991 a major new treaty was concluded between the EC and the members of EFTA: Iceland, Norway, Switzerland, Sweden, Finland, Austria, and Liechtenstein. The new accord will create a market of 380 million people, with the extra 32 million being rather more wealthy per head compared with the existing EC average, as noted in Chapter 2.

Lest we get too carried away by this prospect, we have already pointed out that Finland, Sweden, and Austria have applied to join the EC. Switzerland rejected the treaty in a referendum and so may never take part. This agreement is probably only a stepping-stone to the enlargement of the EC in 1995–1999. The president of the European Commission, Jacques Delors, is already considering the enlargement of the Community.[25]

The EC and EFTA have agreed that there will be a fairly free movement of products from 1993, with special arrangements covering food, fishing rights, energy, and coal and steel.[26] But the new European Economic Area (EEA) will be a free-trade area, not a customs union with common external tariffs.[27] Border controls will still exist between the EC and EFTA, with the costs that are implied by this. Similarly, the EC's high external tariffs, particularly on agricultural products, will not apply to the EEA.

To secure agreement, EFTA had to agree to adopt EC rules on major competition policies, company law, consumer protection, education, the environment, R&D, and social policy. It will not adopt the CAP but will keep its own agricultural regime. All the EC's banking and insurance directives will operate in EFTA from 1 January 1993. But there will be some individually agreed-upon EFTA country restrictions after that time for several years in such areas as real estate, financial services, and takeovers of banks and insurance companies.

After 1993, it might be a potential source of frustration to EFTA members to be subject to changes in laws introduced by the EC without having any right to vote on them. However, this would only become an issue if the member states were not to join the Community; the majority will. Moreover, EFTA consists of countries with a history of political stability: they are likely to seek to make change by democratic rather than revolutionary means. This solid democratic basis may make them more attractive markets than some other potential EC applicants.

After 1995, you will have to look hard to see the join between the EC and EFTA outside of agriculture. Many EFTA companies have already been investing heavily in the EC. Organization for Economic Cooperation and Development (OECD) data show that between 1982 and 1985 28.3 percent of foreign direct investment from EFTA went into the EC. For the years 1986 to 1988, this rose to 58.8 percent, with the U.S. investment figure falling from 47.6 to 12.9 percent. Sharp-eyed readers will note that none of this waited on the agreement to set up the EEA: the EC has always been more important to EFTA than the other way around.

In many respects, the real significance of the EEA agreement lies in the *political* rather than the economic sphere. The EC will grow larger in the late 1990s and will provide useful new EFTA/EC opportunities whose value will lie in the wealth and political stability of the new EC countries rather than the sheer size of their markets. This prospect will be particularly attractive for some North American companies.

THE EC'S MOVES TO INTEGRATION AND THEIR MARKETING IMPLICATIONS

In spite of the doubtful value of some of the economic analysis concerning the single European market, there are real moves toward *political and social integration* in the EC. The main reasons are the following:

- The clear commitment to move toward "ever closer union" at Maastricht.
- Underlying technological, social, and economic trends—for example, in environmental issues, telecommunication developments, and social awareness.
- The success of the EC in providing wealth and protection for its member states.

- The collapse of the COMECON block and reunification of Germany, and the need for these new, potentially powerful forces to be integrated into Europe.
- The Single Europe Act publicity and business commitment to seek its benefits.
- The desire on the part of the EC's most powerful and committed members, France and Germany, for it to happen for political reasons.

Although the move is probably unstoppable, the pace slowed in 1992 because of poor handling by EC politicians. The real question remains what sort of EC will result. Integration is need in the areas of:

- Economic and fiscal activities.
- Political decision making.

Economic and Fiscal Activities

Economic matters were helped greatly in October 1990 when the UK joined the ERM, which, as we have seen, effectively pegs the leading European currencies to the deutsche mark. Progress was hindered when the UK and Italy were forced to leave in September 1992. Further moves to bring about the single currency have now largely been agreed to. But international speculation concerning some weaker members of the ERM has taken its toll. Stability in exchange rates will not return until German interest rates are reduced or the process of monetary union completed. In the meantime, currency uncertainty is a major marketing cost for North American companies. We shall explore its effects in Chapter 10.

The other economic issue is that the EC's budget is only 2 percent of GNP. This is too low for real power, and it will need to rise if power moves toward Brussels. But this raises the dual questions of how such funds are to be raised and what they are to be spent on. These are intimately bound up with political and defense issues.

Political and Defense Decision Making

Policymaking in this area has moved ahead as a result of the Maastricht Treaty of 1992. Actions begun by the Council of Ministers have included joint positions on South African sanctions and the Yugoslavian crisis. However, the latter illustrates how difficult arriving at a common position can be given such disparate national views and with unanimous voting required. It begs the question of how decision making will be handled in an enlarged Community.

The European Commission already has a major role in trade and external relations on behalf of the EC:

- It has a specific mandate from the EC Council.
- The EC president attends the Group of Seven (the United States, Canada, France, Germany, the UK, Italy, Japan) annual summit meetings.
- The Commission coordinates aid to Eastern Europe and some African countries (under the Lomé Convention).
- It directed negotiations on the EEA and the GATT Uruguay Round.

In addition, new proposals will explore a common EC policy on defense, though this is a sensitive issue with countries such as Ireland (which is neutral) and France, which are the only two countries that are not members of NATO.

However, the European Parliament has had only a limited role in such proposals. In spite of being directly elected since 1979, MEPs have not been able to influence legislation to the same degree as their national parliamentary colleagues. Democratic representation has largely been achieved through national governments.

The European Commission has more power than the European Parliament. There has been major concern over this situation because the Commission:

- Is not elected.
- Holds its discussions in secret.
- Has little individual accountability.
- Is difficult to question (even by the European Parliament).

Since voters across the EC gave only narrow endorsement to the Maastricht Treaty and the Danes initially rejected it,[28] there have been moves to deal with these issues by taking power away from the faceless bureaucrats in Brussels. Decisions will be taken at the national level where possible (whatever that means). This is called the principle of "subsidiarity." North American marketers will wonder where future decisions will be taken.

In addition to all these problems, the Community's general administration has been criticized for being slow and awkward. It has a totally irrational system that moves EC Council meetings to Luxembourg for three months and locates the EC Parliament in Strasbourg for part of the time; both are away from the Commission's headquarters in Brussels. Additionally, the EC administration has fewer civil servants than national governments. In the moves to enhance and reform European government, these are all issues that will have to be faced.

Marketing Implications

It must be accepted that further moves toward European monetary, fiscal, and political integration will continue. The Maastricht Treaty will go ahead with or without the UK and Denmark.

Let us summarize some of the main marketing implications:

1. Most EFTA countries will join within 10 years. This will bring continued enlargement of the market.
2. With EC moves toward one market, one set of institutions, and one pan-European decision-making body on key issues, there will be a greater sense of European identity. Pan-European marketing will take on increased meaning for smaller companies. Although there is still some uncertainty over the exact nature of the EC's political structure, such a stronger identity will lend itself to pan-European branding.
3. The strength of regional independence movements around Europe—for example, in Scotland, the Basque country, and the Alto Adige region of northern Italy—is evidence of another trend. There may be a reaction in consumer goods markets in the late 1990s *against* "European" products. Some people may come to resent what they regard as the loss of national sovereignty and identity. Regional products and national brands may still have an important role in national marketing. The Danish rejection of the Maastricht treaty also supports this view.
4. Compared to the 1980s in the UK and the United States, there is likely to be greater emphasis on "social" policies because the political balance of pan-Europe is toward the left of the political

spectrum. It will probably be more interventionist, but competition is enshrined in the Treaty of Rome, so the balance is unlikely to alter radically. The main impact will be on business strategies in areas such as environmental policies, consumer protection, and labor and company law. We shall explore these areas in the later chapters of this book.

Overall, North American marketers will need to consider the possibility of pan-European markets and opportunities. But we should not be over-enthusiastic about the single Europe: for some companies, such as those operating local taxi services in Rome or Munich, marketing strategy will not necessarily be best served by a "pan-European" viewpoint. We shall explore this important topic in Chapter 4.

INFLUENCING THE EC'S POLITICAL AND BUSINESS DECISION-MAKING PROCESS

Whether on behalf of commercial organizations, trade unions, or consumer interests, European marketing may at some stage encounter the need to influence others in the EC. Without doubt, this will include North American marketers operating in the EC. The most obvious targets may be the European Commission and the European Parliament.

More specifically, under the new EC mergers and acquisitions policy, *marketing data* will provide the primary guideline by which major European mergers, joint ventures, and other deals will be approved or disallowed. North American companies such as Pepsi and General Mills, have already had to supply such data.[29] This will inevitably involve the preparation of official submissions on European competition to the European Commission. This cannot be sensibly delegated to company lawyers, economists, or accountants, however much the temptation may exist in some organizations where these professions hold senior positions. Marketing must face up to its European responsibilities.

In addition, marketing and sales may well need to make submissions on other issues likely to arise in EC decision making. For example, new European regulations concerning advertising content, product formulation, and packaging wording will all benefit from marketing input on issues such as customer requirements. It is likely that in the early years of the development of the single European market, marketing will contribute to the formative processes.

Both the EC and national governments have recognized this role and need. Structures have been set up to facilitate this process, for example, the EC's Economic and Social Committee discussed earlier. Guidelines have also been prepared. One example is that issued by the UK government,[30] in which the general advice given can be summarized as follows:

- Get in early, and do not wait until the issues have been virtually resolved.
- Work with others inside the EC and with trade associations *throughout* the Community.
- Think pan-European rather than just about narrow country interests.
- Be prepared with well-researched market information.
- Get involved, and do not just criticize.

All this is excellent guidance. Insofar as marketing represents that part of many organizations directly involved in seeking opportunities throughout the single Europe, it has a special relevance here.

In addition to the preceding general advice, the precise circumstances of European marketing development may suggest the need to appoint *professional public relations advisers* in Brussels to work with a company on a specific area of EC developments. Not every company will need this assistance, but, if the need should arise, there would be nothing more counterproductive than to bumble along in ignorance when experience professionals are available.

With regard to the new EC mergers and acquisitions legislation, it is essential that senior marketing executives acquaint themselves with the main points. Appendix III summarizes the legislation and gives some pointers on how it may need to be handled.

EASTERN EUROPEAN ISSUES

With the upheaval in 1991, not just in the former communist countries of Eastern Europe, but also in the USSR itself, the area presents many marketing opportunities and uncertainties. Many North American companies have made a start. (It should be noted that East Germany is excluded from discussion here because it is receiving special help from the wealthy western part of the reunited Germany.) Already the rush of outside advisers, consultants, and accountants has begun. We shall review some of the opportunities later in this book. We are concerned here primarily with the political implications for European marketing.

According to many commentators, including OECD and the World Bank, the Eastern European economies are likely to decline before they improve (see Figure 3–2). For marketing, this means that entering Eastern European markets in the early 1990s must be considered from a long-term perspective, roughly to the year 2000. Companies requiring rapid returns should not target these countries. For companies willing to invest over the next few years in Eastern Europe, the rewards should come to those willing to pioneer in these new economics. But, naturally, the risks will also be high.

FIGURE 3–2
Wealth Predictions for Eastern Europe
(Wealth per Person in U.S. Dollars, 1989)

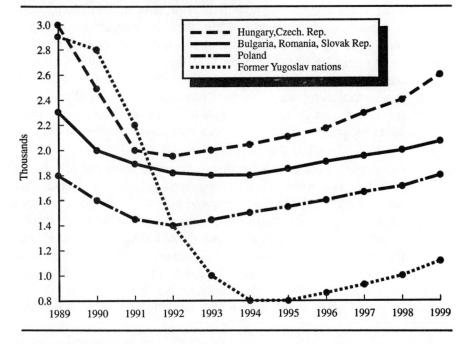

Source: Aldersgate Consultancy.

In many respects, the basic difficulty Eastern European economies face is that too many areas have to be tackled at once to pull these countries out of the morass left by years of state planning and the absence of customer choice.[31] Among the issues to be resolved in economic and political areas for virtually every Eastern European country are the following:

- *Reduction of trade barriers.* Eastern European countries have been operating behind their own tariff walls since the last 1940s. It is not enough just to tear these down, as indigenous industries will just collapse, increase unemployment, and thus reduce spending power. Similarly, there are significant trade barriers with the EC that the East would like to see reduced, but the Community has its own industries to protect, as we have already seen. Poland has already reduced many barriers, but Hungary and Czechoslovakia still have some high tariffs, even though quotas* have been reduced.

- *Privatization of state enterprises.* After the lack of competition and low investment in many state companies over many years, the issue is not whether but how quickly privatization should happen. If these were simply sold quickly, there is no guarantee that they would survive: the quality of many of the goods produced is low by Western European standards. If they are disposed of slowly, then the current inherent inefficiencies are preserved. All the major Eastern European economies have considered rapid privatization. Some, such as Hungary and Czechoslovakia, have made some progress, while others have not, partly because of fears of the social upheaval that may be caused.

- *Reform of the banking loan system.* Over the years, the state banks have lent vast sums to state enterprises. An efficient market system requires banks to lend money to potentially sound companies only. But the state banks have made loans without any market evidence of company profitability to back their judgment. Part of the difficulty with reforming the banking system is therefore to identify which loans are good and which useless. But this cannot be done until a free market operates so that companies can be valued. Hence, the danger is that banking would be "reformed"

---

*A *quota* is a quantitative restriction on imports, for example, a maximum of 40,000 imported cars in any one year. A *tariff* is a tax on products imported, such as 25 percent on the price of all imported cars, but with no restriction on the number brought in.

without knowledge about the quality of the assets banks hold—a true chicken-and-egg situation!

- *Prices governed by market demand with inflation brought under control.* The state has controlled most prices for years. Inflation in the last few years has been high and is growing. The economies are to some extent out of control and need to be stabilized to create the right conditions for growth.[32] This means strict controls over government spending. It also means that prices should no longer be set by the state but by market demand. If inflation can be controlled, this will allow loans to continue from the Group of Seven industrialized nations.[33] Allowing prices to find their own level would also provide evidence of a state company's ability to survive once it had been privatized. Most Eastern European states have therefore decided to allow prices to rise, in spite of the real difficulties this poses for many people.

Unfortunately, all these areas are interlinked, and there is conclusive economic evidence as to which should be tackled first. However, if they are all changed together, the economies of Eastern Europe may collapse completely. It is also possible that some areas will see further public protects at the massive price rises and real hardship resulting from the imposition of new, strict regimes. We do know that these countries are not wealthy. It has been estimated that for them to catch up with the EC average income over the next 10 years would require a US$420 billion investment per annum.[34] Even the former East Germany, which has benefited from massive funds from its wealthy western counterpart, received only US$30 billion in the first nine months of 1991.

Overall, there are real problems in Eastern Europe. Many Eastern European companies have no real valuation of their assets, no useful cash flow analysis, and no long-term marketing plan. Market demand for their products remains to be determined; thus, any marketing investment is high-risk. The difficulties do not stop there. Even if investment is contemplated, there is real uncertainty in the following areas:

- *Property and contract law:* Some states have still not resolved the issue of whether private companies can own property and under what law contracts can be upheld.
- *Unemployment and pension arrangements:* In Western Europe and North America, these areas are clear, but they remain unresolved in the East. They are important if companies wish to follow Tungsram, the Hungarian electric light bulb manufacturer bought

in 1989 by General Electric (U.S.). It has reduced the work force by 4,000 out of 18,000 so far.

- *Banking and financial regulation:* Leaving aside the privatization issues mentioned earlier, the banking system is still in need of a basic overhaul.
- *Accountancy and bankruptcy law:* Much remains to be resolved. In the old system it was not possible to be bankrupt, and accounting was needed for rather different purposes. Company law is also rudimentary.

In addition to these issues, the final collapse in August 1991 of the dominant and binding force in Easter European politics for the last 40 years, the USSR, has brought further political uncertainties. European issues can usefully be summarized under three headings:

1. The breakup of the USSR will lead to a number of powerful *independent republics:*
   a. Latvia, Lithuania, and Estonia may join Sweden and Finland in a Scandinavian alliance.
   b. The Ukraine is large enough, with immense agricultural and energy resources, to stand by itself.
   c. Russia stretches beyond Europe into Asia. It will need immense political skill and Western aid to survive. The fate of other former USSR republics will depend on what happens in Russia and the Ukraine.
2. There are a number of potential *border disputes* in Eastern and central Europe that need to be watched carefully:
   a. The dispute involving Serbia, Croatia, Albania, and other states may take years to resolve.
   b. The Czechs and Slovaks have finally broken their alliance, but the independence of January 1993 will bring its own difficulties.
   c. There is also a potential border dispute involving Moldavia.
3. There is also a potential *flow of refugees and immigrants* across Eastern and central Europe that will bring its own political uncertainties:
   a. From the Baltic states to Russia.
   b. From Poland to Germany.
   Though not specifically related to the collapse of the USSR, there are also two other refugee influxes that will affect Europe:

c. From north Africa to France, Spain, and southern Italy.
d. From the former East Germany to the former West Germany.

All this makes investment by North American companies difficult but not impossible.[35] Marketing will need to watch the politics of Eastern Europe because its effect on markets could be devastating. However, there is a bright as well as a dark side to this picture. The Eastern European countries represent large markets with good natural assets and well-trained people eager to improve their living standards. This all suggests that, for an acceptable level of risk for a North American company, Eastern Europe can have real market potential. But the business risks, and particularly the political risks, need to be assessed carefully.

NOTES

1. D. Gardner and D. Buchan, "EFTA Accord Sees EC on Path to Expansion," *Financial Times,* October 23, 1991, p. 1.
2. H. Arbuthnott and G. Edwards, *A Common Man's Guide to the Common Market* (London: Macmillan, 1989), p. 1.
3. Ibid., p. 7.
4. Ibid., p. 3.
5. Ibid., p. 7.
6. Ibid., p. 6.
7. R. Owen and M. Dynes, *The Times Guide to 1992* (London: Times Books, 1990), p. 48.
8. Ibid., p. 48.
9. Ibid., p. 102.
10. R. Lynch, *European Business Strategies* (London: Kogan Page, 1990), chapter 6.
11. Owen and Dynes, p. 143.
12. See, for example, *The Economist,* October 19, 1991, p. 122.
13. Owen and Dynes, p. 50a.
14. HMSO, *Annual Abstract of Statistics 1988* (London: HMSO, 1988), p. 243, table 14.4.
15. European Commission, *Eurostats: Basics Statistics of the EC,* 27th ed. (Luxembourg: OPOCE, 1990), p. 69.
16. European Community, *Europe in Figures 1989* (Luxembourg: OPOCE, 1989), section 5.

17. Commission of the EC, *White Paper on Completing the Internal Market* (Luxembourg: OPOCE, 1985).

18. P. Cecchini, *The European Challenge 1992* (Aldershot, England: Wildwood House, 1988), p. 4.

19. European Commission, *Research on the Cost of Non-Europe—Basic Findings*, vol. 1 [also gives references to all other volumes] (Luxembourg: OPOCE, 1988).

20. M. Emerson and C. Huhne, *The ECU Report* (London: Pan, 1991), p. 47.

21. P. Geroski, *1992 and the European Industrial Structure of the 21st Century* (London: London Business School, 1988), p. 22.

22. H. Neuberger, *The Economics of 1992* (London: London Socialist Group of the European Parliament, 1988).

23. T. Cutler, C. Haslam, J. Williams, and K. Williams, *1992—The Struggle for Europe* (Oxford: Berg, 1989), p. 5.

24. Ibid., p. 45.

25. *Financial Times*, October 24, 1991, p. 2.

26. "EC-EFTA Treaty: The Key Points," *Financial Times*, October 23, 1991, p. 2.

27. "Lest a Fortress Arise," *The Economist*, October 26, 1991, pp. 105–6.

28. P. Gumbel and M. Nelson, "EC Sidesteps Thorny Issues at Summit," *The Wall Street Journal*, June 29, 1992.

29. "EC Panel to Conduct Routine Probe of Pepsi, General Mills Venture," *The Wall Street Journal*, July 27, 1992, p. 84D.

30. Department of Trade and Industry, "Brussels, Can Your Hear Me?" (London: Central Office of Information, November 1990).

31. OECD, "Economic Outlook No. 50," December 1991, pp. 53–57.

32. J. Lloyd, "Yeltsin's Bitter Pill," *Financial Times*, October 29, 1991, p. 2.

33. S. Colins and D. Rodrik, *Eastern Europe and the Soviet Union in the World Economy*, (Washington, DC: Institute for International Economics, May 1991), pp. 76–80.

34. "A Survey of Business in Eastern Europe," *The Economist*, September 21, 1991, p. 25.

35. "Finding the Hand on the Purse Strings," *Financial Times*, March 20, 1992, p. 3.

4

European customers and market definition

In any area of marketing development, it is essential to examine customer needs and wants closely at an early stage. Since we have looked at European market background issues, we shall now examine European customers.

We first look at the basic question of who European customers really are and what we mean by "European." Once this has been explored, we can undertake the twin tasks of describing customers in more detail and, equally important, determining why they might purchase our products or services. This will take us into the area of market segmentation in Europe. Finally, we shall focus on customers in Eastern Europe, whose 40 years or more of zero customer choice will give the European marketer a particular problem.

The topics explored in this chapter are the following:

- A crucial strategic question: What geographical market are our customers in?
- Exploring European customers.
- Pan-European market segmentation.
- Eastern European customer issues.
- Conclusions.

A CRUCIAL STRATEGIC QUESTION: WHAT GEOGRAPHICAL MARKET ARE OUR CUSTOMERS IN?

The concept of "European" customers for local businesses, such as a baker in Paris, is meaningless for marketing strategy: the *boulangerie* will serve only its Parisian market. To the extent that some local markets are

71

affected by regulations from the EC in Brussels, it might be argued that they are "European." However, this has little to do with European *customers* and simply shows where the decision making on a legislative issue happens to have taken place. The marketing task is no more affected than if the regulation had been enacted in Pisa or Prague. The local bread shop still has local customers.

Similarly, for the multinational North American computer company selling mainframe computers across the globe with developing interests in Japan and Australasia, any particular emphasis on the "European" customer would be largely without meaning. Both here and for Parisian shopkeepers, company profitability and marketing strategy derive in the long term from market definitions outside the "European" dimension as such. This does not mean that Europe is irrelevant but rather that its customers are not the *starting point* for the development of marketing strategy.

To clarify the geographical market in which a company operates, it is useful to identify five positions along the spectrum from localization (e.g., the Parisian bakery shop) to globalization (e.g., the multinational computer company). These are shown in Figure 4–1.

This book is primarily concerned with the three areas on the right of the diagram. However, the single Europe is a *dynamic* entity that may change the markets in which organizations operate. For example, Europe as a whole has reportedly been paying higher prices in those national government procurement markets from which companies in other EC countries have until recently been excluded.[1] These markets are being forced open,[2] and this will result in their moving from being national markets to being European markets. The same dynamics will apply to other market changes in the EC over the next 10 years. The spectrum of Figure 4–1 needs to be considered for its potential from 1993 onward, as well as for the situation existing in the early 1990s.

One of the major advantages claimed for the single Europe is that it will deliver increased economies of scale in production, marketing, and R&D; we shall examine the evidence for this in Chapter 6. In brief, the Cecchini report produced evidence that, up to the present, there has been vast duplication in manufacturing throughout Europe: each country was said to have its own national producers in such items as boilers, turbine generators, and locomotives.[3] On the assumption that some of these companies can be closed down and economies of scale achieved, such savings will be realized only by the remaining companies selling across national

FIGURE 4–1
Where "European" Customers Fit

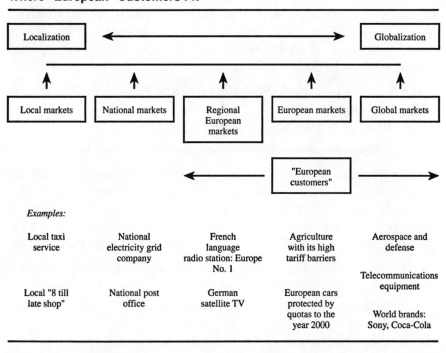

Examples:

Local taxi service	National electricity grid company	French language radio station: Europe No. 1	Agriculture with its high tariff barriers	Aerospace and defense
Local "8 till late shop"	National post office	German satellite TV	European cars protected by quotas to the year 2000	Telecommunications equipment

World brands: Sony, Coca-Cola |

boundaries. Potentially, they have the opportunity to act on a European scale. Again, we need to examine this for its European market potential, even though the reality may be a series of national customers in the early 1990s. By contrast, U.S. companies and possibly some Canadian ones should already be operating with these economies of scale.

To take this even further, Porter has pointed out that some Japanese companies use their highly competitive and large (120 million population) home market as the springboard for global expansion.[4] Europe may well need to do the same, and the single Europe might produce the same highly competitive European market that would be the basis of world expansion. In this case and on the basis of its potential, we might classify our market as a *world* rather than a European one, even though current sales were at the *national* level. We will leave until Chapter 15 the possible implications of this increased global challenge to North American companies.

In more general terms, one of the first steps in European marketing is to define the geographical market of our actual and potential customers. This is entirely consistent with Theodore Levitt's guidance from the early 1960s on careful market definition as the starting point for marketing strategy development.[5] We therefore need to undertake an analysis of current and potential customers, which, for most organizations, starts with an analysis of current sales records:

- Who has purchased? With what frequency? From what geographical source?
- Who has stopped buying? Why?
- Who are the most important customers?

To illustrate the matter, let us take the top 200 companies in Europe as defined by turnover in both public and private ownership. (Note that companies with their headquarters in North America are not included in the sample, even though they may have significant EC sales.) We can locate the sales of the top European companies according to three sources:

1. Their "home market," that is, sales derived from the country in which their headquarters are located.
2. Sales to other European countries, including EFTA and Eastern Europe.
3. Sales outside Europe, including North America.

We shall then classify the companies by their main source of business. The result is shown in Figure 4–2.[6] As companies trade beyond their home (i.e., national) market, some trade elsewhere in Europe and some trade globally. The chart shows that, regardless of size, some companies naturally have national customers, some European, and some global. The location of customers depends primarily on the type of product or market in which the organization is engaged. An important starting point for development of marketing strategy is the company's type of product or service. This is consistent with Kay's view of European strategy development: "The significance of 1992 is almost entirely to be found in measures which are industry-specific."[7]

EXPLORING EUROPEAN CUSTOMERS

If the current analysis and estimate of possible sales indicate that the potential target is "European customers," then we shall want to explore

FIGURE 4–2
Europe's Major Industries (by Source of Sales in 1988)

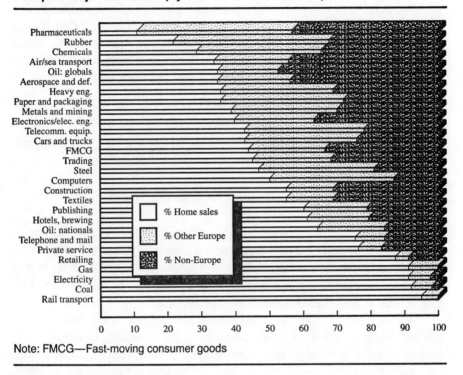

Pharmaceuticals
Rubber
Chemicals
Air/sea transport
Oil: globals
Aerospace and def.
Heavy eng.
Paper and packaging
Metals and mining
Electronics/elec. eng.
Telecomm. equip.
Cars and trucks
FMCG
Trading
Steel
Computers
Construction
Textiles
Publishing
Hotels, brewing
Oil: nationals
Telephone and mail
Private service
Retailing
Gas
Electricity
Coal
Rail transport

% Home sales
% Other Europe
% Non-Europe

0   10   20   30   40   50   60   70   80   90   100

Note: FMCG—Fast-moving consumer goods

what this means for a North American company moving or expanding into Europe.

However, we may have a problem: we know that there are vast differences across the single Europe in customer wealth, language, and culture. For example, the wealth per inhabitant in the Hamburg area of Germany in 1987 was 182.6 compared with the EC average on an index basis (i.e., EC 12 = 100); the equivalent figure for the Norte do Continente region in Portugal was 42.1.[8] One area is more than four times wealthier than the other, leaving aside the language and cultural differences! Even within EC countries, there are vast differences: in the same year, Lombardy in northern Italy had a wealth index of 137.1, while that of Calabria in southern Italy was 58.6.[9] More broadly, anyone who has visited European countries will know that there are significant differences between areas such as northern Germany and Bavaria, and Northumbria and southern England. So how do we reconcile this with our concept of the

"European customer"? Is there any such creature? This apparent contradiction is the subject of this section.

We need to start by reminding ourselves of Levitt's guidance on the formulation of international marketing practice.[10] He argued that it was more influenced by basic *similarities* between countries than by small cultural differences. Applying this view to European markets, we can usefully explore three basic areas about European customers:

1. Do they differ from other customers around the world?
2. Do they differ substantially throughout Europe itself?
3. What factors might draw them together to form the "European customer"?

Differences from Other Customers around the World

We have looked at the global context and seen that Western Europe is richer than many other areas. But when we include Eastern Europe, it is difficult to show that wealth is much higher in Europe than in newly independent countries. Moreover, we have seen that there are important differences within Europe that cannot be ignored.

When Lainder et al., Keegan, and Kotler looked at the issue of classifying world markets, they all came up with inconclusive results.[11,12,13] "Europe" did not emerge from these studies as one area; it had no meaning statistically. However, these were all historical studies up to 1980, and the substance of the single Europe has developed since then. For example, UK exports to the rest of the EC rose from 36 percent of total exports in 1976 to 48 percent in 1986.[14] The same trends applied in other EC countries. EC customers may now be distinguishable from others in the world, but this had not been proven.

Substantial Differences across Europe Itself

From the evidence in this chapter and the previous chapter, there are major disparities in the wealth and consumption patterns of European customers and companies. It might therefore be argued that the "European customer" is a myth. Indeed, Geroski argued precisely this in a paper in 1989: "The benefits to be realized from 1992 arise from the fact that opening up the internal community market will extend and enhance the diversity that can be offered to customers."[15]

There is no point in denying the evidence that Europeans are very diverse, particularly if Eastern Europeans are included. But how, then, do we explain the efforts described by Cote of multinational North American companies, such as Kellogg's in breakfast cereals, Johnson & Johnson in personal products, Johnson in household products, and Procter & Gamble in household and detergent products, to revamp their brands and promote their pan-European status?[16] Similarly, why did the U.S. and European confectionery and pet food company Mars sacrifice investment in national brands to introduce pan-European branding?[17] Are all these companies totally incompetent? And why, according to Keegan and to Terpstra and Sarathy, do many multinational companies have regional European headquarters if this is totally meaningless?[18,19]

The answer must surely be that these companies have good evidence that, in spite of the differences, there are factors that draw Europe together. There is a "European customer" who can be marketed to. In addition, the national differences that exist do not override this vision.

Factors Drawing Europe Together

We should first recognize that it is not just the single Europe that has been bringing companies together in Europe over the last 30 years. The previous chapter outlining the history of the EC supports the view that such a trend has been evident for most of this period for social, political, and security reasons.

Probably the main factor drawing markets together is *industry type*, according to the evidence of Ward.[20] There is a basic distinction between:

- Industrial goods, which are more homogeneous across Europe; for example, the European chemical industry trades regularly on a pan-European basis.
- Consumer goods, which are less homogeneous across Europe; an example is the differing tastes in bread between Germany and the UK.

Within the consumer goods area, it has been found that:

- Consumer nondurables (e.g., food and drink) were less homogeneous than consumer durables (e.g., freezers and refrigerators).[20]
- Within consumer nondurables, food and drink and general con-

sumer goods were less homogeneous than others, such as pharmaceuticals and cosmetics.[21]

It should be recognized that the preceding evidence was gathered to show what product marketing mixes multinational companies develop, rather than their specific activities in Europe. It has also been suggested that the age of the subsidiary company making new products in Europe and the level of wealth of the European country affect the extent of individual European product development: if the company is well established and there is significant local purchasing power, it is more likely that a local development program will have developed.[19]

Let us therefore investigate industry type further. What is the evidence? What types of industry make up the major activities of the EC, and what does this tell us about the similarities or differences among European customers? First we need to define the two main types of marketing:

1. *Industrial:* Buyers are industrial or government buyers purchasing products that are to be incorporated into their own products, resold, or consumed by them in their own organizations.
2. *Consumer:* The ultimate customers are, by and large, purchasing for their own consumption and purchases are smaller in scale compared with industrial markets.

(We shall consider services marketing shortly.) In essence, the marketing task is similar for industrial and consumer markets, but the *balance* of activity between the product, price, promotion, and place is likely to be different for the two types.[22]

If we then examine the main EC markets as defined by output, we can see that some are essentially industrial markets and some are consumer markets. This is shown in Figure 4–3. The evidence suggests that:

1. Many European markets are industrial, not consumer. Hence, many major markets are likely to have more homogeneous European customers, though there may still be significant differences among countries.
2. As for consumer markets, the preceding[20,21] evidence indicates that, even here, the European customer can still be identified. But there are more likely to be national variations.

If we extend the analysis to Eastern Europe and EFTA, the conclusions are unlikely to change substantially. Industrial markets such as electricity

FIGURE 4–3
Ranking of Major EC Sectors by Output (1989)

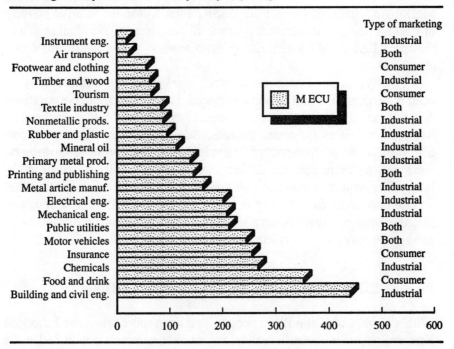

	Type of marketing
Instrument eng.	Industrial
Air transport	Both
Footwear and clothing	Consumer
Timber and wood	Industrial
Tourism	Consumer
Textile industry	Both
Nonmetallic prods.	Industrial
Rubber and plastic	Industrial
Mineral oil	Industrial
Primary metal prod.	Industrial
Printing and publishing	Both
Metal article manuf.	Industrial
Electrical eng.	Industrial
Mechanical eng.	Industrial
Public utilities	Both
Motor vehicles	Both
Insurance	Consumer
Chemicals	Industrial
Food and drink	Consumer
Building and civil eng.	Industrial

Source: European Commission, *Panorama of EC Industry 1991/92* (Luxembourg: OPOCE, 1991).

supply, mining, and machine tools have substantially the same body of European customers. There may be different national levels of wealth, but demand is unlikely to be very different.

To take industrial and consumer marketing further, the evidence suggests that European industrial marketing involves rather different relationships between customer and buyer.[23] The industrial customer may want longer-term contracts and exchanges of technical data on a pan-European scale, leading to closer cooperation and joint involvement in decision making, and there may even be networks of customers. Such relationships are more likely to exist at a pan-European level in industrial marketing than with pensioners buying basic food items such as butter and bread. They also apply to North American companies seeking European opportunities.

In European consumer markets, there may be differences between countries, and the issue is whether such differences are so large that pan-European marketing becomes impossible. The evidence suggests that in some markets there is sufficient commonality of need to form a European common customer base; the successful examples of Pepsi-Cola and McDonald's in Hungary and the USSR, even within the relative poverty of Eastern Europe, illustrate this practical proposition. We shall return to the special issues of Eastern European customers at the end of this chapter.

Finally, as for European *services marketing*, the commonality of need is certainly evident in some services. Larger European corporations deal internationally in banking, insurance, and consultancy; even the relatively poor Eastern European countries have been using Western expertise in these areas. In terms of individual European services customers, there may be more national differences. However, tourism, retail banking, and transport services are all substantially the same, indicating that service customers can often be drawn together across Europe. For example, the U.S. company American Express has used essentially the same product positioning across Europe.

PAN-EUROPEAN MARKETING SEGMENTATION

With a market of 320 million people, and even more when the European Economic Area becomes a reality, any marketing promotion aimed at the whole mass of Europe is likely to be bland in its propositions. Such a large market will lend itself to the identification of market segments, where the persuasion could be stronger and the chances of successful marketing higher. What we are seeking are therefore pan-European segments that are reachable, viable, and different, with common, identifiable needs. It is useful here to make again the basic distinction between European industrial and consumer markets.

European Industrial Markets

There are a number of cross-border customer groups already in operation:

- Twenty-five companies in a number of EC countries in the European chemical industry, including several U.S. companies, were successfully prosecuted in 1989 by the European Court for operating a PVC cartel. This can have meaning only if there was a common demand among customers for the product across Europe— segmentation within the chemical industry.

- The European airbus consortium with the active participation of companies in Germany, France, the UK, and Italy, with sales across the EC (if not profits!), has a range of short- and long-haul aircraft that meet the needs of different pan-European airline customers.
- Europe's leading commercial vehicle manufacturers—Daimler-Benz, Ford, GM, Fiat, Renault, and MAN—all produce ranges of vehicles essentially for industrial customers that sell across European borders to segments identified essentially by engine size and performance.

The European Commission's Cecchini report[3] outlines many areas of common industrial demand across Europe; the Single Europe Act is removing trading barriers in these areas. As the single market becomes a reality, the reduction in national barriers is likely to lead to other pan-European market segments that are reachable, viable, and different.

European Consumer Markets

There have been several attempts over the years to segment the 320 million EC consumers into groups that cross national boundaries and languages. The objective of such work is to form pan-European market segments that can be reached and persuaded to buy particular products or services.

One such market segment project, Socio-Styles-Systeme, initiated by Bernard Cathelat of the Sorbonne and developed by CCA International, was researched in 1989[24] and was published in English by Kogan Page in 1993. Some 24,000 people throughout Europe were asked 3,500 questions about their lifestyle (e.g., "my hero," "my boss," "my world"). From these detailed data, some 16 consumer Eurotypes were developed. The resulting categories are shown in Table 4–1.

By the time of the launch of Socio-Styles-Systeme to the press in September 1989,[25] some 15 companies, including North American companies, had already paid from £35,000 to £100,000 each, depending on how many of the European country results were purchased. Beyond the clients, it met with a mixed response, with criticism made in three areas:

1. Some researchers argued that such typologies are useless unless the cultural and historical background against which they were developed is understood in detail.

TABLE 4–1
The 16 European Socio-styles

Euro-dandy	Euro-gentry	Euro-scout
Euro-rocky	Euro-moralist	Euro-pioneer
Euro-squadra	Euro-strict	Euro-protest
Euro-romantic	Euro-citizen	Euro vigilante
Euro-olivados*	Euro-defense	Euro-prudent

*Poor agriculture workers

Source: B. Cathelat, *Lifestyles* (London: Kegan Page, 1993).

2. The results were judged by some to be so superficial as to be useless for company action.
3. European consumers might react one way in one situation, such as responding to research, and another in a different environment, such as a buying situation. Reactions depended on the context in which the questions were asked.

There are problems that lie not so much in segment viability and differences as in whether such groups are *reachable*: for example, how do you sell to a "Euro-prudent" segment when they do not even speak the same language, let alone see similar media? The contrast with North American market segmentation to English speakers is considerable. Overall, the jury is still out on this form of market segmentation across Europe. Whether it will lead to better marketing has still not been proven.

Another attempt to develop a typology for pan-European consumer marketing is that of Vandermerve.[26] She used conceptual arguments to indicate how the single Europe might evolve. Essentially, she argued that the EC single end-user markets, and the manufacturers, intermediate firms, and retailers that serve them, will change from a culturally complex set of *national* units to a new, equally complex *European* system with three main types:

1. Large *regional mass clusters* of consumers making up the mass Euromarkets and based around the main centers of population (e.g., Paris, London, Milan).
2. Medium-sized *regional niche clusters* making up the mass of customized Euromarkets (e.g., higher socioeconomic classes within the Paris/Brussels region).

3. Small *local niche markets* based on specific locality, lifestyle, and industry differences to form highly customized markets (e.g., a suburb of Hanover or Copenhagen).

By using this outline approach, it was argued, Euromarket groups could be constructed using psychographics, lifestyle, and applications approaches. Once regional or niche clusters had been identified, the next step would be to aggregate these across boundaries into regional Euro-clusters or networks.

Arguably, some of the criticisms applied to the Euro-lifestyle approach could also be made about this approach. However, the key point is that such work is being undertaken to arrive at a better understanding of European customers. None of the authors would suggest that their work is the last word, but, rather, that these are essential matters to be clarified over time.

Perhaps the best evidence that pan-European marketing is possible is the development of brands that are recognizable throughout Europe. According to a major survey undertaken in 1989, the major recognizable European brands included those listed in Table 4–2. There are four U.S. brands in the top 20.

Readers in Western Europe will immediately recognize most of the names on the list. The evidence shows that it is possible to build pan-European brands and gain the marketing strategy advantages that follow. European customers will recognize them and respond accordingly. We shall examine how to build Eurobrands in Chapter 9.

In examining Western European customer behavior, we also need to examine the issue of buying models; these have been used to explain the purchasing process in many national markets. They can be helpful in developing an understanding of the variables and a clarification of the complex customer decision-making process. Many writers have summarized work in national markets.[27,28] However, there have been no major attempts at models of the *European* buying process—or, more accurately, I have not been able to find any. Perhaps this is because of the added complexity of language and culture.

Finally, in examining European customers, there may well be some circumstances where it is evident that a pan-European approach is totally inappropriate. In this case, customer issues need to be tackled on a national basis as usual.

TABLE 4–2
Ranking of Europe's 20 Most Popular Brands

		How Well Known	Esteem
1. Mercedes-Benz	Ger	4	2
2. Philips	Neth	2	8
3. Volkswagen	Ger	3	12
4. Rolls-Royce	UK	15	1
5. Porsche	Ger	10	3
6. Coca-Cola	US	1	66
7. Ferrari	Ita	18	5
8. BMW	Ger	20	4
9. Michelin	Fra	12	26
10. Volvo	Swe	14	25
11. Adidas	Ger	19	21
12. Jaguar	UK	31	11
13. Ford	US	8	103
14. Nivea	UK	16	53
15. Esso	US	11	83
16. Sony	Jap	29	24
17. Nescafé	Swi	6	193
18. Colgate	US	9	141
19. Christian Dior	Fra	38	14
20. Nestlé	Swi	24	45

Source: Landor Associates, First Landor ImagePower Study, as quoted with permission in *European Business Strategies* (London: Kogan Page, 1990).

EASTERN EUROPEAN CUSTOMER ISSUES

For the reasons examined in Chapter 3, the peoples of Eastern European countries are likely to have different levels of wealth, different tastes, and different responses from those of Western Europe over the next few years. Centrally planned command economies have been doing their worst for the last 40 years. Marketing choice has been virtually nonexistent, and the available manufactured products have often been of poor quality. Many Eastern European customers have almost no experience of companies competing for their attention and purchases.

Even the simple wealth and consumption comparisons shown in Figures 4–4 and 4–5 need to be treated with some caution. For example, the East German car ownership statistics are for the notoriously unreliable Trabant model, which some might hesitate to call a "car" at all! However, I can testify to the superior quality of some Polish fruit jams, although

FIGURE 4–4
Eastern European Living Standards: Ownership
(Comparison per 1,000 People)

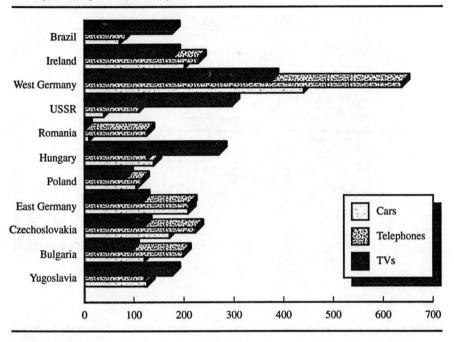

Source: EC data, 1990.

CAP later put paid to their importation into the UK, and I am looking forward to their reappearance as barriers are reduced. So not all Eastern European products are inferior.

We need to look at the underlying issues beyond the wealth and consumption statistics of Eastern Europe. Perhaps not surprisingly, since the question was previously largely irrelevant to the communist parties of the countries concerned, there is relatively little research information on what customers want in Eastern Europe. Indeed, at the time of writing, some of the unfortunate potential customers regard survival as their immediate priority. However, over the next few years, they will surely move beyond this. A marketing priority now must be to prepare for this time by research and understanding of their needs and reactions to marketing concepts.

As an example of the type of research that has already been undertaken and the consumer reactions so far elicited, it is useful to examine

FIGURE 4–5
Eastern European Living Standards: Health Statistics
(Comparison per 1,000 People)

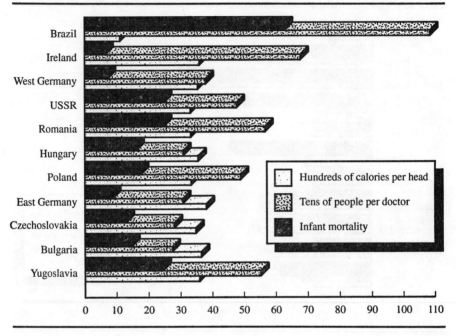

Source: EC data 1990

the work of Millar.[29] She has described some market research evidence conducted by Lintas of consumer reactions in East Germany and considered its implications for Eastern Europe. In May 1990 Lintas Hamburg, one of the largest advertising agencies in West Germany, carried out group discussions in East Germany. The objective was to find out how consumers reacted to the West and to its advertising.

Overall, the first reaction on visiting West Germany was "bewildered amazement." First impressions from the research included:

- Cleanliness.
- Functionality: "everything works."
- Friendliness of the people.

Reactions to the goods for sale were:

- They were incredible, incomprehensible to the point of being oppressive.

- Astonishment that, even at the end of the shopping day, there were still plenty of supplies of goods for sale.

With regard to the market economy, their reactions were the following:

- Being overwhelmed.
- Fear for the consequences.
- Bewilderment on how to cope with the choice available, particularly on wages of only 900 DM per month.
- The realization that a market economy could mean unemployment for some.

While some adults expressed fear and outrage, some young people hid behind the pretense of disinterest and coolness.

Subsequently, there have been reports of similar reactions among Polish workers confronted with the situation. To some extent, these reactions will subside over time, if only because they describe the first responses to a changing situation: people will no doubt move beyond being bewildered. This was confirmed when I visited Eastern Europe in the summer of 1992. Ignatius has described similar evidence in Russia.[30] Nevertheless, the evidence shows that the marketing task in Eastern Europe needs to be treated with caution: Western marketing might work well where there is a desire to experience Western products, such as McDonald's offerings in the USSR or Hungary. But in other product areas basic customer research may be required. In addition, marketing will need to take into account widespread disillusionment as the early hopes of rapidly reaching Western standards of wealth are dashed.

CONCLUSIONS

From the foregoing discussion, it is clear that European marketing strategy must consider customers in a number of stages:

1. What market are we in? What is the correct geographical definition of the customer, both actual and potential?

   It may be useful to make a broad distinction between industrial and consumer markets for the range of products or services.
2. Regardless of the industrial/services/consumer split, we need to consider the European customer by the *product market* in which we operate. Only this will provide the key to successful market-

ing strategy development and to useful customer profiling and purchase-decision analysis.

3. For industrial and services markets and some consumer markets, there may be a pan-European profile of customers. To define this, we need to seek points of similarity across Europe rather than points of difference. Within this pan-European profile, it is then necessary to investigate the purchase decision. There are at present no useful pan-European buying models.

4. When pan-European buying patterns do not indicate a clear route forward, the issue of European customers needs to be tackled on a country-by-country basis.

5. The most likely factors requiring a country-by-country approach will arise from language, culture, wealth, education, and plain, old-fashioned taste preferences. Even where the approach is pan-European, these issues may still be important: in both industrial and services marketing, personal relationships need to be built and maintained, and these are, at least partially, dependent on culture/language.

6. In Eastern Europe, marketers need to look carefully at the special characteristics of the buying decision, including the unfamiliarity with choice, the ignorance, and possibly even the resentment that may be encountered in the process. There is likely to be a need to research the buying process in these countries.

To put some meat on the bones of European customer segmentation, we shall look in the next chapter at European customer marketing research, along with other research matters.

NOTES

1. European Commission, *Research on the Cost of Non-Europe*, vol. 1 (Luxembourg: OPOCE, 1988), chapter 3.
2. L. Kellaway, "Market Beginning to Open up on Bigger Contracts," *Financial Times*, April 4, 1990, p. 14.
3. P. Cecchini, *1992—The Benefits of the Single Europe* (Aldershot, England: Wildwood House, 1988), p. 21.
4. M. E. Porter, "European Companies after 1992—Don't Colloborate, Compete," *The Economist*, June 9, 1990, p. 19.

5. T. Levitt, "Marketing Myopia," *Harvard Business Review*, November/December 1962.

6. R. Lynch, "How International Are Europe's Major Industries?" Working paper at Marketing Education Group Annual Conference, July 1991, p. 682.

7. J. Kay, *1992: Myths and Realities* (London: London Business School, 1989), p. 28.

8. European Commission, *Eurostats: Basic Statistics of the EC*, 28th ed. (Luxembourg: OPOCE, 1992), pp. 53–59.

9. Ibid, p 57.

10. T. Levitt, "The Globalization of Markets," *Harvard Business Review* 61, no. 3, (1983), pp. 92–102.

11. B. Liander, V. Terpstra, M. Y. Yoshino, and A. Sherbini, *Corporate Analysis for International Marketing* (Boston: Allyn & Bacon, 1967), pp. 67–90.

12. W. Keegan, *Multinational Marketing Management*, 2nd ed. (Englewood Cliffs, NJ: Prentice Hall, 1980).

13. P. Kotler, *Marketing Management*, 3rd ed. (Englewood Cliffs, NJ: Prentice Hall, 1980).

14. HMSO, *Annual Abstract of Statistics 1988* (London: HMSO, 1988), p. 288.

15. P. Geroski, *1992: Myths and Realities* (London: London Business School, 1989), p. 45.

16. K. Cote, "1992: Europe Becomes One," *Advertising Age*, July 11, 1988, pp. 46–47.

17. "Why Cesar Has Disposed of Mr Dog," *Financial Times*, October 1990.

18. W. Keegan, *Global Marketing Management*, 4th ed. (Englewood Cliffs, NJ: Prentice Hall, 1989).

19. V. Terpstra and R. Sarathy, *International Marketing*, 5th ed. (Orlando, FL: Dryden Press, 1991).

20. J. Ward, *The European Approach to US Markets: Product and Promotion Adaptations by European Multinationals* (New York: Praeger, 1973).

21. R. Still and J. Hill, "Multi-national Product Planning: A Meta-Market Analysis," *International Market Review* 2, no. 1 (1985), pp. 55–64.

22. M. Christopher, S. Kennedy, M. McDonald, and G. Wills, *Effective Marketing Management* (Bedford, England: Cranfield Press, 1985).

23. K. Hammarkvist, H. Hakansson, and L. G. Mattsson, *Marknadsforing for Konkurranskraft* (University of Lund, 1982). Quoted in P. Turnbull and J.-P. Valla, (London: Croom Helm, 1986), chapter 5.

24. L. Kellaway, "All Fine and Dandy in European Market," *Financial Times*, January 23, 1990, p. 12.

25. G. Bedell, "Marketeers Divided over European Lifestyle Study," *Sunday Times*, September 17, 1989, p. D14.

26. S. Vandermerve, "From Fragmentation to Integration: A Conceptual Pan-European Marketing Formula," *European Management Journal* i, no. 3 (1989), pp. 267–72.

27. Christopher et al., p. 45ff.

28. G. Oliver, *Marketing Today*, 3rd ed., (Englewood Cliffs, NJ: Prentice-Hall, 1990), chapter 4.

29. C. Millar, "Marketing in Eastern Europe: An Analysis," *Proceedings of MEG Annual Conference*, July 1990, p. 733.

30. A. Ignatius, "Life-style Pitch Works in Russia Despite Poverty," *The Wall Street Journal*, August 21, 1992, p. B1.

5

| European marketing research

European marketing research must be regarded as a vital part of the marketing task, both for the single Europe and for Eastern Europe. There are three main reasons for undertaking such research:

1. To identify new European *opportunities*, not only their size but also the reasons why they are attractive.
2. To assist in the *understanding* of existing European marketing processes.
3. To provide data for the *control* of existing and new European marketing activities.

In the last chapter, we saw that "European" customers can vary from separate, disparate groups to those with a common European identity. There may be real problems in researching the smaller groupings on a European scale. In addition, European marketing research will be assessing markets that are still evolving—in some cases, quite rapidly. It may therefore not be possible to provide precise answers to business questions. However, European research should be able to produce important customer evidence from which to develop the answers. If it does not, it will not be cost-effective.

We shall tackle the subject under the following headings:

- European marketing research: some key issues.
- EC current research activity.
- Special issues in European marketing research.
- Data sources for Europe.
- Organization and decision making for European marketing research.
- Marketing research cost-effectiveness: conclusions.

EUROPEAN MARKETING RESEARCH: SOME KEY ISSUES

Whether research is for Eastern or Western Europe, four key questions need to be explored and answered at the outset:

1. What objectives need to be met by the research?
2. What is the organization's commitment to Europe?
3. What resources are available for European marketing research?
4. What is the marketing research task?

Before any research is undertaken by North American organizations, these areas need to be resolved. European marketing research involves resources, time, and usually money. It must therefore be cost-effective, and this, in turn, implies a clear understanding of why it is being undertaken and against what commercial background and commitment.

In practice, there is evidence that some companies make European marketing decisions without the benefit of marketing research. Diamontopolous et al. researched small and medium-sized Finnish design companies in 1989 and established that over 50 percent did not use any export research.[1] Yet they still derived the same proportion of sales from exporting as companies that did use research, and their relative profitability was about the same. The study also showed that, among the sample, export research *users* were more likely to be the following:

- Larger companies.
- Companies that served more export markets.
- Companies that perceived themselves to be more competitive in some elements of the export marketing mix.

A similar survey undertaken of a broader range of French companies by Whitelock et al. produced not dissimilar results: 9 out of the 15 companies in the industries surveyed, ranging from cars to champagne, did not employ *primary* marketing research; that is, they did not commission their own special research.[2] However, this did not mean that such companies were ignorant of their markets: they still used *secondary* marketing research sources such as:

- Knowledge of employees from their own company.
- Questioning of potential buyers at exhibitions.
- French government data sources.

To some extent, the market and its customers affect the type of research undertaken. If it is a European consumer mass-market product, then anecdotal evidence from a few customers will be of limited value. In European industrial markets, which usually involve networks of relationships to make sales, market knowledge is often obtained through current activities in the market.[3] In European industrial marketing, formally commissioned market research reports may be of less value than the direct information exchanges that take place to clarify how markets work, how they are influenced by various external factors, and how the buying network is structured. In particular, such current activities are important in learning about specific customers.[4]

More generally, we do not have much evidence on how firms actually face the key research issues in Europe. However, the experiences described above are consistent with the work of Cavusgil on the broader subject of international marketing research.[5] Cavusgil suggested that the use of export marketing research, including that undertaken by North American companies, depends on the following:

- The stage of a company's internationalization process.
- The nature of a company's products (e.g., industrial or consumer).
- Company size.
- Dependence on foreign markets.

Although such research findings are not specific to either the EC or Eastern Europe, they are largely consistent with our conclusion in the previous chapter that the degree of European customer internationalization (i.e., global, European, regional, or national) is a starting point for all company activity, including marketing research in Europe.

North American companies moving into Europe without marketing research are taking a higher risk in relying on subjective factors to guide their marketing. This may be beneficial in terms of rapid response to opportunities and lower cost, but it runs the risk of wasting resources or missing European opportunities.

Extending the comments made by Christopher et al. to the EC,[6] some types of field market research in Europe may alert sharp competitors to product developments being pursued by the company. When working as a marketing manager in desserts for a U.S. multinational company in the late 1970s, I recall picking up the first warning that a leading European multinational was experimenting with fresh, long-life desserts that would not only be competitive but were technically more advanced than anything in my own company. The multinational had made the mistake of running a large field test in a neighboring town.

In general, in considering key European marketing research tasks, it may be helpful to divide them into two parts:

1. Those where we have no knowledge or experience of the country at all.
2. Those where we have some existing contacts or marketing involvement.

This approach has the twin advantages of making use of any existing information and recognizing that the nature of the entry decision is likely to be different between the two kinds of tasks. On this basis, we can summarize possible European marketing research tasks as shown in Table 5–1.

EC CURRENT RESEARCH ACTIVITY

As a starting point for examining marketing research options open in Europe, it is helpful to look at research activity currently undertaken in the EC. This information is not available for Eastern Europe. To do this, we can use the basic distinction made by the European Commission itself between *ad hoc research*, that commissioned and undertaken as the occasion arises, and *continuous research*, that conducted on a regular basis.

According to European Commission/ESOMAR (European Society for Opinion and Marketing Research) evidence, marketing research within the EC has been subject to an evolutionary process over the last 20 years.[7] In the early years of market research for a new product or service, there was heavy reliance on ad hoc research; this often involved problem solving and the assessment of market opportunities. It may have been accompanied in some EC countries by the use of generalized omnibus surveys and small-scale qualitative research.

As marketing activity has increased in Western Europe, there has been a major change from ad hoc to continuous research. Almost inevitably, this has come from syndicated services, often offered by one or two dominant suppliers, some of which are North American. In more developed EC markets, continuous research may now account for over 25 percent of total market research expenditure, with another 15 percent being spent on other regular services.[8] In both cases, such services substitute for ad hoc studies.

The above data need to be read in conjunction with the associated estimate that some 50 percent of all EC research comes from manufacturers, particularly for consumer products (see Table 5–2). It is, of course, consumer goods manufacturers who are primarily interested in repeat purchase business, which is often monitored on a continuous basis.

Total 1989 EC expenditure on marketing research has been estimated at US$2.04 billion, with the UK accounting for 28 percent of the

TABLE 5–1
Possible Tasks of European Marketing Research

Marketing Decision	Potential Research Areas
For Totally New European Countries	
• Do we enter? If so, which countries?	Assess Europe against North American opportunities: share, competition, costs and risks involved, politics, etc. Rank potential markets for attractiveness and profitability. Develop detailed trade statistics.
	In Eastern Europe, assess country infrastructures: telecommunications, banking, distribution, energy.
• Do we enter on a pan-European or country-by-country basis?	Assess customers: global, European, regional, national. Analyze companies already selling in the markets.
• How do we enter identified countries?	Size of market, trade barriers, competitors, suppliers, government attitudes and contracts, alliances.
• What marketing mix do we employ in identified countries?	Competitive activity and attitudes to new entrants, media available and restrictions, price/value survey, quality.
For European Countries Where We Already Undertake Some Marketing	
• Seek new opportunities? Where?	Market size and trends, technical trends, supplier analysis, distributor studies.
• Monitor competitors	Competitor trends and business performance.
• European Commission initiatives	Monitor and seek representation, consider environmental and other issues, assess national government developments.

TABLE 5–2
Sources of Revenue for EC Market Research Organizations in 1989

Manufacturers	50%
Service industries	15%
Advertising agencies	8%
(Quasi-) governmental	8%
Retailers/wholesalers	3%
Other research organizations	4%
All others (including media owners)	12%

Source: European Commission, *Panorama of EC Industry 1991/92* (Luxembourg: OPOCE, 1991).

total and Germany next with 22 percent.[9] France and Italy were the next two largest countries, with 19 percent and 12 percent, respectively.

Turning to Eastern European countries, the same quality of evidence is not available. According to 1988 EC data, market research activity in Eastern Europe was at that time virtually nonexistent.[8] Since then, there has been regular polling of the popularity of politicians, and some ad hoc in-depth interviews have been conducted. It is likely that the situation will change in these countries during the 1990s; the early years are likely to concentrate largely on ad hoc studies.

As a consequence of the much earlier stage of a market demand–oriented society in Eastern Europe, research respondents may have very different reactions to marketing and its research process from those in the West; we have already reviewed the evidence of nervousness, bewilderment, rejection, and incomprehension reported by Millar.[10] Such reactions will have important repercussions in European marketing research: the phrasing of questions, the piloting of questionnaires, the training and deployment of interviewers, and sensitivity to the aspirations and desires of respondents will all need to be reconsidered for Eastern European research.

SPECIAL ISSUES IN EUROPEAN MARKETING RESEARCH

As the astute reader will have noticed, this chapter has so far avoided the thorny problem of *pan-European* market research: the preceding material relates largely to individual countries, and the unwritten assumption has been that it is possible to take data from one country and compare them with another. Unfortunately, unless the research has been especially commissioned on a common research basis across Europe, this assumption may be false. Certainly, there are a number of potential pitfalls, which we shall examine next. North American market research data are much more cohesive by comparison.

European Data Comparisons

An obvious starting point for any EC analysis would be to employ the data prepared and published by the European Commission under the general title *Eurostats*. There is a vast range of material broken down by country region as well as nationally. However, in some cases, the information has significant problems because it is gathered by individual member governments on behalf of the EC. Unfortunately, the same standard definitions for categories of data are not employed by all governments.

Thus, for the EC we have the following data evaluation problems:

- *Demographic data* are not always collected by government bodies. Some countries use private research agencies, which do not have statutory authority or enforced participation, making the data less reliable.
- *Educational levels* can be used as a measure of social status, but various means of defining levels exist throughout Europe: examinations, numbers of years at school, and college graduate status may all be employed.
- *Marital status* can be important for identifying some household trends. Some Roman Catholic countries, such as the Irish Republic, recognize only three statuses: single, married, and widowed. This ignores those who are divorced or cohabitating or those who are members of a single-parent family.
- *Country source* classification can be a problem with pan-European financial transactions. For example, a funds transfer in which an Anglo-American holding registered in the Netherlands takes up credit in Luxembourg to finance an acquisition in Spain will be recorded as a Dutch direct investment. If the credit is long term, it may also be recorded as a Luxembourg investment.[11]
- *Social class* is measured on different scales in EC countries, such as by occupation, educational attainment, and wealth. These will not necessarily produce the same ranking.

- *Advertising and promotional expenditures* data, according to the EC Commission, may be incomplete or doubtful in four ways:
  —Some countries use estimates; others use actual data.
  —Media coverage for compiling data is not always complete; for example, cinema advertising may be excluded, and print media may cover only major titles.
  —Some countries include commissions paid to advertising agencies and costs of producing the advertising in turnover data; others do not.
  —Classified advertising expenditure (e.g., job advertising and houses for sale) is included only in some countries.[12]

So much for the single Europe! North American companies will need to be wary.

ESOMAR publishes material that assists in making cross-country comparisons within the EC: a contact address is provided after the references to this chapter.

With regard to Eastern European countries, the differences are even more marked, if the data are available at all. Certainly, there is no coordinating institution like the European Commission available to gather marketing data. The OECD "Economic Outlook" and the World Bank annual report make useful comments on the lack of available data and the major weaknesses in the comparative data that exist.[13,14] The matter of data sources for Eastern Europe is discussed later in this chapter.

Consumer, Industrial, and Services Research

In researching Europe, a clear distinction in the issues that will arise in research needs to be made between the different types of market:

- *Consumer markets* may involve demographic and population problems, and interviewer and questionnaire structuring problems. There may well be difficulties in identifying any form of "European" customer or user in some markets.
- *Industrial markets* often do not involve the large-sample interviewing of consumer markets. They thus avoid some of the difficulties just cited. They may need to explore a much closer relationship between buyer and seller: both may be involved in the buying decision and be particularly interested in developing long-term relationships.[15] This means that the marketing research is likely to be characterized by:

—Longer time scales.
—More cooperative research techniques.
—Fewer definitional difficulties.
These comments apply both to the EC and to Eastern Europe.

- *Service markets* are conditioned by the people providing the service, who influence greatly the value and benefits offered by the service approach. This makes marketing research in service industries more difficult, particularly in the following respects:
—Attitudes in service organizations toward marketing research.
—Quality of secondary data sources.
—Intangibility of services (i.e., they can be difficult to define).

Although these comments can be applied to all services markets and not just those in Europe, they will certainly make the European task more difficult.[16] Eastern Europe has special problems after 40 years or more of the absence of a tradition of service; the concept may not even be understood, so care will be needed.

Questionnaire Design and Responses

The use of questionnaires is likely to involve problems in three main areas:[17]

1. *Languages*: Research questionnaires are expensive to translate and may lose something in the process. There are nine official languages in the EC alone.

2. *Social organization*: This encompasses the role of individuals, groups, and organizations in society. This can affect not just consumer research (e.g., the role of the woman in the home), but also industrial research, where the study of interrelationships between customer and seller require an understanding of social patterns, values, and expectations (see Chapter 4).

3. *Obtaining responses*: Among businesspeople, the level of research response may depend on the willingness to reveal data. For example, in Italy, it used to be said that each company kept three sets of accounts: one for the tax authorities, one for the shareholders, and one for the truth! Which set will be revealed in research? In addition, respondents in some countries are more willing than those in other countries to talk about certain issues; for example, Scandinavians have a more open attitude toward sexual matters than the British.

Availability of Professional Researchers

Trained, professional researchers are essential for high-quality marketing research: there is no point in collecting data if their accuracy is doubtful. The EC is reported to have some 23,000 permanent employees of market research companies in 1989 and over 100,000 freelance interviewers.[18] Thus, in general terms, there is no shortage of research personnel in EC countries.

The situation is totally different in Eastern Europe. There is simply no professional background in this area: the central planning officials of the last 40 years have not used any subtle means to determine what people would like to buy. Other methods of obtaining data are therefore needed. Hill[19] investigated this issue for the former USSR in 1978 and suggested the following substitutes, which might be adapted for use elsewhere in Eastern Europe:

- Meetings with Soviet import organizations.
- Involvement in trade exhibitions in the USSR.
- Sessions with state committees in a region.
- Setting up an office in a particular state.
- Taking part in trade negotiations.

Such approaches would be more likely to work with industrial than with consumer marketing. All of them would suffer from the dead hand of continuing state bureaucracy. In addition to these approaches, it may be possible to use published data as a substitute for information that is not available. For example, the number of TV sets per household in the USSR, which is published,[20] provides some indication of TV component availability (or the lack of it) in that country.

Data Sources for Europe

There are five main marketing research sources for Europe:

1. *World Data*: In seeking opportunities in both the EC and Eastern Europe, it is essential to consult basic country trade statistics. These include:
   a. UN statistics: import/export data for each country published annually.
   b. OECD: biannual survey of economies for major Western countries plus some comment on Eastern European countries.

    c. World Bank report: can provide basic trends and insights into world economies.

2. *EC data*: There is now substantial material from the European Commission. Among the leading sources are the following:
   a. *Eurostats*: both summary statistics and individual areas.
   b. *Panorama of EC Industry*: useful pan-European market summaries for many industrial goods and services, but not so useful for consumer goods and products.

3. *National data*: Many governments now publish useful European information, for example:
   a. UK: *Annual Abstract of Statistics*, as well as on-line and off-line computer databases.
   b. France: Centre Français du Commerce Extérieur (statistics).

Unfortunately, U.S. and Canadian authorities publish only a limited amount of EC data. However, data for individual countries are widely available.

4. *Industry sources and organizations*. There is a very wide range of information available from these sources (more details are listed in Bennett[21]), which include:
   a. Chambers of commerce.
   b. Industry associations (many with pan-European links are listed in *Panorama of EC Industry*).
   c. Exhibitions—an excellent source.
   d. Personal visits.

5. *Publishing sources*: Publications are another rich source of marketing information. The following are only a few examples:
   a. EC: *Cronor's Europe*,[21] *Financial Times*, "Europe's Top 500 Companies,"[22] *Fortune's* Top 500 annual survey.
   b. Eastern Europe: *Business Eastern Europe* from Business International and PlanEcon Business Reports. Bilmes[23] has produced a useful summary of published sources in Eastern Europe.

ORGANIZATION AND DECISION MAKING FOR EUROPEAN MARKETING RESEARCH

An important issue for North American companies is how to organize the responsibility for specific tasks in marketing research: should the initiative for research rest at the country level or at European headquarters level? Naturally, for companies that are simply exporting from a home country, the same questions do not arise. But, as national offices are set up elsewhere in Europe, such companies may have to face these issues. The pros and cons associated with each level of decision making are summarized in Table 5–3.

There are no easy solutions to this problem. I worked in Unilever's Economics and Statistics (E&S) department more years ago than I care to admit; essentially, it was the UK market research headquarters of one of Europe's largest companies and a true multinational, with some 40 percent of sales outside Europe.

Unilever faced the issue of how to organize the balance of its research activity. The E&S department had around 70 people who were mainly professionals and experts in key market areas. There was thus much concentrated expertise to support worldwide decision making. In addition, there was a major library and database in London. While international data were collected and coordinated by the E&S department from the Unilever national operating companies, each main company was also able to take the initiative in its own market research.

For some North American companies, the balance of decision making may lie elsewhere. It will depend on the number of markets involved and their size, the customers and the purchase decision, and the scale of decision making required: global, European, regional, or national.

TABLE 5–3
National versus European Headquarters–Level Market Research

For	Against
National	
Closer to market data	May duplicate other studies
Can react to local concerns	Cannot take broad, pan-European view
European Headquarters	
Takes true international view	Too far away
More concentrated expertise for comment and evaluation	Unable to provide detailed guidance
Closer to HQ strategy so central issues known	Slow decision making
No duplication of research	

MARKETING RESEARCH COST-EFFECTIVENESS: CONCLUSIONS

In practice, all European research has a cost in terms of time as well as salaries and fees for outside market research agencies. Perfect knowledge is usually not necessary for making decisions on Europe. All marketing research therefore must be evaluated against these costs and against the contribution that will be made to the *European decision-making* process. Often one of the key problems is not the shortage of data but rather what to make of the excess: "we need to market-research the issue" may even be a substitute for making marketing decisions.

European market research in companies must be cost-effective. Researchers are more likely to be so if they not only use well-developed research techniques but also:

- Use existing distributors as a source of information.
- Seek out material at trade fairs.
- Visit the countries concerned.
- Investigate the hidden barriers to entry.

Ultimately, cost-effective European research means undertaking only studies that have usable results, not those that are merely interesting or chosen through some equally vague criterion. When used effectively, research is a powerful weapon for continuing improvement in European marketing and for the basic development of European marketing strategy, the subject we examine in the next chapter.

NOTES

1. A. Diamantopolous, B. B. Schlegelmilch, and C. Allpress, "Export Marketing Research in Practice: A Comparison of Users and Non-users," *Journal of Marketing Management* 6, no. 3 (1990), p. 257.
2. J. Whitelock and S. Bainbridge, "The Practice of International Marketing Research," *Proceedings of MEG Conference*, July 1991, p. 1306.
3. J. Johanson and J. E. Valne, "The Internationalisation Process of the Firm," *Journal of International Business* 8, no. 1 (1987), pp. 23–32.
4. J. Johanson and B. Wootz "The German Approach to Europe." In P. Turnbull and J.-P. Valla, *Strategies for International Industrial Marketing*, (London: Croom Helm, 1986), chapter 3.

5. S. T. Cavusgil, "International Marketing Research: Insights into Company Practices," *Research in Marketing*, 7, (1984), pp. 261–288.

6. M. Christopher, S. H. Kennedy, M. McDonald, and G. Will, *Effective Marketing Management* (Bedford, England: Cranfield Press, 1985).

7. European Commission, *Panorama of EC Industry 1990* (Luxembourg: OPOCE, 1990), pp. 20–28.

8. European Commission, *Panorama of EC Industry 1991/92* (Luxembourg: OPOCE, 1991), pp. 27–59.

9. Ibid; pp. 27–58.

10. C. Millar, "Marketing in Eastern Europe—An Analysis," *Proceedings of MEG Conference*, July 1991, p. 733.

11. European Commission, *Panorama of EC Industry 1990*, p. 83.

12. European Commission, *Panorama of EC Industry 1991/92*, pp. 27–42.

13. For example, see OECD, "Economic Outlook No. 50," December 1991, p. 56.

14. For example, see World Bank, *World Development Report 1991* (Washington, DC: World Bank, 1991), p. 270.

15. M. T. Cunningham, "The British Approach to Europe." In P. Turnbull, and J.-P. Valla, *Strategies for International Industrial Marketing* (London: Croom Helm, 1986), chapter 5.

16. D. Cowell, *The Marketing of Services* (Portsmouth, NH: Heinemann, 1984), chapter 5.

17. V. Terpstra and R. Sarathy, *International Marketing* (international edition) (Orlando, FL: Dryden Press, 1991), chapter 7.

18. European Commission, *Panorama of EC Industry 1990*, pp. 20–28.

19. M. R. Hill, "Desk Research Methods for the Soviet Capital Goods Market," *European Marketing Journal* 13, no. 5 (1979), p. 271.

20. European Commission, *Eurostats: Basic Statistics of the Community* 27th ed. (Luxembourg: OPOCE, 1990), p. 283.

21. R. Bennett, *Selling to Europe* (London: Kogan Page, 1991) chapter 2.

22. "Europe's Top 500 Companies," *Financial Times*, January 13, 1992.

23. L. Bilmes, "Guides to the New Frontier," *Financial Times* 6 (December 1991) (business book supplement), p. 7.

Contact address: ESOMAR: European Society for Opinion and Marketing Research, Central Secretariat, J J Viottstraat 29, 1071, JP Amsterdam, The Netherlands. Telephone: +31 20 664-2141.

6

Developing the options for European marketing strategy

In studying the development of European marketing strategy, we start by taking an overview of the whole process. We then look at the factors that will deliver profit and meet other objectives of the organization. We also need to examine competitive advantage and its implications for Europe; market-based competition is explicitly supported in the Treaty of Rome. In addition, to ensure that we have chosen the best strategy, we need to look beyond the obvious solutions. Essentially, these subjects add up to an exploration of the *marketing strategy options* available. We shall leave the task of selecting among the options until the next chapter and the matter of developing the immediate entry and country strategies until Chapter 8.

The subjects explored in this chapter are the following:

* The European marketing strategy development process.
* Identification of European critical success factors.
* Sustainable competitive advantage in Europe.
* Developing the options.
* Special strategies for the EC and the European Economic Area.
* Special strategies for Eastern Europe.

THE EUROPEAN MARKETING STRATEGY DEVELOPMENT PROCESS

Any North American marketer relying on a "formula" for European strategy development is highly likely to fail: there is no such recipe. The process is complex, subtle, and wholly dependent on the unique circumstances of an organization's starting point and history. Nevertheless, this does not mean that the process cannot be structured with clear stages. For example, Jauch and Glueck indicate that it is usual to start with the organization's objectives which may be subsequently modified by the strategy development process.[1] Let us follow the outline process through from this point.

As Ohmae has observed, one of the crucial early aspects of strategy development is to pose the right questions.[2] This means understanding those factors in the European marketplace that fundamentally influence the objectives, such as profit, earnings per share, sales growth, market share, and other, similar measures of service satisfaction in the public sector. For the sake of brevity, we shall refer to the answers to such questions as the market *critical success factors* (CSFs) (Ohmae calls them "key factors for success"). We shall examine how these might be derived in the next section.

For the next stage of the strategy development process, we need to remind ourselves of its whole purpose. Most organizations, both in Europe and North America, compete for customers. Competition is fundamental to articles 85 and 86 of the Treaty of Rome.[3] Much of the reason for marketing strategy development is to achieve long-term survival and growth for the organization, and this is more likely if we are able to develop *sustainable competitive advantage* for the company. Over the last few years, Ohmae, Porter, Day, and many other writers have developed and set out the analytical techniques in this area.[2,4-6] We shall explore these for Europe in the second section of this chapter.

In principle, such writers refer to three main strategy areas that need to be explored: the *company* or organization for whom the strategy is being undertaken, its actual and potential *customers*, and its *competitors*. We shall add a fourth area in this book: *channels* of distribution. Our particular perspective of European marketing strategy will benefit from highlighting this aspect, rather than hiding it within the customers or competitors definition. The consideration of the complexities of European marketing strategy using these "four C's" will lead to the development of strategic options for the company. This process is shown diagrammatically in Figure 6–1; note that it is only an enlarged and elaborated version of part of the diagram used at the beginning of this book. The fourth section of this chapter looks at option development.

Having developed the basic options for European markets—and, frankly, this process is, in principle, no different from developing the options for any other market—we shall then look at special strategy op-

FIGURE 6–1
European Marketing: Decision-making Process
(Enlarged Section on Strategy Development)

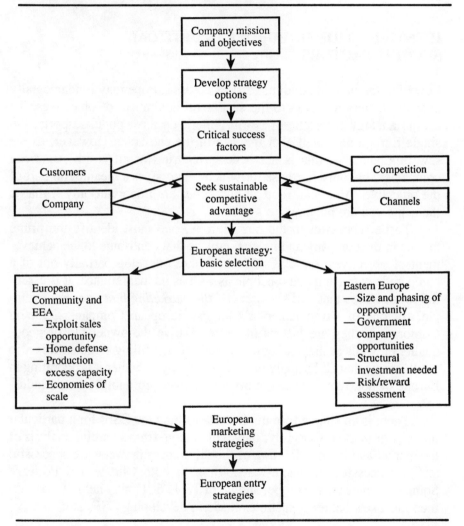

tions for Europe. As with the previous chapters, we shall split this into Western and Eastern Europe because the markets and the associated risks are so different. The main areas for consideration under this heading are shown in Figure 6-1. We tackle these issues in the last two sections of this chapter.

In summary, we have the outline of a process for developing the options for European marketing strategy. But no one should think of this as a 'formula': as we shall shortly see, it is far too imprecise for that.

IDENTIFICATION OF EUROPEAN CRITICAL SUCCESS FACTORS

Lowering the national trading barriers across Europe may fundamentally alter the factors that lead to the successful attainment of objectives. To use an analogy from one of North America's most popular sports, the single Europe may well alter the size of the end zone. However, as we saw in Chapter 4, this is not necessarily true for all North American companies, but only for those for which "Europe" is a meaningful part of the objective. American football end zones are important only if that is the game you are playing!

To be successful in the new Europe, one must identify the prime factors in the company and its marketplace that contribute to the achievement of objectives: the CSFs. Because these develop partially out of a company's own capital and people as well as its marketplace, it is essential to recognize that CSFs *go beyond the marketing function*. For example, for one of North America's largest European Companies, Exxon Corporation, they are just as likely to involve the ownership of good-quality oil wells as the marketing of well-located filling stations. It is also worth noting that CSFs apply in every company, whether it is operating in Europe or not: they are the factors that deliver profitability in the industry.

There is no simple formula for establishing the CSFs for a particular industry or market. Certainly, they will emerge from a careful analysis of the market and the highlighting of the differences between the successful and unsuccessful companies, according to both Ohmae and Porter.[2,4] Some examples from Europe, shown in Table 6–1, may help. Two common mistakes that are sometimes made in developing CSFs are:

1. Showing just one main factor for a market: it is usually a *combination* of three or four key factors that make up the CSFs. Table 6–1 is misleading in this respect.
2. Producing a "recipe ingredients list" of every conceivable factor that could possibly contribute to CSFs. Only *critical* factors should be listed.

TABLE 6–1
Examples of Critical Success Factors in European Industry

Critical Success Factor	Market	Example Companies
Raw material sources	Oil	British Petroleum (UK) Mobil (US)
Product design	Aircraft	Dassault (Fra) McDonnell Douglas (US)
Capital-intensive production	Chemicals	Du Pont (US)
Product range	Some food	Nestlé (Swi) Philip Morris (US)
Service	Commercial vehicles	Ford (US) Daimler-Benz (Ger)
Location	Fast food	McDonald's (US)
Sales force	Insurance	Allianz (Ger)

The CSFs are usually devised by a multifunctional team in a company, rather than merely by the marketing department. Such a team may well take several weeks to reach their conclusions, but the effort is worthwhile. *The strategy options that follow then need to address these areas.* CSFs thus set much of the agenda for European strategy development. But there is another factor that needs to be examined before considering option development: sustainable competitive advantage.

SUSTAINABLE COMPETITIVE ADVANTAGE IN EUROPE

As we have already seen, competition is encouraged by the single European market basic treaty. The resulting laws are directed at both private firms and national governments. The European Commission is charged with the task of ensuring that community law on competition is adhered to. However, it is allowed some discretion where there are special national needs, as, for example, during an economic recession.[3] The two principal competition clauses in the Treaty of Rome that guide and shape competitive strategy for individual companies are as follows:

1. Control of any agreements between companies or governments that "have as their object or effect the prevention, restriction or

distortion of competition within the common market" (article 85).

2. Prevention of any enterprise with a "dominant" position from abusing that position (article 86).

The principles are not unlike U.S. legislation. From a marketing viewpoint, we need to accept that such laws mean that competition is inevitable in the EC: the key issue is therefore how to gain the maximum benefit. Hence, the main reason for developing European marketing strategy is likely to be to gain a sustainable advantage over competitors.

From the work of Porter and others, sustainable competitive advantage can be seen, in simple terms, as deriving from one of three main routes:[7]

1. *Low-cost leadership*: A company has lower costs than its competitors. It seeks to maintain this position by further investment and innovation. It may use its position not just to reduce its prices but to invest in promotion and market development. *Example*: Japanese car manufacturing operates at lower costs than U.S./European operations such as Ford and General Motors[8]—hence the European nervousness over reducing quotas on Japanese cars imported into the EC by the year 2000.

2. *Product differentiation*: A company produces products for a mass market that are significantly different from competitors in their performance, quality, or some other aspect of the product recognizable as important by the customer. *Example*: The new laundry detergent "Radion" has been launched across much of Europe by Unilever. Unlike other washing powders, it claims to remove both dirt and odors. It has taken market share from its international rival, Procter & Gamble (U.S.).

3. *Niche markets*: A company produces a product or service that fills a special need of a small part of the total market. A niche can be based on either lower cost or product differentiation. *Examples*: any of the up-market global brands of specialist clothing and fashionwear, such as Dunhill, Yves Saint Laurent, and Gucci.

Each of these three areas has a customer dimension: cost leadership is meaningful only when it is significant to customers; product differentiation and niche markets must also be explored in a customer context. The importance of this in the new Europe is that the *customer base* may well have changed, or be about to do so, as the single market develops. This means that marketing strategy must be looked at afresh. Sustainable competitive advantage may change as a result of the single European market or Eastern European opportunities and threats.

Four principal areas need to be examined by North American Companies:

1. New European customers may mean:
   a. Larger markets: economies of scale.
   b. Geographically more distant customers.
   c. More diverse customer needs and tastes.
   d. New market segments.
   e. Different stages in the product life cycle.
   f. Different combinations of marketing product, price, promotion, and place in different EC countries.
2. New European competitors may mean:
   a. New competitors with lower costs.
   b. New competitors with higher quality or a better-differentiated product.
   c. New niche market opportunities or threats.
   d. New allies and partners.
3. New European channels to the market may mean:
   a. New or partially new routes to customers.
   b. Existing routes totally dominated by established competitors.
4. European national issues will almost certainly mean:
   a. The skills and resources of some countries will put them ahead in ways that will be difficult to overcome; for example, the Netherlands' cheap off-shore natural gas gives it a competitive advantage in areas where this resource is used as a feedstock or for cheap energy;
   b. Government support will act to cushion competitive pressures and support industries that might otherwise fail—for example, EC support for the consumer electronics industries of France (Thomson SA) and the Netherlands (Philips NV).

We shall explore strategic options for Europe in more detail in the next section, but what do they imply for developing sustainable competitive advantage in Europe? Where might it be obtained? To answer these questions, we can usefully extend and apply the ideas developed by the Japanese strategist Ohmae[9] to a European context. European sustainable competitive advantage might be achieved by the following methods:

1. Identify the CSFs across Europe and then reallocate company resources to provide a concentrated advantage in one (or more) areas. For example, British Steel's investment in modern plant and technology has made it one of the lowest-cost steel producers in Europe.[10]

2. Use the unique links and associations that all companies have developed to form the basis of advantage. For example, the French company Alcatel Alsthom has developed a strong position in the European telecommunications equipment industry as a result of its unique links with France Telecom, its joint venture with Fiat telecommunications (Italy), its acquisition of Philips telecommunications (the Netherlands), and so on.[11]

3. Against an entrenched competitor in a slow-moving market, analyze the CSFs and then aggressively alter the whole balance of the CSF. For example, the Japanese car industry used higher reliability and higher standard car specification to spearhead its entry into Europe.[8]

4. Innovate. For example, Glaxo, UK, in pharmaceuticals, outspent many European companies in R&D to develop an anti-ulcer drug that it claimed was superior in performance to those of its rivals.[12]

5. Build on *national* skills, resources and infrastructure not available to others. For example, German engineering companies, such as Bosch, Krupp, Thyssen, Siemens, Mercedes, BMW, and Mannesmann, have developed real strength and skill in a network of investment and training programs that are mutually supportive.[13] Other countries, such as the UK, have partially withdrawn during the 1980s from similar heavy engineering industries, thus losing national advantage in this area.

6. Use the resources and grants provided by national governments and the EC. For example, the French government and its wholly owned subsidiary, France Telecom, invested some US$3 billion to produce the world's largest home videotext system, Minitel, and provide a real boost to French technology and telecommunications growth in this area.[14] (It should be noted that this method has also been used to preserve and promote "national

champions"[14] that would otherwise have no sustainable competitive advantage such as Rover cars, UK.[15] Rover has struggled to survive ever since. This option can be a route to business problems.)

European examples were deliberately given above to indicate the strength of competition faced by North American companies. In practice, the development of European competitive advantage also depends on factors such as the growth prospects in an industry and whether a company dominates a market. We shall continue with the principles and then explore some of these aspects more fully in Chapter 7.

DEVELOPING THE OPTIONS

As Day has pointed out, the whole business of developing strategic options can be a slow and tortuous process.[7] He quotes the director of a major British food processor who described the planning process in his company as:

Griping→Groping→Grasping (for solutions)

To define the process, it may be better to focus on some strategy areas and make them *issue-driven*; they then become the center of a shorter, directed study, in contrast to a laborious search through every conceivable option. While this runs the risk of missing some key strategic area, it has the merit of avoiding the strategic-planning indigestion occasioned by the director's description above.

Let us look at three ways that issue-driven European marketing strategy options may be generated.

Strategy Questions

European marketing managers need to formulate strategy-related questions around the CSFs and other relevant market development areas. Some examples of the types of questions might be the following:

- What are the implications of Spanish company X entering our existing European markets?
- Which German market segment would be best tackled by our

product range? Do we need to innovate further to take market share? What promotional support will be required?

- Will Italian labor costs be significantly lower than our own? If so, will Italian companies use the advantage gained? Where? What action can we take to reduce our costs?

- How will our potential Austrian customers view our narrow product range as compared with those of domestic and southern German producers?

- What might persuade a potentially valuable Dutch customer to switch to us? Can we afford it?

- How crucial are difficulties over foreign currency facilities for our potential Polish customers? How will we be paid?

Clearly, the difficulty with such an approach is that important areas may not be investigated.

The Ansoff Matrix

Marketing options outlined by the Ansoff matrix will be familiar to many marketers.[16] The format can be used in Europe to structure the possible ways that a company might wish to develop its products or markets. The matrix of choices in Figure 6–2 indicates, in general terms, the options available to the company.

There are three difficulties with the matrix: It says little about the company's skills and resources, it does not directly consider customers, and it provides only a very limited view of competitive activity. Its benefit is its clarity on the European *outcome*, but it is less helpful on the means of getting there.

The Four C's

Both the use of strategy questions and the Ansoff matrix involve significant weaknesses in approach. In developing options for European marketing strategies, there is a more general, albeit time-consuming, approach that complements these two and provides a more structured methodology. This is to develop *European marketing strategy options using the four C's*: the company itself, its customers, its competitors, and its channels of distribution.

Naturally, the four C's need to be explored against the company's

FIGURE 6–2
European Options: Ansoff Matrix

		Product	
		Present	*New*
Market	Present	Withdraw Penetrate market Consolidate	Product development
	New	Market development	Diversify into related area (i.e., backward or forward) Unrelated diversification

marketing objectives; there are no rules for generating the options in these areas. A summary of the issues that might be explored in the process is shown in the following box. Essentially, the procedure begins by raising some basic questions about European marketing objectives. In practice, the brief summary in this box would need to be developed further with some really searching questions about Europe, what the company is trying to achieve, and why the European dimension is being considered.

Company
The *company* factor encompasses the skills and resources possessed by the company (or nonprofit organization) and any possible unique linkages between parts of its businesses that are relevant to customers in a European context and might build sustainable competitive advantage. (The latter is related to Porter's concept of horizontal strategies.[17])

Marketing strategy makes sense only when set in the context of the skills and resources available to the company.[18] Thus, such investigations need to go *beyond the marketing function*. Two areas deserve particular attention. The first is the company's *financial resources* to develop and sustain European marketing developments. The detail of this area is beyond the scope of this book. The second is the *human* resource implications of European marketing; this is explored in Chapter 13.

Single European Market Strategy

Company objectives:

- Company growth and profit objectives?
- What is our advantage over competitors?
- Will we also protect our North American home base?

Company strategy:

- Seek to maximize existing skills and resources of company.
- What market are we in?
- In the marketplace, what are the critical success factors that produce high profits?

Customer strategy:

- Profiles of actual and potential customers in terms of size, number, growth, needs.
- Identify customer profile either on a pan-European basis or by country.
- Who really are our customers?
- Investigate why and how they buy: what persuades customers?
- Targeting and market segmentation?
- Implications for product quality, technical development, product differentation.

Competition:

- Investigate market growth and shares.
- Lower costs than competitors.
- Product differentiation relative to competition.
- Whether competitors operate across the market or concentrate on a niche.
- Any opportunity to build alliances?
- Likely competitive response to new entrants.
- Changes expected over a long time scale (e.g., five years).

Channels:

- Explore existing and new channels.
- Importance of intermediaries.
- Customer service required.

Overall factors:

- Desirable to keep things simple and not overstretch company resources.
- Build on company strengths if possible.
- Seek competitive advantage.
- Seek excellence rather than just an average performance.

Customers

The *customer* dimension includes actual and potential customers, their reasons for purchase, and market segments across Europe that the company already serves or might develop.

The next important area in the development of options is clearly the customer. It is usual to start with an organization's current customers, whether they are "European" or not. This analysis is then extended to identify who the customer really is; it may well be that a European sales agent, distributor, or retailer is just as important a "customer" as the final purchaser of the goods or services.

Including potential European customers, we then need to thoroughly analyze why they purchase. It is only by this means that their needs can be identified and the reasons they may be persuaded to switch from competitors can be discovered. This process may lead to the further consideration of customer targeting and possibly new market segmentation, which we examined in Chapter 4. The implications of this process for product quality, innovation, and differentiation will be explored further in Chapter 9.

In his identification of three generic strategies, Porter uses the customer categories "industrywide" and "particular segment only" to structure his three business strategy areas: product differentiation, low-cost leadership, and niche strategy.[19] Although this customer structuring may be satisfactory for developing general concepts, the idea of defining customers as *either* "industrywide" *or* "particular segment only" is unlikely to be sufficiently precise for the development of a European marketing plan. For example, there may be several market segments into which the company decides to launch products. Moreover, broad, "industrywide" groupings do not usually lend themselves to the type of customer targeting and persuasive campaigns that develop effective marketing.

Porter's generic strategies concept has been of real benefit to the development of business strategy, but the widely quoted broad/narrow customer aspect may be too simple for use in European marketing. For related reasons, no attempt has been made to explore some of the more detailed aspects of generic strategies.[20]

Competitors
Consideration of competitors should include actual and potential competitors in the new Europe—their resources, skills, plans, and market shares. Sustainable competitive advantage, discussed earlier in this chapter, needs to be explored here. That means a thorough analysis of competition on a country-by-country, pan-European, or global basis. There is really no shortcut to this process, other than to identify two or three typical or major competitors who can act as examples for the rest.

Channels
Channels are the means by which the product or service actually reaches customers. Like all other aspects of European marketing, channels must be examined in depth. This may mean considering radical solutions beyond the more conventional approaches of seeking an import agent or setting up a direct sales force. As an example of radical alternatives that might be considered, we can take the options outlined by Lynch in European business strategy development to "secure the means of distribution":[21]

- Appointing an agent or distributor.
- Buying an existing distribution chain.
- Buying sites and building a distribution chain.
- Buying a manufacturing company with well-developed distribution arrangements.
- Negotiating a long-term contract with a retailer or other distributor.
- Franchising.
- Exclusive arrangement and shareholding in a regional or national distributor.

These options certainly go well beyond the usual practice of choosing between an agent and a distributor to export the product into Europe. It is not that there is anything wrong with the agent or distributor option, but it is important to consider unorthodox solutions, at least at an early stage. They may turn out to be more effective in developing real, sustainable competitive advantage in the long term. Some of these options are not necessarily beyond the resources of North American companies.

Naturally, the concept of radical solutions should be extended to all the four C's. In addition, it is usually worthwhile in marketing strategy development of this kind to build on strengths rather than worry about weaknesses.

SPECIAL STRATEGIES FOR THE EC AND THE EUROPEAN ECONOMIC AREA

Based on studies commissioned by the European Commission, we can identify four main areas that may lead to special marketing strategies for the single Europe during the 1990s.[22] Because many members of the EEA will join the EC during this decade, it is convenient to extend these principles to these other countries, though in practice this would need careful validation. The first two areas clearly have marketing implications. The remaining two areas will have some impact on marketing, but they are really strategy issues in which other functional areas of the company will take the lead, and so they are covered only briefly here.

Exploiting the Single Europe

Since the Single Europe Act of 1986, the EC has made great efforts to bring down the remaining national barriers to trade and to encourage more active trading across the Community. If this is successful, there will inevitably be new marketing opportunities to be explored by North American as well as European companies.

Six questions can be usefully addressed under this general subject area:

What Market Are We In?
Are we in a world, European, regional, or national market? We have already explored this area in Chapter 4.

Are There Any Special Sales Opportunities That We Need to Exploit?
As a result of the single Europe, government procurement is now being encouraged across national frontiers.[23] North American companies, who have been pressing for inclusion in this area, need to recognize that even EC companies have problems. Also, the European Commission has been using its considerable resources to stimulate pan-European projects that

may well have sales implications—for example, in the environment and pollution control.[24]

More generally, the reduction in barriers may bring other business opportunities that will need to be examined.

What Will Our Company Bring to Potential Customers?
For most European companies, the reduction in trade barriers will emphasize that many products across the EC are basically similar. Customers in new countries will need a reason to change; this suggests that marketing to this target will need both to satisfy their needs *and* to offer something different. These considerations apply in the same way as for North American countries. We explore this further in Chapter 9.

Which of the Main Ways Shall We Choose for Single-Market Expansion?
There are four main routes: launch (using the company's own sales force or a distributor), joint venture, alliance, or takeover of a company in the target country. Although some might argue that options involving takeovers, for example, are beyond the responsibility of marketing management, this is clearly nonsense. We shall explore this area in Chapter 8 for European markets. Young et al. have provided a more detailed study for international markets.[25]

How Shall We Tackle Existing Competitors?
In most European markets, new entrants will encounter existing competitors and, strategies must be devised for tackling them. From the work of Kotler and Singh, we can identify four main methods relevant to Europe:[26]

1. Frontal attack: a head-on assault on existing companies. This is usually expensive and likely to require substantial resources. The Jacobs Suchard attack on the UK chocolate market in 1988 was largely unsuccessful for these reasons.
2. Flanking attack: picking off an area of the market that may not be so well defended by existing competitors.
3. Bypass attack: developing a new product through innovation that will totally alter the battleground. According to Ohmae, the Japanese are particularly keen on exploring this area.[27]
4. Guerrilla attack: a quick entry into a new country to pick up opportunistic sales. Only certain types of companies and markets lend themselves to this approach (e.g., fashion textiles).

How Shall We Gain Distribution and Keep It?
We will explore the issue of acquiring and retaining distribution in Chapters 8 and 12.

Defending the Home Market

For North American companies already established in Europe, their business will be threatened as barriers come down. For U.S. and Canadian companies new to Europe, this threat is irrelevant as far as Europe is concerned. However, those North American companies involved in *global* markets may still need to defend their U.S. and Canadian markets from European companies.

In static markets, the only way to exploit the single Europe is to steal sales at another company's expense. In growth markets, the issue will be more complex but may still involve beating existing companies in their home markets. Every company's sales opportunity in the single Europe may be someone else's problem; a strategy for defending the home market may therefore be important to survival.

The issues are explored more fully by Lynch.[21] There are five questions to be answered in developing home defense strategies:

What, Precisely, Are We Defending?
To avoid wasting resources, the best defense should start by identifying precisely what aspects of the home market need defending. It may be a special group of customers, possibly market share, perhaps market profitability; two of these are the same, and they require different strategies that may be mutually exclusive. Clarification of objectives is at the heart of successful strategy.

Why Are We Undertaking the Defense?
There is likely to be a cost to mounting the defense. It is important to be able to set this cost against the benefits, which must therefore be understood.

Shall We Defend Everything We Own?
If some product ranges or key customers are more important than others, it may be particularly vital to defend these. The cost of defending others

may exceed the benefits obtained. This deserves to be carefully investigated.

How Shall We Mount the Defense?
Based on the principles of warfare, Lynch suggests a number of ways of mounting the defense:[21]

- Be clear on the objectives for the reasons outlined above.
- Sharpen market intelligence: knowing the attacker's plans leads to better defense. For marketers, this means quality monitoring of competitors.
- Launch your own product into a market niche. If it is evident that the new entrant is likely to launch into a market segment that is only partly served at present, it is better for a company to attack rather than allow another to gain entry.
- Look after the main customers. This is fundamental to any strong marketing company.
- Stop the competitor from becoming established. New entrants are at their weakest in the very early days. That is the time to stop them.
- Bold competitive moves demand a bold response. A new entrant undercutting the current price of products by 20 percent is ignored in a price-elastic market only at the consequence of its becoming established.
- Make entry difficult and unprofitable; this follows from the preceding discussion.
- Consider a counterlaunch into the home territory of the new entrant. This may drain the resources of the new entrant and divert attention.

Are There Any Longer-Term Solutions Beyond Mere Defense?
Some European markets, such as the cola soft drinks market dominated by Pepsi-Cola and Coca-Cola, are likely to see an offensive war that may last for years. For other markets it may be more profitable to seek solutions that encourage entry by the more acceptable competitors—for example, those that will be less aggressive in their actions than others. Porter calls this "competitor selection" and explores it in some detail.[28]

Seeking Lower Costs from Single European Market
Economies of Scale

As a result of the Single Europe Act, Cecchini argues that there will be economies of scale in production, research and development, and some areas of marketing.[29]

> The trigger point for all these gains [+4.5 percent on GDP, −6.1 percent in consumer prices] should not be forgotten. It is the removal of non-tariff barriers. This is synonymous with the reduction in production which, under the pressure of the strengthened competition, exerts downward pressure on prices. From this starting point come:
>
> - purchasing power gains, which stimulate economic activity;
> - competitivity gains, which, in addition to providing another growth stimulant, improve the external balance;
> - the initial lowering of prices, not just inhibiting demand-push inflation, but actually leading to deflation.
> - the easing of public deficits, under the dual impact of open public procurement and economic regeneration.

Marketers will certainly wish to question the simplistic economic view implied in the above statement that lower costs lead only to lower prices. Nevertheless, the evidence from the studies backing the Cecchini report suggests that there should be economies of scale resulting from the single market in some markets.[30] This has already been put into action by some leading European producers: for example, Ford has concentrated its European manufacturing sites over the last few years so that each now specializes in certain products, and Mars built one factory in 1990 at Steinbourg in France for the pan-European production of Mars ice cream.[31,32] These two U.S. companies clearly show that not just European companies can benefit from the single Europe.

Consideration of production economies of scale across Europe is beyond the scope of this book, but we need to examine marketing economies of scale in the single Europe. For products or services that will benefit from pan-European marketing, there may well be such cost savings in marketing effort—for example, in avoiding the national duplication of some marketing staff or in some form of European branding. We examine these most important aspects of European marketing in Chapters 9 and 13.

Tackling Overcapacity Arising from Removal of Barriers in the EC

The Cecchini report argued that certain industries in individual EC countries had been protected behind national barriers.[33] When the barriers came down, these combined industries would provide the EC with more production capacity than was needed. For example, the study found that only 50-80 percent of total EC production capacity in electric locomotives was currently being utilized. The EC estimated that the number of main manufacturers was likely to be reduced from 16 to 4. This would inevitably mean that some companies would have to close their production capacity in the single market, if the proposed benefits across the whole EC were to be achieved.

Strategies for handling such activities are important in European business strategy and are described in Lynch.[21] One of the possible strategies is for such companies to seek new customers and new markets and thus avoid factory closure. Such an examination can be structured by the Ansoff matrix (Figure 6–2).

SPECIAL STRATEGIES FOR EASTERN EUROPE

As we have seen, there will be fundamental differences in marketing strategies in Eastern Europe compared with the West. After 40 years or more of a command economy, the whole structure and fabric of Eastern Europe countries needs to be renewed; the only country to which this does not fully apply, Yugoslavia, has been engaged in a destructive war since 1991 that has made reinvestment essential here as well. If other Eastern European countries needs to be renewed; the only country to which this does not fully apply, Yugoslavia, has been engaged in a destructive war since the development of marketing strategy for Eastern Europe difficult and complicates the assessment of risks.

In addition to ethnic and religious tensions, the people of some countries may lose patience with the renewal process. Certainly, there will be real suffering as painful adjustments are made; for example, prices rose 400 percent in Romania in 1991, and hundreds of thousands of workers were on short time.[34] Such difficulties may lead to major political instability and possibly the threat of revolution. This is a very stark background against which to plan marketing strategies.

Beyond the political uncertainties, there has been little competition in these countries, and it has been of dubious quality. Arguably, this might provide an opening for Western marketing. In addition, government privatization may provide some unique opportunities for development. Perhaps the major potential benefit is that such markets may have great long-term potential. But they need to be assessed against the real difficulties of the 1990s throughout the region.

Pulling these issues together, we can structure the analysis of the special marketing strategies for Eastern Europe under the following four headings.

Size and Phasing of the Opportunity

The potential size of the market is likely to be the key consideration and so it deserves careful exploration in the following areas:

- How big potentially? Compared to what current size?
- Rate of growth?
- Growth factors?
- Other potential entrants from Europe, the United States, and Japan?
- How certain is the time scale?

Government Company Privatization Opportunities

Privatization has already provided PepsiCo (U.S.) with a chocolate company in Poland and BASF (Germany) with a chemical company. However, both of these examples illustrate the poisoned chalice that may be purchased.

The U.S. company PepsiCo, owner of Pepsi-Cola and a range of North American and Western European snack companies, has had real difficulties in distribution.[35] Its entire system collapsed overnight when all the small retail shops were privatized and the former state-owned wholesale network disappeared. Europe's second largest chemical company, BASF of Germany, acquired Synthesewerk Schwarzheide in October 1990 for nothing.[36] It has already earmarked US$300 million for fundamental restructuring. But there have been management problems, gross overstaffing, lack of any real financial accounts, major plant inefficiencies, and environmental problems. It is hardly a bed of roses.

In more general terms, privatization issues that deserve investigation include the following:

- Assets and assessment of their quality.
- Links with other government institutions and banks.
- Assessment of any future government plans.
- Assessment of what is *really* being acquired.

Structural Investment Needed

Because of the run-down state of much of Eastern Europe, there is a need to provide items that are taken for granted in the West.

The U.S. bicycle maker, Schwinn, bought 51 percent of a Hungarian bicycle company in 1989 for US$2.1 million. It has had some success because its product has had little competition. But it has also had major problems.[37] It needed to import some parts, and the Hungarian authorities raised import duties. There were no computers in the customs office, so extra staff had to be employed to undertake the task. VAT was repaid on exports, but it took up to six months for the government to make the payments. As the Hungarian economy has struggled, rising interest costs and currency devaluation have also cut profits. Production has not met its target, and quality is still not satisfactory. There have been real structural problems that may well have contributed to Schwinn's subsequent bankruptcy.

Some questions that might be raised on structural issues include:

- Beyond the company itself, what other investment is needed to make the systems work?
- How much investment? On what time scale? What international grants are available to assist (if any)?
- How important is financing of the venture? What are the consequences of rising interest rates?
- What are the foreign currency implications of the deal?

Risk and Reward Assessment

Most of the company problems that have been described can be overcome, given time. There is no point in applying a short Western time scale in Eastern Europe. The major risks are those connected with basic political stability. These require a more fundamental assessment and recognition that business exposure will be high for the next 10 years in such countries as the Ukraine, Byelorussia, and Russia itself. Questions and issues that deserve exploration as part of any marketing assessment include:

- The balance between early entry and realistic profit delivery (assuming the possibility of delaying profit for several years).
- The extent of business exposure if complete withdrawal must be undertaken.
- An assessment of political risk.

In general, for Eastern European countries, there are no easy options. There will inevitably be much greater risk than applies in the West. However, the rewards should also be higher; if they are not, there is no point, commercially, in making the investment.

NOTES

1. L. Jauch and W. F. Glueck, *Business Policy and Strategic Management*, 5th ed. (New York: McGraw-Hill International, 1988), chapter 2.
2. K. Ohmae, *The Mind of the Strategist* (New York: *Penguin*, 1983), pp. 15ff.
3. H. Arbuthnott and G. Edwards, *A Common Man's Guide to the Common Market*, 2nd ed. (London: Macmillan, 1989), pp. 105ff.
4. M. E. Porter, *Competitive Strategy* (New York: Free Press, 1980), chapter 3.
5. M. E. Porter, *Competitive Advantage* (New York: Free Press, 1985).
6. G. Day, *Strategic Market Planning* (St. Paul, MN: West Publishing, 1984), p. 60.
7. Porter, *Competitive Strategy*, p. 39.
8. "Car Makers Face the Pain Barrier," *Financial Times*, January 26, 1990.
9. Ohmae, pp. 216ff.
10. British Steel, *Annual Report*, 1990.
11. R. Lynch, *European Business Strategies* (London: Kogan Page, 1990), p. 30.
12. Ibid., p. 76.
13. Ibid., p. 263.

14. Ibid., p. 239.
15. Ibid., p. 156.
16. M. Christopher, S. Kennedy, M. McDonald, and G. Wills, *Effective Marketing Management* (Bedford, England: Cranfield Press, 1985), p. 66.
17. Porter, *Competitive Advantage*, chapter 10.
18. Christopher et al., p. 3.
19. Porter, *Competitive Strategy*, p. 39.
20. J. Hendry, "The Problem with Porter's Generic Strategies," *European Management Journal* 8, no. 4 (1990), pp. 443–50.
21. Lynch, chapter 25.
22. European Commission, *Research on the Cost of Non-Europe*, vols. 1–16 (Luxembourg: OPOCE, 1988).
23. P. Cecchini, *1992—The Benefits of the Single Market* (Aldershot, England: Wildwood House, 1988), chapter 3.
24. European Commission, *Panorama of EC Industry 1990* (Luxembourg: OPOCE, 1990), pp. 133ff.
25. S. Young, J. Hamill, C. Wheeler, and J. R. Davies, *International Market Entry and Development* (Brighton: Harvester Wheatsheaf, 1989).
26. P. Kotler and R. Singh, "Marketing Warfare in the 1980s," *Journal of Business Strategy*, Winter 1981, pp. 30–41.
27. Ohmae, p. 216.
28. Porter, *Competitive Advantage*, chapter 6.
29. Cecchini, p. 98.
30. European Commission, *Research on the Cost of Non-Europe*, vol. 1.
31. Ford Motor Company, *Annual Report 1990*.
32. P. Rawsthorne, 'How Mars Took Ice-Cream in Hand,' *Financial Times*, October, 1990.
33. Cecchini, p. 21.
34. "Romania—and So to Winter," *The Economist*, December 14, 1991, p. 66.
35. F. G. de Jonquieres, "Home-Grown Produce on Multi-National's Shopping List," *Financial Times*, August 8, 1991.
36. "The Money Pit," *The Economist*, June 22, 1991, p. 96.
37. "A Bicycle Made for Two," *The Economist*, June 8, 1991, p. 99.

7

Selecting the best option

Having generated the European marketing strategy options, we now need to select among them. We shall look at the techniques available and explore the factors that will influence the choice. However, as part of the final decision, we must also examine such options in a broader encompassing context, the potential for global markets, the attraction of pan-European activity, and the scope for expansion into Eastern Europe. These three areas all have special implications for the final option selection. The subjects covered in this chapter are as follows:

- Selecting the best option: the basic steps.
- European marketing strategy guidelines.
- Options selection in global markets.
- Implications of pan-European markets for marketing strategy selection.
- Marketing strategies for Eastern Europe.

SELECTING THE BEST OPTION: THE BASIC STEPS

In Chapter 1 we saw that all European marketing activities undertaken by an organization need to be judged against its mission and objectives. As Jauch and Glueck have stated, company objectives are usually developed at the corporate level rather than at the marketing functional level.[1] This is particularly important in allowing *all* business functions, rather than just the marketing area, to contribute to corporate European goals; multifunctional activity is a vital early part of the strategy process. After this, corporate objectives may be revised as a result of feedback from the marketing function and other business areas.

Ultimately, European marketing objectives derive from corporate objectives. The best marketing strategy then needs to be selected to deliver them. According to Jauch and Glueck, the selection of the best strategy option derives from two sources:[2]

1. Strategy analysis, which identifies a company's marketing environment (Chapters 2 and 3);
2. Strategy options, which outline possible areas for development (Chapter 6).

Having examined these two areas, our task now is, essentially, to bring them together. It is useful to categorize this process into the following four stages.

Preliminary Study

We certainly want to start by weeding out the "no hope" options. There is no point in leaving them in purely for the sake of a symmetrical strategic analysis. Beyond this, we may want to undertake a rough examination of each option's contribution to corporate objectives. If there are any that are substantially remote, it may be worth considering whether they deserve to be pursued: there is little point in chasing the irrelevant to achieve the challenging.

European SWOT Analysis

Strengths, weaknesses, opportunities, and threats (SWOT) with respect to competitors across Europe should be summarized in a SWOT analysis. This should be short, sharp, and to the point, not a long, rambling report that runs to several pages. Bowman and Asch as well as Day provide ideas and structure to attain this.[3,4]

The SWOT analysis may again suggest that some options should be dropped: they may require too many resources or too high a level of risk to achieve the overall objectives. Certainly, it is vital to begin to consider at this stage the balance between the risk that the organization is willing to undertake and the possible rewards; sometimes these are insufficiently clear when translated into the marketing objectives that have been agreed upon. A European SWOT analysis, with its examination of competitive positions, may help to bring this issue out.

Scenario Building

For the remaining options, a useful next step is to explore the consequences of various combinations of courses of marketing action and external effects, for example:

- Single Europe barriers after 1992:
  —Come down fast.
  —Reduce slowly.
- Potential European Competitor:
  —Attacks our home market.
  —Stays in existing markets.
  —Moves into other European markets.
- Market growth:
  —Slows in home country.
  —Grows faster in other EC countries.

Oliver has a long, useful description of scenario building, its uses, and its consequences that can be applied to European marketing.[5]

In some cases, it may be inappropriate to build detailed scenarios—for example, where there is only one major outcome. Even in these more limited circumstances, there is a strong case for some exploration around the recommended option to answer two related questions:

1. What is our best and most optimistic outcome beyond this recommendation?
2. What is the worst outcome and our highest level of exposure?

Most North American marketers presenting the marketing director with European recommendations should expect to be asked to provide answers to these two questions.

Estimated Financial and Human Consequences and Risks

For the main options, it is important to investigate the main financial consequences and risks. Issues such as the effects of tax regimes, currency, and any EC special or regional investment grants need to be considered at this stage. This will ensure that no opportunities are missed and that the risks are adequately understood.

Moreover, any proposals are very likely to have a human dimension; this might range from the need to recruit new personnel in other European countries to an option involving company takeover, with its important human consequences. Such considerations are heightened where language, culture, and law aspects differ from those of the home country.

Although the UK has not signed the EC social protocol of the other 11 EC countries at Maastricht, companies operating in *any* of the 12 need to consider the implications of EC law as soon as they move outside their home countries. We shall look at this and other human resources considerations in Chapter 13. But there may be implications that need to be considered *before* marketing options are resolved and final recommendations made.

EUROPEAN MARKETING STRATEGY GUIDELINES

Having examined some of the likely steps in evaluating the options, we can usefully explore what might emerge for European strategies. Naturally, the precise option chosen will be unique to an organization and its circumstances. But some general guidelines based on commonly accepted evidence and principles may provide some clues on both the European marketing strategy development process and the potential results achieved.

Ultimately, we are seeking guidelines that will provide clues to the correct marketing strategy for different situations that may arise in the single Europe. We shall develop them from evidence in the areas discussed below. We shall then show how these can be combined to produce some guidelines for European marketing strategy.

The PIMS Evidence on Quality, Market Share, Marketing Expenditure, and Capital Investment

Let us first use the Profit Impact of Market Strategy (PIMS) evidence on what delivers profitability to companies in the United States and, to a lesser extent, Europe. The continuing work of the Strategic Planning Institute and its PIMS data bank provides data on the experiences of some 3,000 businesses in terms of both products and services. The data record the activities undertaken by the organizations over a number of years, their markets, and their competitive moves, as well as the resulting business profitability.

The main PIMS evidence, quoted in Buzzell and Gale and in Johnson and Scholes, that can be applied to European marketing strategy suggests the following principles:[6,7]

1. The most important single factor affecting business performance is the *quality* of the products or services relative to the competition. In the short run, high quality means that high prices can be sought, and, in the long run, high quality will lead to high profitability and thus allow businesses to grow. The significance of quality in the single Europe may be that, as barriers come down, new competitors with new, high-quality delivery will suddenly present themselves. For companies that already have high quality, new markets may well open up. Either way, this could be a serious long-term threat to profitability for poor-quality performers in the EC. We explore product marketing and quality issues further in Chapter 9.

2. Market share and profitability are related: high market share is correlated with high return on investment. Buzzell and Gale say that the main reason for this, apart from quality, is that large businesses gain from economies of scale. Jacobson and Aaker have questioned the relationship, pointing out that the fundamental cause (of which share would be just a symptom) might be luck or management skill.[8] However, the PIMS evidence is strong and deserves to be considered carefully. In the single Europe, the elimination of entry barriers will substantially reduce a company's market share unless it takes the same share in all other EC markets: either a company sells its products in other EC countries or it will simply become a smaller fish in a bigger sea. Market share could be crucial to profitability, so we shall return to further evidence in this area later in this chapter.

3. An increase in marketing expenditure (as a percentage of sales) has a positive effect for companies that are already strong in the marketplace. For companies with a weak market share, this relationship does not hold; the evidence suggests that low-brand-share companies will not increase profitability by increasing market spending as a percentage of sales. Again, with the potential redefinition of some market shares in the single Europe as barriers come down, the data suggest that some companies may need to examine carefully their marketing expenditure in the new, larger market. If the same sums are invested as previously but spread over more countries, the evidence suggests that this investment might be a waste of money. Clearly, since market share depends on how a market is defined, it will be important to define carefully the European market.

4. Companies with high-fixed investment (as a percentage of sales) have great difficulty delivering profits. In the single Europe, there is much discussion of major investment in plant and equipment—for example, in steel, cars, and machine tools. The discouraging evidence on fixed investment does not mean that such investment should not be undertaken, but rather that the resulting profitability may be less than anticipated. The reason is that in some industries, such as European steel, political factors have stopped the necessary reduction in production capacity that would normally result from the investment in new equipment.[9] In others, such as the car industry, competitive activity has been such that the results of extra investment have been partly negated.[10]

The Distinction between Market Leaders and Market Followers

Looking beyond the PIMS evidence, we can develop the guidelines further by considering the work of Porter on competitive advantage.[11] We have already addressed his assertion that sustainable competitive advantage derives from:

- Low-cost leadership.
- Product differentiation.
- Niche positioning.

Porter has also pointed out that such strategies will vary depending on whether a company is a leader or a follower in a market, that is, whether it has a dominant market share or must follow market initiatives taken by other companies. Rather than rely simply on a basic distinction between leaders and followers in markets, we can refine this in the context of the single European market: we can explore whether companies are leaders or followers on a *pan-European scale* or whether they are leaders or followers in *one or two countries only*. (In fact, as we shall see later in this chapter, the evidence suggests that the latter is highly likely.) We shall assume that followers operating in only one or two countries have at least a viable share in those countries.

Finally, we can also extend the scope to take account of those companies that have developed a market *niche* across Europe or in one or more countries.

The Concept of Product Life Cycle

Porter also uses the marketing concept of the product life cycle to refine the scope for strategy: markets may be growing, mature, or delining.[12] In growing markets, the market growth itself will present sales opportunities, but there will also need to be investment to persuade buyers to try the product. In mature markets, the only way to increase sales is to steal from competition, a method that may be expensive. In declining markets, there may be a real struggle for survival. We can apply these basic concepts to marketing strategy in the single Europe.

The Reduction of Barriers to Entry as the Single Market Becomes a Reality

We also need to take into account how the single Europe will affect barriers to entry. In some cases, the Single Europe Act has already brought barriers down; in others, this has yet to happen. Moreover, Lynch has pointed out that in some cases present EC barriers to trade will not just disappear when 1993 arrives: hidden barriers will remain.[13] For example, the natural knowledge that some regional and nationalized European companies have of their existing suppliers will not disappear just because of legislation in Brussels. We therefore include in the definition of barriers those that are *hidden* as well as those that are openly stated.

In looking at the implications, we can consider two situations: (1) the barriers will remain up for several years to come, (2) the barriers have come down. Clearly, this oversimplifies the situation, but it may provide the essential clues to action.

European Marketing Strategy Guidelines

This basic structure can then be used to develop guidelines for the single Europe. It will spell out possible courses of action in different sets of circumstances. The results are shown in Figure 7–1. It should be stressed that they are not necessarily the "right" actions for all circumstances, but they may provide a useful indicator. Clearly, some of the actions go beyond European marketing strategy as such: for example, divestment is a possibility in some situations. But the marketing department is not an island within an organization and should be prepared to look beyond its immediate functional area at strategy level.

FIGURE 7-1—European Competitive Strategy Options

		European Market Growth					
		High Market Growth		Slow or Static Market		Declining Market or Weak Growth and Excess Production Capacity	
		EC Barriers Up	EC Barriers Down	EC Barriers Up	EC Barriers Down	EC Barriers Up	EC Barriers Down
European market share	Dominant across Europe	• Hold barriers • Invest in marketing • Keep ahead	• Keep ahead in single market • Hold quality • Invest in marketing	• Hold quality • Deter competitors • Seek cost leadership • Hold barriers	• As left	• Help EC to negotiate departures • Redefine market scope	• Long-term view essential • Divest or hold?
	Niche across Europe	• Hold barriers • Invest in marketing • Seek quality	• Hold niche in all countries • Build alliances	• Hold niche • Seek quality	• Hold niche if possible • Seek new opportunities	• Redefine niche • Seek new opportunities • Hold quality: add service	• Hold if attractive • Redefine niche • Hold quality: add service?
	Strong in one or two EC countries only	• Review single market timing • Explore quality • Build links with other EC companies	• Imitate at lower cost • Expect home market threat • Raise marketing in home countries	• Deter competitors • Hold quality • Seek national government help • Invest in marketing	• Differentiate products • Build from critical success factors • Build EC share	• Seek alliances • Negotiate with EC and other companies	• Seek new opportunities • Reduce marketing expenditure • Differentiate
	Niche in one or two EC countries only	• Review single market timing and prospects • Seek quality • Maintain niche	• Investigate niche status in EC • Possibly raise marketing in home countries	• Build alliances • Review single market prospects	• Investigate EC links to hold niche • Maintain marketing spending	• Expect new entrants • Hold while barriers remain	• Seeking new opportunities • Major issue: divest or hold?
	Viable in one or two EC countries only	• Seek links with other EC companies • Probe quality	• Expect home market threat • Develop niche?	• Hold barriers short term • Consider takeover or being acquired: build share • Hold quality	• Differentiate, niche, or takeover essential	• Differentiate? • Build niche? • Exit from industry?	• Prepare to exit

We shall explore single market strategy further after we have explored global strategy and its possible implications for Europe.

OPTIONS SELECTION IN GLOBAL MARKETS

For those North American companies engaged in global markets, such as aerospace and defense, selecting among options takes on a wholly new meaning. There may be barriers across Europe, but, essentially, the customer base is worldwide. In addition, the production, technology, and logistics are likely to have global dimensions. In developing the single Europe, EC countries have always seen themselves as providing the base in some global industries to compete on equal terms with the United States and Japan—for example, in semiconductors and advanced electronics.

In 1989 the European Commission produced the chart shown in Figure 7–2 to indicate where the EC stood in terms of the overall "triad": the EC, the United States, and Japan. The Commission argued that the chart shows that:

- The EC is still strong in its traditional "cash cows," mature products with limited growth prospects, such as machine tools, steel, cars, and textiles.
- The EC is weak in "stars," high-growth markets with a strong position, such as semiconductors and consumer electronics.

Although the EC may be too large to treat as a single trading area in product portfolio terms, the evidence of the EC share in growing and declining markets cannot be denied. The European Commission goes on to argue that this means Europe needs to invest further in production investment in some areas, such as microelectronics in the EC machine tool industry and new products in iron and steel. However, Porter's studies of the way nations stimulate industrial growth and development indicate that investment may not be the best way to achieve this growth; it is much more important to "compete rather than collaborate," according to Porter.[14] From a European marketing viewpoint, this may mean that:

1. European Commission grants are unlikely to provide the lifeline for struggling companies to find success in global markets; they may just prop up the inefficient a little longer. North American companies have little to fear.

FIGURE 7–2
The European Portfolio—Annual Volume Growth of the Triad's Production 1987–1993 (%)

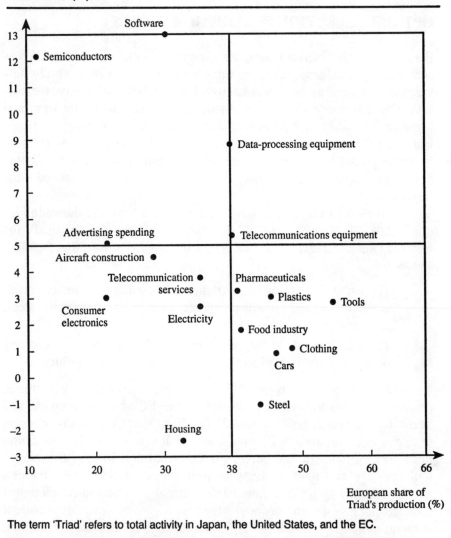

The term 'Triad' refers to total activity in Japan, the United States, and the EC.

Source: European Commission, *Panorama of EC Industry 1989* (Luxembourg: OPOCE, 1989), p. 11.

2. The chances of success from EC funding initiatives on electronics developments and high-definition TV are slim if we accept Porter's evidence.[15-17] However, it should be clearly acknowledged that governments such as France and Italy do not agree. They point to the fact that Japanese success is based, in part at least, on the influence of its Ministry of International Trade and Industry and the need for "critical mass."

More generally, it has been argued by the European Commission that pan-European sales will provide the basis for European companies to achieve the essential economies of scale to compete globally.[18] But, according to other evidence, size for its own sake is unlikely to bring success. According to Porter, "overall size is largely irrelevant to competitive advantage."[14] Kay has written, "It cannot be repeated frequently enough that the larger relative size of American and Japanese companies . . . is the *result* of their success, not the *cause of it*."[19]

From a marketing viewpoint, global markets do not necessarily imply global operations. European activity justified purely on the basis of global expansion may not be successful. Cvar, in a study of global activity case studies, concluded that effective global strategy emerges from those companies taking the *initiative* to move an industry to a global scale.[20] Moreover, such companies are more likely to be successful if they take a clear global viewpoint on strategies to achieve globalization. This suggests that both North American and European companies considering global opportunities need to tackle the issues boldly if they are to succeed. Half-hearted tinkering is unlikely to bring substantial rewards. The bold move to unite the Swedish ASEA company with the Swiss Brown Boveri in 1987 to produce an engineering company of international size is an example of the strategy required. But bold moves mean higher risk.

In an article on Citizen Watch, Rodger points out that this highly successful Japanese company operates in world markets.[21] However, its success has come partially by *avoiding* competition with the big multinationals. The company steers clear of sectors where the global competition is intense and where the group would be a late entrant.

Doz points to the extensive evidence showing that, in developing a global strategy, it is essential to analyze *government politics*.[22] His studies were undertaken in 1985–1986 but no doubt also apply to European Community policymaking in the 1990s. He shows that governments can affect:

- Entry into a national market.
- Public procurement by nationally owned organizations.

He also says that governments can influence the performance requirements needed for successful competition to the extent that they may make such markets unattractive. Thus, global marketing strategies need to explore these aspects in some detail, particularly in certain industries. He identifies the following markets as particularly subject to these influences:[23]

- Military aircraft.
- Electricity generation equipment.
- Telecommunications equipment.
- Civil aircraft.
- Aero engines.

In 1993 the U.S. government began to recognize its own role in this area. It called for greater openness in European public procurement. This may help North American companies, but it encourages equal openness in U.S. markets.

IMPLICATIONS OF PAN-EUROPEAN MARKETS FOR MARKETING STRATEGY SELECTION

The European single market may represent a unique opportunity and a new challenge for some corporations. As discussed earlier, Cecchini summarized the research of a small army of consultants employed by the European Commission to investigate the impact in a series of industries.[24] Although Cecchini may be overenthusiastic and there will be losers as well as winners, we have good economic evidence that lowering trade barriers has a positive effect; see, for example, the World Bank's *World Development Report 1991*.[25]

We are concerned here about the impact of the single Europe—and, to a lesser extent, the European Economic Area—on marketing strategy development for *pan-European* operations rather than for national markets. Lynch pointed out that of Europe's top 250 companies in 1987–1988, only some 100 were actively trading in *all* the EC countries.[26] The main reason is that many European companies, such as national rail systems, are inherently structured to operate mainly in national markets. Even allowing for further developments in the early 1990s, there is clearly still some way to go in achieving broad-based pan-European activity such as that already seen in the United States.

But how do we identify pan-European marketing opportunities? The evidence suggests that there are five important indicators.

Start with Markets, Not Industry Structures

The starting point is likely to be a pan-European industry and its customer requirements rather than the common needs of similar customers across industries.

For example, identifying the needs of telecommunications equipment customers or computer industry customers across Europe will be more productive than analyzing the needs of "large company" or "small company" customers. The great variability of wealth, language, and cultures in Europe is more quickly traversed by focusing on some common customer need rather than on more general characteristics such as industry size. This is consistent with Kay's view of European strategy development: "The significance of 1992 is almost entirely to be found in measures which are industry specific."[27]

Seek Emerging Pan-European Segments

There will be a need to reexamine pan-European, regional, and national market segment opportunities. Introduction of new pan-European brands or a realignment of regional brands to serve these opportunities may be required. The segments will emerge from new pan-European demand. They will benefit from the consequent savings in marketing economies of scale across the EC from a pan-European or regional approach.

Many more markets are taking on a pan-European, regional, or even global approach. McGee and Segal-Horn point to the gaps in the pan-European market in own-label suppliers and pan-European branders.[28] They argue that this will lead to a new configuration of strategic groups, which currently consist mainly of national branders (e.g., brands only in Germany) and multinational branders (e.g., brands common to the United States and the EC).

Arguably, in terms of consumer goods, U.S. companies have already made much more progress across Europe in building pan-European brands than EC companies; examples range from Kellogg's breakfast cereals to McDonald's fast food. Outside of the top three EC food companies (Unilever, Nestlé, and BSN), there has been only limited activity. Similarly, in consumer electronics, only Philips stands out as a pan-European brand against the ranks of the Japanese: Sony, Toshiba, NEC, and so on. North American companies seem to have largely given up on consumer electronics.

Concentrate the Product Range

In order to build market dominance on a pan-European scale, there may be a need to narrow the product range and extend the remaining products throughout the EC. For example, a food company with a strong share in biscuits in a couple of European countries and a weak share in cakes in several countries might sell its cake companies and use the funds to purchase biscuit companies, or, more simply, it might build its biscuit brands and ignore its cake brands across Europe with the aim of building dominance in the former product group.

The evidence to support this strategy comes from Gogel and Larreche's study on product strength and geographical coverage.[29] This work is, in turn, related to research commissioned by the European Commission and produced by the MAC Group.[30] We have already observed that high market share is correlated with high profitability.[6,7] The research from these two sources extends this observation to a study of how companies have been building brand share in the United States by the means described above (for biscuits and cakes) and how this could be applied to Europe. The main marketing strategy that has been used in the United States is shown in Figure 7–3. The obvious disadvantage of such a strategy is the increased exposure to one market.

At the time of the study, in 1988, out of a sample of 46 large EC-based food companies, one-half had a presence in two EC countries or less. The research also showed that U.S. companies such as Coca-Cola, Mars, and Kellogg's were significantly further advanced already across Europe compared with many European companies.

Innovate

Pan-European marketing will benefit from innovation rather than just repeating in other countries what is already present in one country. As

FIGURE 7–3
Portfolio Adjustments by a U.S. Food Manufacturer

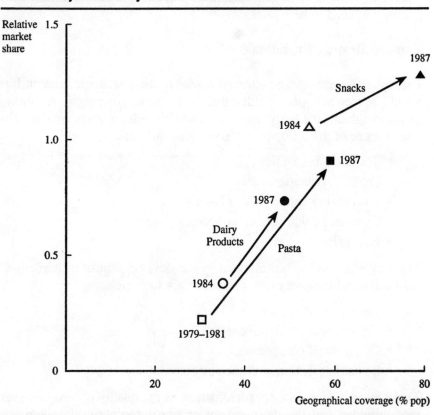

Source: European Commission, *Research on the Cost of Non-Europe*, vol. 1 (Luxembourg: OPOCE, 1988), p. 435.

Ramsey has observed for fast-moving consumer goods (FMCG), increased per capita income will provide the opening for innovative companies to develop some really exciting added-value products:[31]

> Whilst it is true that consumers and retailers are conservative and demanding, it is really up to FMCG manufacturers to find out more about their markets and their consumers in order to capitalise on the new product opportunities offered by the single market. It may be the last opening for the survival and renewal of branded manufacturing as it has been known in the 20th century.

His comments on the value of *innovation* for FMCG products can also be extended, without doubt, to industrial products. North American companies will need to be innovative.

Explore Strategy Evolution

Particularly in European industrial markets, many strategic relationships should be seen as *evolving* rather than being created overnight. According to Cunningham, the early stages in customer relationships may involve one or more of the following offers to gain business:[32]

- Technical innovation.
- Product adaptation.
- Availability and security of supply.
- Conformity with customer-specific requirements.
- Low price.

But they will need to be followed by the development of customer/supplier relationships over many years through such areas as:

- Customer orientation.
- Organizational effectiveness.
- Commercial competence.
- Social integration with the customer.

These areas, which concern such matters as the quality of long-term service provided and the development of trusting relationships with customers, do not always appear in marketing strategy because they are not so easy to quantify and specify. But they are no less important for that.

MARKETING STRATEGIES FOR EASTERN EUROPE

Because of the speed of change in Eastern Europe over the years 1989–1992 and the business risks that still remain, there has not been the same market-research-based analysis as in the West. Evidence on marketing strategy is more anecdotal and is likely to remain so for several years.

In addition to all the other upheavals, the reunification of Germany has taken place during this period. Massive investment is now under way to improve the infrastructure, environment, and living conditions in the former East Germany. A major privatization program to sell off the nationalized East German companies is also being undertaken, and the main purchasers have been West German companies. In devising marketing strategies for East Germany and other Eastern European countries, it would be wrong to underestimate the turmoil now taking place.

Commenting on German reunification in July 1991, the OECD said:[33]

> Forty years of development under two contrasting economic systems have not only led to vastly different economic structures and behavioural patterns in the two post-war Germanys but has also opened up a much wider gap . . . in terms of capital endowment, productivity levels and living standards than was suggested by official statistics.

> The full and abrupt exposure of the structurally-weak eastern German economy to competition from western Germany and from abroad . . . resulted in a virtual collapse of production and employment in the five new federal Länder.

Similar descriptions could be given of other Eastern European countries. East Germany has at least had its rich West German partner to assist in the recovery process. For other economies, the same resources and expertise may be much slower to arrive.

In many respects, this is a government-to-government matter, and individual companies may expect to react to events rather than take the lead. However, four important implications for marketing strategy in Eastern Europe follow.

Planning for Uncertainty

The considerable upheavals of Eastern European countries are still not fully resolved, and North American marketing strategists would be naive if they did not recognize this reality. Three areas are particularly relevant:

1. *Lack of reliable market data*: The preceding OECD quotation suggests that even official statistics may be inaccurate. In addition, in many areas there is simply a lack of information that would normally be available in the West. Strategies building on such poor data need to allow greater margins of error than would apply in the West.
2. *Long time scales*. Marketing strategies that rely on significant

positive results within two years are unlikely to work. It may well take 5 to 10 years to see any real return.

3. *False expectations of Western values*: Eastern European expectations of Western wage levels and quality of life have in some cases been dashed as the reality of unemployment takes hold.[34] Alternatively, these issues have yet to be faced as privatization proceeds. Either way, marketing strategies need to allow for a long period of adjustment by consumers in the East and possible resentment when the results fall short of expectations.

Careful Distinction between the States and within the States of Eastern Europe

In marketing terms, there is no such market as "Eastern Europe." There are a number of sovereign states such as Poland, Hungary, and Romania, each with its own language, culture, history, and resources. Unlike the EC, where it is possible to think in pan-European terms, Eastern Europe is merely a convenient way of grouping states previously under the domination of the USSR. By late 1991, even the USSR had broken up into a series of major individual countries set upon individual paths to growth and freedom.

Eastern European countries need to be treated separately. Hence, there are unlikely to be many significant "marketing strategies" for the whole of Eastern Europe. In addition, there are some movements for the further breakup of individual states; for example, Czechoslovakia has split into Czech and Slovak states. Similarly, parts of other countries within states may desire to secede, with possible consequences as severe as those seen in the Yugoslavian conflict. Marketing strategy must recognize the political sensitivities among potential customers.

Levels of Exposure in Early Market Initiatives

Over the next 10 years, the EC agreements with Poland, Hungary, and the Czech and Slovak republics will establish free trade.[35] Eventually, this could lead to full EC membership, but that is likely to be further away. As these countries move closer to the EC, the level of exposure to business risks faced by Western companies trading with them may diminish.

More generally, North American companies moving into Eastern Europe have limited their exposure by two means:

1. They have concentrated on introducing service industries from the West.
2. They have limited acquisitions to familiar areas and at affordable levels of investment.

Real business exposure rises quickly when significant capital investment for plant and equipment is involved. For service industries relying on the skills and knowledge of individuals, the business exposure is lower: they can simply pull out if the situation deteriorates. Their presence is also consistent with the early needs of Eastern European countries: the drive to introduce Western-style market economies, privatization, and related measures has provided a major demand for Western advisers. Many consultants, banks, and accountancy companies have set up branches in Eastern European capitals. Acquisitions by Western Europe and the United States have been made mainly by companies having similar interests and market knowledge in the West. Thus, many of the leading U.S. and European food companies have bought similar companies in the East.[36] North American car companies have also negotiated deals of this kind.[37]

One of the real attractions of such deals is that the companies being purchased were previously monopolies. Thus, if such companies can be bought cheaply, Western companies are buying a large market share at a relatively modest cost.[38] We have already discussed the importance of market share. This would be an argument for raising the early exposure because the potential profits are very high in the long term.

Unfortunately, business exposure begins only with acquisition. As discussed earlier, the U.S. company GE bought the Hungarian lighting company Tungsram in 1989. It has already reduced the work force from 18,000 to 14,000 and believes its needs to shed another 4,000 to reach Western productivity levels. It has taken out some six levels of management between the main directorate and the shop floor. In spite of these painful changes and a 25 percent increase in production, the company was still not profitable in 1991.[38] Although these are not strictly marketing issues, such structural problems will inevitably affect the development of marketing strategy.

In principle, if it is decided to limit exposure in these circumstances, the level of Eastern European investment needs to be kept to a small share of the company's total investment in both East and West.

Infrastructure Problems

One of the main problems encountered by companies entering Eastern Europe has been an unreliable or possibly even collapsing infrastructure. This can be seen in two areas: energy and distribution systems.

For many years, Eastern European countries have received supplies of oil from the USSR. From mid-1990, supplies were withheld either because the oil was needed inside the USSR or because it had to be sold for hard currency, which was in short supply everywhere in Eastern Europe. Since that time, there have been major oil supply shortfalls and increases in costs for the other countries involved.[39] Eastern European distribution systems have proved to be unreliable and inadequately developed. They have also been at the center of much of the upheaval from privatization: 70 percent of the retail trade in Poland has been transferred to the private sector.[36] Though there is nothing inherently wrong with this, it has led to problems for companies such as PepsiCo and BSN.

In conclusion, probably the best strategy over the next few years for Eastern Europe is to assume that the infrastructure does not exist and that demand will be limited, as economies struggle to control inflation and currency and maintain basic living conditions. Developing detailed marketing strategies in these circumstances is likely to involve:

* Long time scales for payback.
* Limiting risk to affordable exposures as compared with total levels of investment in the West.
* Investment in marketing infrastructure.

NOTES

1. L. Jauch and W. F. Glueck, *Business Policy and Strategic Management*, 5th ed. (New York: McGraw-Hill International, 1988), chapter 10.
2. Ibid., chapters 3–6.
3. C. Bowman and D. Asch, *Strategic Management* (London: Macmillan, 1988), chapter 8.
4. G. S. Day, *Strategic Marketing Planning* (St. Paul, MN: West Publishing, 1987), p. 52.
5. G. Oliver, *Marketing Today* (Englewood Cliffs, NJ: Prentice Hall, 1990). p. 180.

6. R. Buzzell and B. Gale, *The PIMS Principles* (New York: Free Press, 1987), chapter 1.

7. G. Johnson and H. Scholes, *Exploring Corporate Strategy*, 2nd ed. (Englewood Cliffs, NJ: Prentice Hall, 1988), p. 192.

8. R. Jacobson and D. Aaker, "Is Market Share All It's Cracked up to Be?" *Journal of Marketing* 49 (Autumn, 1985), p. 11.

9. R. Lynch, *European Business Strategies* (London: Kogan Page, 1990), p. 265.

10. Ibid., p. 175.

11. M. E. Porter, *Competitive Advantage* (New York: Free Press, 1985), chapters 14 and 15.

12. M. E. Porter, *Competitive Strategy* (New York: Free Press, 1980), chapters 8, 10–12.

13. Lynch, chapter 6.

14. M. E. Porter, "European Companies after 1992: Don't Collaborate, Compete," *The Economist*, June 9, 1990.

15. A. Hill, "Electronics Plan for Debate," *Financial Times*, November 18, 1991.

16. A. Hill, "Fresh Doubts on HDTV Strategies," *Financial Times*, November 20, 1991.

17. A. Hill, "MEPs Back More Flexible HDTV Strategy," *Financial Times*, November 21, 1991, p. 2.

18. European Commission, *Panorama of EC Industry 1989* (Luxembourg: OPOCE, 1989), p. 11.

19. J. A. Kay, *1992: Myths and Realities* (London: London Business School, 1989), p. 26.

20. M. R. Cvar, "Case Studies in Global Competition: Patterns of Success and Failure." In M. E. Porter (ed.), *Competition in Global Industries* (Boston: Harvard Business School Press, 1986), chapter 15.

21. I. Rodger, "Clocking on to Diversity," *Financial Times*, July 18, 1990.

22. Y. Doz, *Strategic Management in Multinational Companies* (Elmsford, NY: Pergamon Press, 1986), chapter 6.

23. Ibid., p. 147.

24. P. Cecchini, *1992—The European Challenge* (Aldershot, England: Wildwood House, 1988).

25. World Bank, *World Development Report 1991* (Washington, DC: World Bank, 1991), pp. 96ff.

26. Lynch, p. 109.

27. Kay, p. 28.

28. J. McGee and S. Segal-Horn, "Strategic Space and Industry Dynamics," *Journal of Marketing Management* 6, no. 3 (1990), pp. 175–93.

29. R. Gogel, and J.-C. Larreche, "The Battlefield for 1992: Product Strength and Geographic Coverage," *European Management Journal* 7, no. 2 (1989), p. 132.

30. European Commission, *Research on the Cost of Non-Europe*, vol. 1 (Luxembourg, OPOCE, 1988), pp. 29–36.

31. W. Ramsay, "Challenges and Opportunities for New Product Development in the FMCG Industry," ESOMAR seminar, 1990, Barcelona.

32. M. T. Cunningham, "The British Approach to Europe." In P. Turnbull and J.-P. Valla, *Strategies for International Industrial Marketing*, (London: Croom Helm, 1986), chapter 5.

33. OECD, "Economic Outlook No. 49," July 1991.

34. "Survey of Business in Eastern Europe," *The Economist*, September 21, 1991, p. 25.

35. A. Hill and C. Bobinski, "EC Paves the Way for Free Trade with Eastern Europe," *Financial Times*, November 23, 1991, p. 2.

36. G. de Jonquieres, "Home-Grown Produce on the Multi-Nationals' Shopping List," *Financial Times*, August 8, 1991.

37. "A Fast Autobahn to Unity," *Financial Times*, March 13, 1990.

38. "A Survey of Business in Eastern Europe," *The Economist*, September 21, 1991, p. 25.

39. J. Dempsey, "Eastern Europe Struggles to Fill Energy Gap," *Financial Times*, February 1, 1991.

8

European market entry and country selection

Having discussed the overall direction of European marketing strategy, we now need to consider the first two or three years—the entry period and country choice. Some readers might argue that this should be determined *before* resolving long-term strategy. But choosing the entry route into Europe before knowing the destination and the vehicle that will get you there is usually unwise. However, there is nothing absolute in marketing strategy, so the entry route and country considerations may well have a significant effect on overall strategy.

We shall examine the opening moves in European strategy under the following headings, which are in some respects interrelated:

- European market entry strategy.
- European country selection.
- Competitive reaction to European entry.
- Conclusions and action.

EUROPEAN MARKET ENTRY STRATEGY

In approaching market entry, it is convenient to explore two questions:

1. What are the basic options for entry?
2. How do we choose among them?

Basic Options for Entry

In international marketing development, it is normal to start with the option that involves the business in the lowest exposure to overseas activity and then build international involvement in stages; see, for example, Root and Bilkery, who both describe this process.[1,2] This option has the basic advantage of limiting business risk while developing European export sales; it is shown in Figure 8–1.

The only difficulty about the evolutionary nature of such an approach to European export development is that, in some cases, it may not reflect reality. We have already seen that some markets such as cars, aerospace, defense, and telecommunications equipment simply cannot exist on demand from one European country; for these markets, it is largely irrelevant to consider some of the early stages shown in Figure 8–1. Other European markets that might be considered capable of this carefully phased approach may be blown apart by the momentum created by the "1992 single market" campaign, which has been vigorously pursued in most EC countries apart from Germany.

In the more general context of international marketing, Rosson and Reid have argued that the flow process is likely to be too structured and generalized to be of use.[3] Turnbull surveyed 24 companies in France, Germany, and Sweden and showed that, even where foreign sales were a small proportion of total turnover, half the companies in the subsample were still using direct selling from local sales offices (i.e., partway along the spectrum in Figure 8–1).[4] From further analysis, he concluded that it was the *market* that determined the entry strategy, not the degree of risk exposure.

In theory, all the European entry options shown in Figure 8–1 may be present, but, for an individual company, some of the lower-risk options may not be available in practice. Moreover, Lynch has documented that the staged approach would miss a whole series of options that have been used extensively in the EC and Eastern Europe:[5]

- Philip Morris (U.S.) *acquired* Jacobs Suchard in 1990 to extend its coffee franchise in Europe.
- GE (U.S.) *merged* its domestic appliances business with GEC (UK).
- Corning Glass (U.S.) has a series of *joint ventures* with European and U.S. companies in Europe.
- PepsiCo (U.S.) has been *franchising* its Pizza Hut restaurant chain to major brewers and retailers in the UK and Belgium.

Other European entry options might include licensing and turnkey contracts. Young et al. provide more detailed descriptions of these than is possible in this text.[6]

FIGURE 8–1
Evolution of European Market Entry

	Example of Method	Business Risk to Producer
Indirect exporting	Exporting house buys from home firm and sells in Europe	Low
↓		
Direct exporting	Agent in Europe: does not take title to goods *or* European distributor who does take title	
↓		
Direct selling	Send sales team from home country	
↓		
Local sales office	Permanent sales team plus administration	
↓		
Overseas sales and production	Involves highest capital commitment and permanent presence	High

There is one further option that the European Commission itself has been keen to promote: the *strategic alliance*. This might involve a long-term contractual relationship or even a minority shareholding:

> The exchange of goods and services on an arm's-length and ad-hoc basis, ie trade in a textbook sense, between independent firms in two different countries is becoming the exception rather than the rule and contractual relationships between links in the chain of value-added are becoming essential features of the modern economy. Transborder links of this kind can involve one or all of the elements of the chain of value-added, from basic R & D, organisational know-how, production or procurement of intermediate and final products, to marketing and other services.[7]

Interestingly, among the four countries studied (Germany, the UK, France, and Italy), there was significant variation in the enthusiasm to form such alliances. France was the most enthusiastic and Germany the least.[8]

Although there are clearly arguments in favor of strategic alliances, it is important not to underestimate the difficulties of this route and the special types of management required by both parties; see Lynch.[9] Relationships need to be flexible, trusting, relaxed, and organized. They might be difficult to hold together for a North American company without a European base.

It might be argued that some of the above options are beyond the scope of North American marketing management; certainly, they will mean working with other functions within the company. But to conclude that marketing should not take the initiative in developing strategies in these matters would be to take a narrow and parochial view of the interface between marketing and business strategy.

In examining the possible options for European entry, there are two main conclusions. The first is that entry strategy based merely on exporting may not exploit the advantages of the single Europe in the long run. The second is that the difficulty lies not in generating the options but in choosing among them.

Choice among Options

In essence, the best option is the one that delivers the company's objectives at the lowest risk. Since most marketing management entails a mix of different elements, this is easier to state than to achieve: many factors need to be balanced, and there is no formula that will provide the best solution. Each option has advantages and disadvantages that need to be explored. These are summarized in Table 8–1.

In practice, some routes can be quickly eliminated on the basis of the resources, objectives, and capabilities of the company. For example, there is no point in attempting to acquire a competitor if all the best companies have already been bought; this is the case in some EC markets now. Similarly, an option may be quickly ruled out if the company to be acquired is asking a high price but has such poor-quality assets that acquisition for anything but a pittance is irrelevant; this is the case in some Eastern European markets now. We shall return to the selection process when we have looked at country selection.

Readers may be wondering to what extent any of the above options have actually been used in the EC. According to a 1990 study by the London Business School, the number of mergers in the EC tripled between 1983 and 1987.[10] However, many involved UK companies alone, with the proportion of *cross-border* deals actually declining over the period. It is possible that the study may have underestimated the effect on the EC because it concentrated on the numbers of deals rather than their quality, but this judgment is difficult to substantiate.

The researchers argued that many of the advantages of mergers could be gained by other forms of deals, such as alliances and joint ven-

TABLE 8–1
Advantages and Disadvantages of Routes into Europe

Advantages	*Disadvantages*
Exporting	
Cheaper	Slow
Lower risk: less commitment	May miss opportunities through lack
Good route for unique product	of knowledge
Allows slow buildup and learning	Allows home competitors to assess
about market conditions	and build response
More control	Building scale economies may be
Keeps economies of scale at home	high-risk and expensive
base	
No need to share technology	
Strategic Alliance	
More permanent than mere exporting	Slow and plodding approach
Close contact	Needs constant work to keep relation-
Uses joint expertise and commitment	ship sound
perhaps not available to exporter	Partners have only limited joint com-
Allows potential partners to learn	mitment to success
about each other	Unlikely to build economices of scale
Locks out other competitors	
Joint Venture	
Build scale quickly	Control lost to some extent
Obtain local knowledge and distribu-	Works best where both parties con-
tion	tribute something to the mix
Cheaper than takeover	Difficult to manage
Local entry where takeover not possi-	Share profits with partner
ble	
Can be used where outright takeover	
not feasible	
Can be used where similar product	
available	
Takeover	
Can be relatively fast	Premium paid: expensive
Useful for national expertise acquired	High risk if wrong
Buys presence	Best targets may have already gone
Buys size and market share	in some markets
	Not always easy to dispose of un-
	wanted parts of company

Source: R. Lynch, *European Business Strategies* (London: Kogan Page, 1990).

tures, which have the advantage of being less permanent and thus lower-risk. They warned against ill-considered mergers: "Those who rise too quickly on the dance floor for fear that there will be no nice girls left, risk waking in the morning beside unsuitable partners."

EUROPEAN COUNTRY SELECTION

In addition to considering country entry routes, it is essential to look at which countries to select; the two issues are interrelated. We can usefully structure country selection with three questions:

1. Should we adopt a pan-European or country-by-country approach?
2. Should we concentrate on certain countries or spread our marketing effort across many countries?
3. Which countries do we choose?

Pan-European versus Country-by-Country Approach

There is no point in attempting to select individual European countries if the marketing strategy needs to be directed to *pan-European* customers and resources. Note that this issue is not the same as deciding whether to enter a few or many European countries. We are examining solely the implications of pan-European demand—for example, companies requiring transport or delivery services throughout Europe, not just to a few destinations, or an advertising agency whose clients already have subsidiaries across much of Europe.

There are two criteria against which to judge the matter:

1. *Customers*: Actual or potential customers may or may not purchase on a pan-European basis.
2. *Company*: Corporate resources may or may not lend themselves to handling the additional strain imposed by dealing across the much greater geographical area.

The considerations that will lead to the decisions in this area are set out in the following box. Naturally, if it is decided to seek entry on a truly pan-European basis, the only question that follows is whether some countries should receive priority; this is discussed below. For many companies, a combination of available resources and lack of true pan-European demand may make this entry route unlikely. If the example of entering U.S. markets is any guide, then entering a European region (for example, Eastern Holland and the Ruhr) and extending from this base throughout the EC is likely to prove more practical.

Pan-European or Country-by-Country Approach?

Customer Considerations

Pan-European when:

- Same need in all 12 EC countries
- One country cannot provide sufficient sales

- Pan-European image enhances product
- Product has relatively few buyers
- Product bought for rational performance rather than psychological reasons

Country-by-country when:

- Culture and language are significant in purchase decision
- Costs of building Eurobrand are higher than benefits from country approach
- Product or service has many buyers
- Distribution varies widely across Europe
- Product essentially provides local service

Company Considerations

Pan-European when:

- Company already selling on this (or global) basis
- Company already has extensive skills and experience across Europe
- Company has resources to handle work involved

Country-by-country when:

- Company's main experience comes from country approach
- Company has historical, cultural, or language link with specific countries
- The home country of the company has established links with specific countries

Concentrating Effort on Certain Countries or Spreading It across Most of Europe

Even though there may be no clear case for pan-European entry, the issue may remain of the number of European countries that should be entered in the early years: do we concentrate on a few or spread our effort across many, possibly even some from Eastern Europe?

The questions of spreading or concentration of effort in international marketing have been researched in detail.[11] The checklist shown in the following box applies these arguments to Europe. Clearly, the conclusions to be drawn for an individual company will depend on its resources, markets, and the apparent risks and opportunities.

Country Choice

Now, at last, we tackle the obvious question—which countries to enter. A rational marketing approach for large and small North American com-

---

Cover All 12 EC Countries or Select a Few?
Market Concentration or Market Spreading?

Concentration when:

- Wish to limit span of control for dealing with administration and problems
- Want better market and agent knowledge
- Company sales improve with high-quality selling
- High market share important to strategy and profits
- High relative expenditure is needed to gain and hold market share

Spreading when:

- Competition is mainly on price with nonprice factors unimportant
- Low after-sales service content
- Only limited data to select concentrated markets correctly
- Low market share is acceptable objective
- More important to specialize in products across many countries than to have geographical concentration

Key point: Northern European "industrial triangle" may be useful starting point for all entry strategies.

panies would entail collecting data in each market across Europe. The information to be collected, according to Douglas et al., can be summarized as follows:[12]

- Market size and growth potential.
- Competitors.
- Associated risks of operating in a particular market.
- Factors relating to the costs of being in each country.
- Channels of distribution and media availability.

They have suggested that even small and medium-sized companies should consider these matters. Larger companies with more resources may want to extend their searches further. For example, when working in a large company, I recall spending weeks analyzing the economies of individual countries in South America prior to extensive visits and the final selection of Brazil from a shortlist.

In the context of Europe, it is certainly worthwhile to be rational. However, there are some 18 countries in the EEA and another 20 or so in Eastern Europe, which implies a potentially large task. Douglas et al. suggest that subjective elimination of some countries might be undertaken, possibly using desk research (i.e., data available from libraries, computer databases, etc.). Such an early stage might also be used to apply any other criterion (e.g., a company's irrational dislike of all things Mediterranean, which might as well be faced early in the process).

Objective evaluation might then follow the process shown in Figure 8–2: desk research followed by more detailed analysis of selected countries. For the final list, there may even be some primary research (i.e., specially commissioned data), and there would almost certainly be a series of company visits. Figure 8–2 illustrates this approach in more detail.

For the smaller company with limited resources, it may be better to replace elaborate studies conducted in stages by some desk research coupled with:

- Individual overseas visits and key meetings.
- Overseas trade fairs and exhibitions.
- Surveying existing company customers and distributors for their overseas contacts.
- Trade audits (e.g., surveying actual shop distribution) in potential markets.

FIGURE 8–2
Country Selection and Evaluation for Large Companies

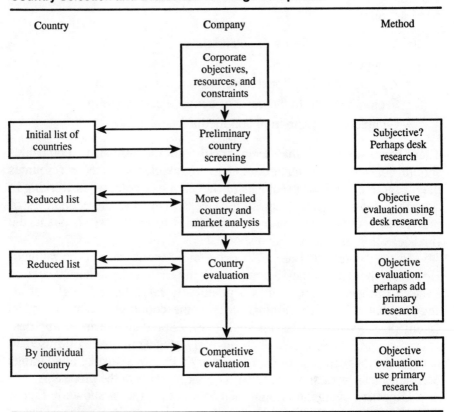

Country	Company	Method
	Corporate objectives, resources, and constraints	
Initial list of countries	Preliminary country screening	Subjective? Perhaps desk research
Reduced list	More detailed country and market analysis	Objective evaluation using desk research
Reduced list	Country evaluation	Objective evaluation: perhaps add primary research
By individual country	Competitive evaluation	Objective evaluation: use primary research

According to Johansson and Nonaka, this approach has been particularly popular with Japanese companies.[13] More generally in international marketing, the evidence suggests that the small company research described above is probably closer to reality.[14] Many companies do not employ a strictly rational process based on evidence in international markets. Although no specific research has been done, it is likely that the same may apply to European country selection. However, it is important to note that the European Commission and national governments have filled some of the potential gaps by supplying material that may not otherwise be so easily available for world markets:

- Background data.
- Embassy contacts.

- EC regional offices.
- European credit and insurance.
- European literature.

Indeed, the European network of contacts that has developed over the last few years does make the country selection process different from markets further afield. Other organizations worth contacting would include:

- European trade associations.
- EC organizations to provide ministerial contacts, resolve trade disputes, and so forth.

Some of these groups are listed with telephone numbers in EC publications.[15] North American companies have the same access as EC companies to this general material.

COMPETITIVE REACTION TO EUROPEAN ENTRY

If European market entry has any significant impact, then a competitive response is likely, particularly in Western Europe. Porter argues that such responses are best foreseen and forestalled, if possible.[16] For small companies aiming to take a small share of a fragmented market, such considerations may have little practical effect. But for larger North American companies entering oligopolistic European markets and seeking a significant market presence, there is a need to explore this matter or face trouble on entry. To illustrate, note the maneuvering by U.S. airlines during 1992, when British Airways (UK) and KLM Airlines (Netherlands) acquired shares in U.S. airlines to enhance their access to the U.S. market. Both companies were forced to back away from their initial entry.[17] The U.S. domestic market was still largely secure from outside invasion in 1993.

Porter suggests investigating five areas when seeking market entry:[18]

1. How likely is the retaliation?
2. How soon will the retaliation come?
3. How effective will retaliation potentially be?
4. How tough will it be, where toughness refers to the willingness of the competitor to retaliate strongly, even at its own expense?
5. Can retaliation be influenced?

Plotting these potential reactions to entry deserves careful thought and analysis. Bleeke investigated the U.S. deregulation of trains, banking, and plane markets during the 1980s.[19] He suggested that the lessons learned could be applied to the formation of the single European market. He observed the following in the United States:

- Large numbers of new entrants, most of which fell by the wayside.
- Deterioration in industry profitability as new entrants shatter pricing for all competitors for at least five years.
- Moves to launch into the most attractive market segments, thus making them less attractive.
- The weak becoming weaker.
- Merger and acquisition activity often occurring in two compressed waves—the first consolidating the weak, the second combining the strong.

But all this happened in the United States where there is a truly single market in at least some products and services, and also an aggressive belief in beating competition. Even though the "single Europe" has now been under way for some years, many of these phenomena are still to appear; this may suggest that the single Europe is still not a reality, rather than that the U.S. evidence cannot be applied to Europe.

Nevertheless, the research showed that some entry strategies had a higher likelihood of success in the United States than others; Bleeke suggests that they might be applied to Europe in the 1990s. We shall pick out two examples here to stimulate the type of strategic thinking that needs to be undertaken. The strategies can best be summarized according to the type of single Europe entry proposed.

Low-cost new entrants should:

- Target the most profitable segments.
- Focus on price-sensitive customers and price-oriented media campaigns.
- Avoid attacking core markets of existing major companies.
- Not have ambitious growth plans in the early years, which would take them away from their core strength.

An example of single Europe low-cost entry would be the successful launch by Dell Computers (U.S.) of its mail-order computer range into Europe in 1990.[20] It successfully used the knowledge and well-tried techniques of its U.S. home market.

Focused, segmented new entrants attacking a specific market segment should:

- Target nonprice segments.
- Deepen customer relationships in the target market by providing a range of customer services and products.
- Develop information systems and databases for superior customer service.
- Seek new ways of providing products or services to lock in customers through specialist product attributes.

A successful example of this approach is the move by Nynex (U.S.) to acquire 11 cable franchises in the UK.[21] The deal will make the company Britain's largest cable franchise owner with a carefully targeted and exclusive service in parts of the UK.

Finally, on the matter of competitive reactions, we should refer briefly to Eastern Europe. With these countries, the likelihood of competitive response is much lower: Western investment is still being actively sought. However, there is some evidence of national reactions against the privatization process, for example, in Poland.[22] This may have an impact on potential new entrants but would involve very different strategies from those described above. Essentially, political support would be vital, possibly coupled with local negotiation to ease the genuine difficulties faced by the people after years of incompetence.

CONCLUSIONS AND ACTION

As in most other marketing, it is not possible to derive easy solutions for North American market entry. However, the main considerations are likely to include the following:

- Number of Markets to be Covered.
- Penetration required.
- Market feedback needed for product development and long-term growth.
- Whether experience is needed before further expansion is attempted.
- The level of control required.
- Profit potential: smaller markets need lower-cost methods.

- Local infrastructure: Eastern European and some markets in southern Europe may demand heavy investment.
- Risk and feasibility.
- Type of product: some are clearly international, and some are very dependent on culture and language.

Beyond the general considerations of entry, the detailed marketing entry process will also need to be undertaken. Entry strategy may need to be plotted carefully, especially where potential customers may have unfavorable expectations of or experiences with similar approaches. Turnbull and Valla have described the detailed steps undertaken by the Dorkan Company (UK) when entering the German market for small castings in the automotive and consumer durable industries.[23]

1. First, the marketing director establishes contact with the most senior purchasing executive of the customer. No business is negotiated at this point.
2. The director then contacts the buyer in order to gain access to the customer's engineers, who specify the product.
3. A sales representative and engineer from the supplier then take over the negotiations and establish contacts with the buyer and customer's junior engineers.
4. The sales representative progressively raises the level of contacts to senior buyer and older engineering staff who were previously opposed to the process.
5. The supplier offers to quote for a small order and sends over technical staff to liaise with the customer's engineers and buyers on the correct choice of trial component.
6. At the trial contact stage, the supplier's quality control, engineering, and marketing staff visit customers to make sure that the trial is conducted satisfactorily.
7. If a contract is likely to be placed, the customer's buyers, engineers, and quality inspectors are invited to the supplier's factory.

In the preceding preplanned entry sequence, the underlying aims were to overcome resistance to innovation and to a new source of supply. The two authors also described other entry techniques more suited to other situations:

- A specific French entry strategy where close relationships needed to be established quickly with a potential customer. The quickest route was to acquire an existing French supplier of the customer.
- Making the customer excessively dependent on the supplier's technical problem-solving and product application skills. This will subsequently make the cost of changing to a new supplier prohibitively high.

These examples are based on a prepared entry plan using etiquette appropriate to the EC country involved. Strong professional and social links are sought across the various functions in both organizations. I can vouch for the success of this carefully planned process from my own experience setting up a highly successful relationship between Barker & Dobson (UK) and Marabou (Sweden) for the importing of Dime chocolate bars into the UK.

In terms of action, specific procedures on documentation, warranties, and after-sales service will also need to be planned; we shall examine these in Chapter 9.

NOTES

1. F. R. Root, *Entry Strategies for International Markets* (Lexington, MA: Lexington Books, 1987), figure 3.
2. W. J. Bickley, "An Attempted Integration of the Literature on the Export Behaviour of Firms," *Journal of International Business Studies* 9 (1978), pp. 33–46.
3. P. J. Rosson and S. D. Reid, *Managing Export Entry and Expansion: An Overview* (New York: Praeger, 1987).
4. P. W. Turnbull, "A Challenge to the Stages Theory of the Internationalisation Process," chapter in Rosson and Reid.
5. R. Lynch, *European Business Strategies* (London: Kogan Page, 1990), p. 274.
6. S. Young, J. Hamill, C. Wheeler, and J. R. Davies, *International Market Entry and Development* (Herts, England: Harvester/Wheatsheaf, 1989), chapters 4–6.
7. European Commission, *Research on the Cost of Non-Europe*, vol. 1 (Luxembourg: OPOCE, 1988), p. 218.
8. Ibid. pp. 209–11.

9. Lynch, pp. 302–3.

10. Centre for Business Strategy, *Continental Mergers are Different: Strategy and Policy for 1992* (London: London Business School, 1990).

11. N. Piercy, *Export Strategy: Markets and Competition* (Winchester, MA: George Allen & Unwin, 1982).

12. S. P. Douglas, C. S. Craig, and W. J. Keegan, "Approaches to Assessing International Marketing Opportunities for Small and Medium-Sized Companies," *Columbia Journal of World Business* 17, no. 3 (1982), p. 26.

13. J. K. Johansson and J. K. Nonaka, "Market Research the Japanese Way," *Harvard Business Review*, May-June 1987, p. 16.

14. Young et al., pp. 56–58.

15. European Commission, *Panorama of EC Industry 1991/92* (Luxembourg: OPOCE, 1991).

16. M. E. Porter, *Competitive Strategy* (New York: Free Press, 1980), chapters 3–5.

17. A. Lorenz and J. Harlow, "Global Air Wars," *The Sunday Times*, November 22, 1992, p. 3.3. See also M. DuBois and B. Coleman, "EC Takes Major Step to Opening Skies to Free Pricing for Member Airlines," *The Wall Street Journal*, June 23, 1992, p. A17.

18. Porter, p. 95.

19. J. A. Bleeke, "Strategic Choices for Newly Opened Markets," *Harvard Business Review*, September–October 1990, p. 158.

20. A. Cane and L. Kehoe, "New Order Forces the Pace of Change," *Financial Times*, November 8, 1991.

21 A. Kupfer, "Ma Bell and Seven Babies Go Global," *Fortune*, November 4, 1991, p. 85.

22. "Survey of Business in Eastern Europe," *The Economist*, September 21, 1991, p. 9.

23. P. W. Turnbull and J.-P. Valla, *Strategies for International Industrial Marketing* (London: Croom Helm, 1986), pp. 200–1.

9

| European product decisions

After all the customer analysis, market research, and strategy development, it is worth reminding ourselves that the actual objective for a North American company is to market a European product or service,* that is, what the European customer will purchase. Thus, product decisions are fundamental to all marketing activity.

With barriers coming down across the EC and trade developing with Eastern Europe, we start by investigating what this means for existing products. We look first at the EC trading and legal framework within which we must operate. We then examine the central issue of how the product benefit needs to be defined in the context of the single Europe, before considering how it will change. New products will also be developed for EC markets and may well provide the innovation needed to make real headway in Europe. Again, Eastern Europe presents its own special challenges and difficulties. The subjects covered in this chapter are the following:

- EC basics: the trading and legal framework for the single Europe.
- Defining the European product benefit.
- Developing benefits for existing products to beat European competitors.
- New product development in the single Europe.
- Product marketing decisions for Eastern Europe.

To help clarify the European product decision-making process as described in this chapter, we diagram it in Figure 9–1.

---

*For the sake of brevity, throughout this chapter I shall refer to a "product" when I mean "product or service."

FIGURE 9–1
European Product Decisions

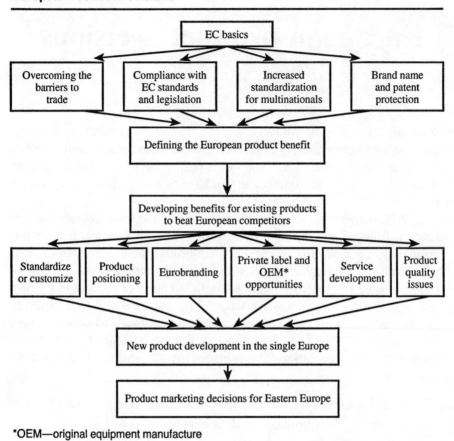

*OEM—original equipment manufacture

EC BASICS: THE TRADING AND LEGAL FRAMEWORK FOR THE SINGLE EUROPE

From a marketing viewpoint, the single Europe product opportunities will become reality only when set in the context of the changes in trading regulations, product harmonization, and product legal issues. We examine these in this section. Some legal issues concerned with product descriptions and product claims are discussed in Chapter 11.

Overcoming Barriers to Trade

Because the EC is made up of sovereign governments, each with its own laws, history, industries, traditions, and pressure groups, there have been few common technical product standards across the area until recently. This has meant that during 1950–1980 it was only in theory that products for sale in one EC country could also be sold elsewhere. In practice, there were countless barriers to cross-border trade. The 1988 Cecchini report found, for example:

- *Automobiles:* "The trouble is that the world's largest car market is single only in name. The range of obstacles hindering its effective integration provides a quintessential roll-call of Common Market disunity."[1]
- *Foodstuffs:* "More than 200 non-tariff barriers . . . were identified as applying to intra-EC trade on 10 product sectors in the five largest countries."[2]
- *Telecommunications equipment:* "The costs imposed on the EC telecommunications equipment industry by national regulation and practice are substantial, as is their ripple effect throughout the economy."[3]

Essentially, products to be sold across the EC had to be modified for many individual EC countries. The Commission identified the following three barriers as having a possible impact on products.[4] Marketing managers both in and outside of the EC had to examine them for each EC country and decide whether any basic product modifications were necessary.

1. *Physical barriers:* intra-EC border stoppages, customs controls, and associated paperwork. Product modifications here chiefly concern the need to generate new documentation and more robust packaging for longer distances than for home markets.
2. *Technical barriers:* meeting divergent national product standards, technical regulations, and conflicting business laws. Product modifications here might mean reformulated or redesigned products with new labeling.
3. *Fiscal barriers:* especially different rates of value-added tax (VAT) and excise duties on tobacco and alcohol. Product mod-

ifications in this situation might mean new sizes to accommodate different price points. We shall discuss the pricing aspect in Chapter 10.

To summarize, it has been essential for marketing managers to investigate in detail the situation across the EC country by country and make any necessary product changes. This has been compounded by *hidden barriers* to entry to other EC countries: these are the unrecorded reasons that national firms can continue to pick up the bulk of some contracts in their home countries beyond meeting the technical specifications. Lynch has recorded some examples.[5] The best-known is the case of Europe's largest construction company, Bouygues, France, which attempted to bid for a Danish public bridge contract in 1989. The company was unsuccessful and complained that bias by the Danish authorities did not allow the company to make a fair estimate. After intervention by the European Commission, the company was allowed to resubmit its bid.

Other hidden barriers operated by the national country have involved the slow processing of technical approval applications, obscure product-testing procedures, the inconsistent application of test results on products, and the need for extensive retesting when equipment was modified. The UK government complained to the Spanish authorities about all these during 1991 on behalf of UK companies. North American companies should therefore not be surprised if they meet similar difficulties.

For North American companies, there is one more basic issue: The EC has detailed rules for products to qualify as local (i.e., EC) products. Products that are not local may carry heavy EC quota restrictions, designed to protect EC markets. The rules will need to be checked on an individual basis; U.S. and Canadian embassies can help.

Compliance with EC Standards and Legislation

Over the last 20 years the EC has made considerable efforts to bring about a single market in products. In the early years, it undertook the slow, laborious process of roundtable discussions between countries in an attempt to determine common standards; this was unpopular, bureaucratic, and time-consuming.[6] It was replaced by a two-pronged attack during the 1980s comprising:

1. Mutual recognition.
2. Selective technical harmonization.

Mutual recognition means that "if a product is lawfully manufactured and marketed in one member state, there is no reason why it should not move through the Community."[7] This followed a famous ruling by the European Court of Justice in 1979 concerning the French liqueur Cassis de Dijon, which could not be imported into West Germany because it allegedly did not conform to that country's standards for liqueurs. The case was overturned by the court.[8]

Subsequently, there were other, similar disputes; the German beer purity laws, the *Rheinheitsgebot*, were used to stop the importation of beers that did not meet German national standards.[9] This case was overturned only in 1987, so it has been a long war of attrition! And all EC countries have been at fault at various times.

Selective technical harmonization has also been required. It has not been enough just to employ mutual recognition: there would still have been too many anomalies. Technical committees have been set up to produce common pan-European standards on key EC products, and these have now emerged in many areas.

There has also been another problem in obtaining common standards: They needed unanimous approval by member states, and this was a recipe for delay and obfuscation. The Single Europe Act of 1986 therefore allowed majority voting in this area. It also effectively empowered the Commission to move ahead to create common standards.

But development in Brussels of new product standards has created its own inefficiencies. In the UK, for example, *The Sunday Times* campaigned vigorously with well-documented evidence against some truly daft harmonization ideas from the Commission. Its story "Crisp-Crusher Turns His Bureaucratic Blitz on Britain's Soccer Heroes" referred to the EC industry commissioner's proposals in the interests of single European harmonization to ban certain ingredients in British prawn-flavored crisps and to stop UK football teams having more than two "foreign" players.[10] No doubt other EC countries will experience similar absurdities, and the Commission will claim it was misrepresented.

More generally, many North American managers will recognize that each EC country has had its own laws, for example, on product safety. They have often differed widely with national authorities reluctant to accept the results of checks on products conducted elsewhere. The only long-term solution is to have one set of rules across the EC. The Commission must ultimately pursue common standards. Marketers must investigate the resulting standards for compliance by their own products and services.

gate the resulting standards for compliance by their own products and services.

One particular area of product standardization is *packaging*. Compliance here will need to be verified with national and EC regulations. North American companies will need to check these on a country-by-country basis.

However, changes needed in European packaging are likely to go beyond this with:

- Additional languages being required.
- New packaging design to accommodate the extra words.

There is a real trap for the unwary marketer in the second of these; let us take the 1989 box design for Nabisco's Cookies Belin from France as an example. The pack had two main panels, each with identical illustrations and brand names. One panel had English and German product descriptions, the other French and Dutch. There is a reasonable probability that an unsuspecting grocer would shelve the pack the wrong way around! Bahlsen Biscuits from Germany designed better packs, relying almost totally on the pack illustration alone. The words were on the sides.

The other area of standardization likely to become increasingly important during the 1990s is *environmental developments*. There may be increasing EC pressure to upgrade environmental standards. In December 1991 EC environment ministers agreed to introduce a Community-wide "Eco-label" to identify for consumers those products that do the least damage to the environment. In addition, German laws to be enforced by 1994 require packaging manufacturers and retailers to take back used bottles, cans, and general packaging material. This may well be extended across the EC by the late 1990s. North American marketers used to coping with state as well as federal laws can easily deal with all of this.

Increased Standardization for Multinational Companies

Beyond EC requirements, there are other forces bringing about product standardization in the single Europe—principally, efficient working practices as applied by the larger multinationals. Until recently, Europe's largest consumer goods company, Unilever, had 15 different shapes of ice cream cone in its supposedly standardized Europroduct, Cornetto ice cream. Similarly, it was using 85 flavors in the chicken soups it sold in Europe.[11]

Unilever is in the process of standardizing and rationalizing these products by centering product development on a pan-European rather than a national European company basis, but that runs the danger of offending some national companies in the group. The company has said that it is easier to harmonize impulse purchases such as ice cream, but the nearer a food product is to being a part of the national customer's staple diet, the more difficult it has been to obtain a European standard. The converse of this is that where demand is similar across borders, as for some industrial products, the easier it should be to establish pan-European product standardization and development. North American multinationals such as Gillette, Colgate, and Kellogg's do not seem to have experienced the same confusion, probably because their branding and packaging has always been more uniform.

EC Progress on Standardization

All the preceding issues will no doubt be resolved in the 1990s. Certainly, the internal market is slowly taking shape and was largely complete by 1 January 1993. The Commission undertook its own study of progress as of November 1990:[12] 200 of the 282 decisions had been adopted by the Council. Many were already in operation with some states ahead of others, according to EC data. Italy was the worst country in terms of implementation.[13] But, even in those countries were the standards had been adopted, there were still problems: in 1990 the Commission dealt with 1,758 complaints that governments had ignored EC laws and treaty articles, a total that was up from 1,074 in 1986.[14] So all is not over yet in product marketing and the need to investigate *individual countries* in the single European market.

European Brand Name, Trademark and Patent Protection

There is little point in investing in European brand name development if there is no legal protection. Unfortunately, this is an area in which the single Europe does not operate, and there will be anomalies for the next few years. Expert legal opinion is essential.

European brand names and trademarks can be registered, but there are 10 separate systems in the EC, all with different criteria. The European Commission has proposed an EC trademark with single EC registration.[15] But national registration would still be allowed for those companies uninterested in selling across the EC.

There is another reason national registration will remain important: for reasons of history, some brand names are owned in one EC country by one company but have different ownership in other countries. For example, Unilever owns the Persil washing powder brand name in the UK, where it is a market leader. However, in Germany and most other EC countries, the same brand is owned by the German chemical and consumer products company Henkel.

Patent protection can support powerful unique product benefits and enhance competitive advantage. The law is much like that for trademarks—national registration with the possibility of a single EC convention in the early 1990s. In addition, there are a few other methods of registration, including the European Patents Convention, which includes some non-EC countries such as Austria and Sweden but excludes Ireland and Portugal. Yes, the situation is complex.

DEFINING THE EUROPEAN PRODUCT BENEFIT

Although mutual recognition and technical harmonization may not be fully achieved, the way forward is at least clear and reasonably predictable. For North American marketers, a more fundamental problem in the single Europe may be that, even when barriers come down, there is no automatic incentive for customers to move from their existing suppliers. This is a more subtle and potentially longer-lasting issue than that of technical matters. How do U.S. and Canadian companies seeking European expansion persuade potential European customers to switch from their current suppliers?

The 19th-century British economist David Ricardo, in his "theory of competitive advantage," argued that international trading allows countries to specialize in certain products. If Germany is better at making engineering products and Ireland is better at producing agricultural products, then it would be more profitable for Germany to concentrate on engineering and export some engineering products to pay for importing Irish agriculture. Ricardo argued that nations should produce and sell what they do best and discontinue what they do least well. Arguably, the marketing extension of this is that, where no obvious advantage exists for a new European entrant, an EC country and its customers have no incentive to switch to suppliers from other EC or North American countries.

Undoubtedly, the single market will throw together products and services that have existed in national markets for years and have relatively small differences from each other. Ramsay has suggested that there will be a period of discontinuity as barriers come down in the single Europe: markets will need to be redefined across national boundaries with new competitors and redefined market shares.[16] The challenge in both industrial and consumer markets for existing products moving across Europe and new products entering from North America will be to persuade customers to switch their product loyalties. But how can this be done?

The starting point must be to seek a product benefit over potential European competitors, what Peckham calls a "demonstrable and merchandisable consumer plus."[17] In basic marketing, product benefits have usually been founded upon a "core" benefit; see Kotler, for example.[18] The corollary is that benefits beyond the core, such as quality, service, and warranties, can be used to "augment" the basic core benefit, *if so required*.

In European marketing, this approach is unlikely to be satisfactory. Because they have become well established, all the existing products are likely to have the core benefits, so it will be essential for U.S. and Canadian producers to look beyond these; "augmenting" core benefits will not be sufficient. One way of categorizing this process is shown in Figure 9–2. The implication is that *all the elements of product benefits* will need to be developed for successful European marketing. For example, it has not been enough for Whirlpool (U.S.) to develop well-branded domestic

FIGURE 9–2
European Product Benefit Definition

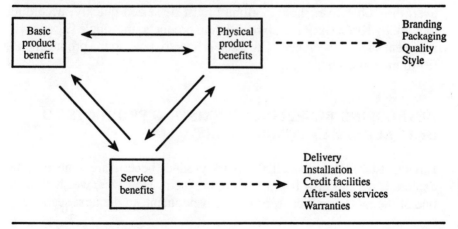

appliances across Europe: the company has also needed to offer extended warranties, delivery policies, and service schedules to stand any chance of making headway.[19,20]

Against this it might be said that a good many European companies already regularly update their existing products with simple improvements and occasional technological advances. Indeed, there is good evidence to indicate that the main reason for losing market leadership is a competitive technological advance by a competitor.[21] Although there is nothing new in this for the single Europe, it does not follow that normal continuous product improvement is all that is necessary for success, and other companies are already undertaking this across Europe. The real EC winners will be those who start thinking in terms of the complete range of potential product benefits in addition to the regular product improvements.

For existing products, it may be argued that the amount of effort on new development depends on where a product is in its life cycle: the convention view is that products in the early stages justify more effort than those in later stages.[22,23] But this ignores the significance of Ramsay's comment about the discontinuity resulting from the single Europe: as barriers come down, there may be no conventional rise and fall of sales with life cycle but rather a sudden influx of new competition. This would accelerate any changes unless action were taken.

The whole problem is compounded by the shorter product development cycles being obtained by leading competitors in recent years. Xerox halved its development process between 1982 and the later 1980's, and Glaxo cut the development time on its anti-ulcer drug Zantac from a conventional 10 years to 5.[24] Where a fast-moving "market window" is the overriding objective, the opportunity must be seized quickly, according to work by Krubasik.[25] For some existing products, the single Europe will represent such a watershed. The issue is how to develop the product benefits to meet this challenge.

DEVELOPING BENEFITS FOR EXISTING PRODUCTS TO BEAT EUROPEAN COMPETITORS

Having established that all the main product benefit areas need to be explored, we can now begin to examine them. However, we shall leave one of the most significant, product development, to the next section.

Customization versus Standardization

Some products for new European markets are likely to be at least slightly different from those in North America—for example, because of extra languages, more robust packaging needed to travel longer distances, branding variations, or different warranties (e.g., Heinz ketchup has the same label design but a slightly different taste between European countries—sweeter in some, sharper in others). Conversely, for other products, profitability and competitiveness will depend on their being standardized; for example, Ford Mondeo cars are essentially the same in each European country. There may be a need to strike a balance between the desire to customize the product for a local market against concerns about the extra costs involved in moving away from a standard product. This issue is shown in Figure 9–3, along with its implications for the European product benefit.

The key issue is where to strike the balance; there is no universal answer for all markets. The arguments are summarized in Table 9–1. Until Europeans all speak one language, some changes will always be needed, if only to translate the sales literature. Ultimately, it will be matter of costs against benefits and of which option delivers the company's objectives best.

Although the standardization/customization issue clearly has rele-

FIGURE 9–3
Product Benefit Options in Europe

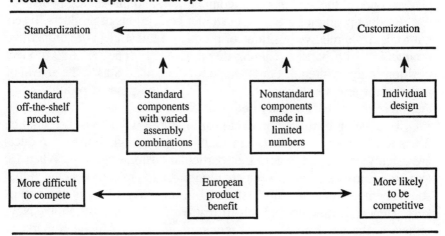

TABLE 9–1
European Standardization versus Customization

For standardization	For customization
Economies of scale in production and R&D	Varying customer needs
Savings in marketing costs on advertising production, sales training, and servicing	Differing conditions of usage (e.g., climate)
	Customers will pay extra
Lower inventory and more rapid response to spare parts delivery	High skill levels in local country to make changes
High technical specifications more easily satisfied	Government requirements

vance to Europe, a more meaningful long-term approach may be to consider European product positioning versus competition.

Positioning Products in Europe

Eventually, the single Europe will cease to be a market in which European companies "export" products to other EC countries, just as U.S. companies do not consider that they are exporting when products manufactured in New York are sold in California. There is simply a larger market for existing products. In the new Europe, the surviving products will therefore need to *reposition* themselves over all or part of Europe to take account of the new markets, competition, and market segments.

Product position starts with customer perceptions of products. It sets out to describe relative positions of products against ideal or competitive products.[26] With barriers coming down across Europe, relative product positions may be altered. For example, in the United States, the arrival of luxury Japanese sports cars in 1991 affected the product positioning of German Porsche cars already in that market.[27]

To develop European product positioning, it will almost certainly be necessary to examine market segmentation in the single Europe: products are usually positioned to appeal to particular customer groups. When we explored European market segmentation in Chapter 4, we concluded that some segments may remain ill defined in the early 1990s in some markets. Hence, it may be difficult to resolve European positioning. Nevertheless, the basic process will remain as in North American markets, with the following steps:

- Determining the competitive products.
- Establishing the relevant product attributes, as seen by customers, to profile the positioning factors defining the market.
- Mapping relative product positions.
- Deciding where to position the product across Europe or a region of Europe.

It should be noted that the process of European product positioning is rather different from "international marketing," where the debate is rather about whether products should be adapted to local markets or kept to a standard international format; the well-respected book on international marketing by Terpstra, for example, does not explore product positioning.[28]

In practice across Europe, it may be easier to define a product position than to launch a successful product. Unilever (Netherlands and UK) has tried twice to launch a gourmet frozen fish dish that is highly successful in Germany into the UK; each time it has failed.[29] The company has had more success with a range of convenience foods positioned as healthy options, which were launched in Germany in 1989 under the brand name *Du Darfst* ("You may"). This was successfully adapted in 1990 for France under the Effi brand name and for the UK as the Delite product range.[29] Kellogg's (U.S.) has had more success with its range of breakfast cereals, where positioning has largely been dictated by the type of product and a common brand name, regardless of language (e.g., Fruit 'n' Fibre is used unchanged on German and Scandinavian packaging). North American readers may care to note that, in Europe, this is a Kellogg's and not a Post cereal.

European Branding Opportunities

European positioning may in practice be associated with European branding; the issue here is not whether national brands can be developed but, rather, in the context of European marketing, the scope for *pan-European branding*. The economies of scale in advertising, packaging, production, and international positioning make this an inherently attractive marketing area worthy of consideration. Moreover, brands are a powerful method of obtaining sustainable competitive advantage.

Even where it is likely that the same pan-European customer demand exists across the continent, Lynch has suggested that there are three primary conditions for the development of European brands:[30]

1. *Resources across Europe:* A minimum of US$75 million in advertising and promotional funds are required every year for five years to build the brand name across the whole of the Community.
2. *Quality:* Consistent quality has to be delivered and maintained in each EC country.
3. *Timing:* At least five years will be needed to build a pan-European brand. Company objectives and investment criteria must allow for this.

On this basis, the initial attempts to relaunch the Philips domestic appliances business by the U.S. Whirlpool company as the "Philips Whirlpool" brand may succeed: the first year's advertising budget was reported to be US$75 million across 14 European countries, which may be enough.[31] More broadly, the list of top European brands in Chapter 4 shows that many have built consistent quality and have been building their brand franchises for many years. However, they are not necessarily the largest or the most profitable: Rolls-Royce and Jaguar may be well known but have small market shares. Similarly, Michelin and Ford may be strong Eurobrands, but they have an uneven profit record.

If the company has the resources, the potential rewards from Eurobranding may well produce real product benefits across Europe. The Mars confectionery and pet food company (U.S.) took the difficult decision in 1989–1990 to drop years of investment in some national brand names in order to develop Eurobrands:[32]

Mars UK Brand		Mars New Eurobrand
Mr. Dog	became	Cesar
Marathon	became	Snickers
Treets	became	M&Ms

North Americans will recognize the new names as being part of a global branding initiative.

But this does not mean that all companies see Eurobranding as the route forward. One of Europe's largest brewery companies, Heineken (Netherlands), has chosen to preserve local products, local brand names, and local recognition in some countries: the brand names Dreher (Italy),

Aguila (Spain), Amstel (Canada), Murphy (Ireland), and Heineken (the Netherlands, the UK and the United States) are all employed by the company.[33] Indeed, the alcohol market may be one where standardized, pan-European products could be contrary to European tastes. The growth of smaller individual beer brands in the UK and the survival of many local beers in Germany, coupled with the many regional brands of wine available in France, Italy, and Spain, suggest that Eurobranding may have its limits: customers in some markets prefer the individuality of small-scale brands. It might be argued that the Budweiser (U.S.) launch into the UK is the start of a pan-European platform, but it has been positioned as a U.S. premium-priced, specialty beer. There will always be room for pan-European alcohol brands if their segment is defined narrowly enough. Gucci and Calvin Klein will always appeal across Europe.

Naturally, there may be a case for *multiple branding*, that is, a company's operating more than one brand in the same European market. For example, Electrolux (Sweden), the world's second largest domestic appliance manufacturer, relaunched its European range under two brand names positioned at different market segments across Europe: Electrolux (up-market brand) and Zanussi and Frigidaire (mass-market brands).[34] It should be noted that this branding activity has been combined by Electrolux with over US$1 billion investment to upgrade its plant capacity and products across Europe. This must have an effect on product quality, whose importance we will explore later in this chapter.

A possible classification for brand development options in Europe has been suggested by Wolfe.[35] He makes a distinction between mass and niche markets for brands across Europe: in mass markets branding may be accompanied by lower margins and cost leadership, whereas in niche markets higher margins should be possible, but sales will reflect the smaller market opportunity. The three brand categories are the following:

1. *Euro-mass brands*: high volume, basic quality, low margins. *Example*: Natrel deodorant was launched by Gillette (U.S.) in each EC country with the same brand name, formula, pack, and advertising. It has achieved economies of scale through heavy promotion.

2. *Euro-niche brands*: medium volume, high added values, high margins. *Example*: American Express Card is the same product worldwide, appealing to a narrow target group in each country (i.e., the international business community).

3. *Local brands*: tailored to specific national or regional tastes. *Example*: The UK's biggest selling newspaper, *The Sun*, is tailored to a specific national target group that is quite distinctive to that country. The same would be true of many other national newspapers.

There are relatively few true Eurobrands at present because consumer tastes vary so widely, consumer laws are different, and media availability is not consistent throughout the EC. Most important, multinationals have placed responsibility for brand development largely with national companies and given them profit objectives. The result is that Eurobranding may exist in name only: a well-known brand of toothpaste may taste of peppermint in France and be sold on a platform of whiteness, yet in Germany it tastes of spearmint and is promoted to keep the breath fresh.

Overall, it is important not to be carried away by the concept of Eurobranding. It can justify itself only if customers judge that European branded products are more attractive than national ones or if there are cost savings or other business advantages that make it more profitable.

Private-Label and Original Equipment Manufacture Opportunities in Europe

As an alternative to branded goods, some manufacturers have made headway in Europe by supplying goods to retailers under the *retailer's brand name*: private-label goods. Similarly, manufacturers of industrial products and components have gained entry by supplying *original equipment manufacturer* (OEM) products, which are then used in the manufacture of other industrial finished products.

In both cases, the marketing usually involves long negotiations with the buyer; it was described in Chapter 7, on entry strategies. The process can represent a long-term, profitable route in some product categories. In industrial marketing, it is a route that has been used for many years.

In consumer goods marketing, it depends partly on the acceptance of private-label consumer goods in a European country. According to 1986 data from A. C. Nielsen, the share of private-label consumer goods varies from a low of 5 percent in Italy to a high of 25 percent in the UK.[36] There has been no consistent Europe-wide trend over the 1980s, but where the interest is high, the single-market opportunities are clear.

Service Development across Europe

In the search for additional product benefits, North American marketers will certainly wish to explore the possibility of providing extra service with existing products. Some Japanese car and electronics companies have used this method, coupled with better product reliability, as a major European entry strategy. There are two main aspects:

1. *Warranty*: a guarantee prior to the sale that the product will perform as it is meant to.
2. *After-sales service*: creating a complete network to ensure performance and backup once the sale has been completed.

Warranties can, in principle, be standardized across the EC, and this is increasingly likely. There are several reasons for this:

- Where the product is totally standard, warranty variations make little sense.
- Where the product is taken regularly across country borders, a standard warranty is highly desirable (e.g., commercial vehicles working across the EC).
- Increasing legal standardization across the EC points to warranty standardization.

Problems arise where the manufacturing source or operating conditions vary between countries (e.g., differences in climate adaptations for cars between northern Sweden and southern Spain).

After-sales service is more complex because it involves investment in physical service facilities, personnel training, and distribution networks. Probably because of the large size of the individual purchase and the strength of competition, U.S. and European car companies have invested as much as any in the development of this aspect of their business. Their difficulties result because most of them do not own the main import agents of individual dealerships responsible for distributing their products within the country.

Typical after-sales issues for European car manufacturers are:

- How do dealers handle any customer problems arising immediately after delivery?
- How do manufacturers ensure consistent service standards through dealers in the long term?

- How do customers obtain consistent quality of service across the EC from different importers in different countries?
- How do manufacturers motivate importers and dealers to take responsibility in individual countries while attempting to achieve common standards across the Community and greater coordination of activity?

These difficult issues need to be tackled by careful understanding of the customer, who may well be not only the final purchaser but also the importer. Beyond the main importer, there are individual dealers responsible for specific regional areas. All these will need to be considered.

As an example of the effort required, Volvo trucks used the following methods to begin creating a pan-European before- and after-sales network:[37]

- Marketing information systems to a standardized format across Europe.
- Volvo truck dealer European task force to represent importers and dealers and develop common standards.
- Appointment of a manager responsible in each dealership for the achievement of the common European standards.
- Three-day training seminars for the main importers and Volvo headquarters staff.

Beyond this, it was judged important that individual country contributions be seen to be useful and that the whole process not be dominated by headquarters staff from Sweden. Similar considerations no doubt have been applied by Ford (U.S.) and General Motors (U.S.) in building their European operations.

In some industrial products, after-sales service may take on even greater importance. For example, continuous operation of plant and machinery may be crucial to customer profitability in some oil refineries and chemical plants. Service in the form of preventive maintenance may therefore be required. This is achieved either by a special parts service from stocks strategically placed around Europe or by rapid transit from a central location; certainly, good communications are crucial for this to work.

In some industrial markets, the trend is now moving firmly toward much closer relationships between the supplier and the customer.[38] One of the driving forces is the increased emphasis on product quality and re-

liability. To this extent, the description "after-sales" service may be misleading: "*continuous*-sales" service may be more accurate!

European Service Quality

In our search for European product benefits that will provide competitive
advantage, we must consider product quality. We saw in Chapter 7 that
PIMS evidence links profitability with product quality. Moreover, we
know that product quality and total quality management (TQM) have
been identified as one of the distinguishing features of Japanese success
in world markets.[39]

Over the last few years, there has been a tendency for the production
or operations function in Europe to grasp the TQM standard and leave
marketing to handle promotions and advertising in terms of European
TQM developments. Certainly, it is true that quality has to imbue all
production activities inside the company. But it is also the case that "quality" has meaning only when related to *customer* expectations, and here
marketing is surely in a strong position to contribute to the process. In
reality, production and marketing need to work together to plan the way
ahead; this is much closer to best Japanese practice, as described, for
example, by Cusumano and Takeishi in their comparative work on the
U.S.-Japanese car industry.[40]

Lest North American marketers think quality is largely a U.S.-Japa-
nese battle, a study of 224 large companies in 14 European countries has
provided detailed evidence of European marketing and quality activity.[41]
The study showed that two-thirds of respondents wanted to build market
share over the years 1991–1993; this contrasted with previous surveys
that considered maintaining market share more important. This aggressive approach to markets was to be accompanied by *continuous upgrading* of manufacturing facilities. The priorities set by European manufacturers, in descending order, were:

1. Quality.
2. Delivery.
3. Dependability and reliability.
4. Price.
5. Flexibility (in customizing products).

Economists reading this evidence will note that price appears some
way down the list. Quite rightly, they would argue that the low position

of pricing does not hold for all cases, but only in this sample. But North American marketers will want to respond to evidence of customer requirements as a starting point, and quality is first on this European list. The implications are the following:

- Close links between production and marketing.
- Cross-functional teamwork beyond even these two areas.
- Special training programs at all management levels.
- Translation of customer quality standards into meaningful measures and targets for the factory floor.
- Quality emphasis throughout the organization as well as in European marketing.

European marketing needs to explore the implications of quality both for its contribution to enhanced product benefits and for its links with customer satisfaction and overall company profitability. In the long term, the two routes will converge.

North American marketers should also note that new EC regulations on quality are now being introduced. Only those companies that reach a certain *quality threshold* will be able to bid for certain EC contracts. The new procedures to validate quality require time and management resources. North American marketers may wish to investigate the implications carefully; the European Commission in Brussels has the details.

NEW PRODUCT DEVELOPMENT IN THE SINGLE EUROPE

The thrust of this chapter is that North American companies involved in European markets need to reconsider every aspect of their product benefits. European new product development can contribute to this process, possibly by adding a new dimension to an existing range.

New Product Development Process in a European Context

Probably because it is too early, there is little evidence on the success rate of new product introductions across the single Europe. Nevertheless, because it is so difficult to obtain success in this process, chances are that the relatively high failure rates seen in national markets will apply in Europe. If this is true, a key task for North American marketing will be to explore the advantages of new product development on a European scale. Ramsay points to several possible implications in consumer goods markets:[42]

- Products may be developed for more than one market.
- New products may be launched simultaneously across countries, not sequentially as before.
- The size of major products will be larger—perhaps US$100 million rather than the more typical US$10–20 million from one country.

He concludes that the potentially larger payoff will justify higher new-product development resources. However, it should be added that pan-European research will also be more complex. This may make it more difficult to evaluate the results.

In terms of the new-product development process for the single Europe, there are two broad routes:

1. Adopt the *comprehensive route* used in national markets (e.g., see Oliver[43]).
2. Take the *incremental route* recommended for some international markets (e.g., see Terpstra and Sarathy[44]).

The comprehensive route is shown in Figure 9–4. In involves a thorough and sequential evaluation across Europe of each stage of the development process.

The incremental route takes as its starting point products developed for the *home country*. From this range are selected those with European potential. These are then tested in one or more countries for customer reactions. Clearly, this route is less comprehensive, but it may well represent a lower-cost and more practical European approach in the early 1990s. It also has the merit of building on the experience and economies of scale already operating in North America.

EC Funding of Research and Development Initiatives

Highly relevant to some areas of potential pan-European development are the initiatives generated and funded by the Community itself. The EUREKA pan-European research program has been running since 1985. By 1991 it had generated around 470 projects with a value of 8 billion ECU.[45]

FIGURE 9–4
Comprehensive Route to European New-Product Development

Stage	Activity
Concept development	Generation of a broad range of early ideas
Screening	Early removal of "no-hopers" and those ideas quite outside the company's objectives
Concept testing of screened products	Qualitative research techniques used to test the basic propositions in several European countries
Business evaluation of successful concepts	In-company analysis to weed out concepts that may test successfully but be unprofitable
Product testing	Small-scale samples used to obtain European customer reactions
Test market	Large-scale test to evaluate sales potential in several countries
European launch	

Individual projects range from the European semiconductor research program, with a final cost of US$4.8 billion when it finishes in 1996, to a modest research study on synthetic alternatives for leather shoe uppers, at a cost of US$43 million.

Some North American companies will consider whether they wish to take advantage of this generous funding. Well-established U.S. companies, such as IBM, have benefited from the grants and contributed to these projects. More generally, the activity raises the vital contribution that R&D will play in pan-European development and how this is organized. For the majority of firms, scale would suggest that it be concentrated in a few locations rather than spread across the EC. However, this does depend on the nature of the task.

Objectives and Organization of New-Product Opportunities

As Unilever (Netherlands and the UK) has discovered, the single market will provide opportunities both to launch similar products across Europe and to eliminate duplication of products and brands.[46] Much of its development effort in detergents over the next five years at a cost of £195 million will actually go toward rationalization and restructuring into larger and more productive plants at an estimated annual savings of £250 million.

Although Unilever has no intention of reducing the number of brands in which investment has been made over many years, the company is moving to greater European coordination with less national autonomy for its operating companies. This raises the fundamental question of how to organize European new-product development—on a national or pan-European basis?

For Unilever, the common interests of customers and the potential cost savings have propelled the company into one pan-European development effort on detergents. But this carries the potential cost of demotivating individual-country marketing managers who have had decisions removed from their companies. So a bargain has been struck: more managers from individual countries become involved across Europe and have responsibility for product areas on behalf of Europe. Thus, the regional headquarters in Brussels will have nationals from 11 countries.

Unilever's main European rival is Procter & Gamble (U.S.), which has used a pan-European marketing strategy for years: common brand names, standard packaging, and central management. Unilever now appears to be moving in the same direction.

Other companies may choose different approaches. In industrial marketing, the organization may focus not so much on a move from national to pan-European development, but rather on the development of links between customers and suppliers on a pan-European basis. Certainly this has been the Japanese approach to new product development in the car industry.

Cusumano and Takeishi characterize the development process for the Japanese-U.S. car industry as being more involved with close relationships, for example, in the sharing of ideas, cost information, and technology between suppliers and customers.[47] Much discussion, then, focuses on such matters as quality improvements and annual contract price reductions of perhaps 10 percent through greater efficiencies and cost savings; specifically, price increases for the purpose of passing on wage increases are unlikely to be acceptable. These development pressures will inevitably extend to Europe during the 1990s if only because of the greater Japanese involvement in Europe over this period. They represent a radically different focus for product development that many European companies may not understand. Indeed, there is a clear case for European companies to adopt them now: Fiat is already reported to be taking up some Japanese ideas.⁴⁸ North American companies may be better placed to meet this challenge.

Some marketing purists may argue that Japanese developments have little to do with European marketing and new-product development, and more to do with production techniques. But this would be to miss the point: Japanese new-product initiatives are less concerned with pushing back the frontiers of science and more focused on the practical issues of applying technologies to obtain product improvement and quality—fewer new-generation European Community semiconductor projects costing US$4.8 billion and more spending to improve plant efficiencies and product quality. The results show that the Japanese product development emphasis has had considerable success.

Test-Marketing and Sales Estimating

European marketers may wish to consider the use of test markets across Europe to estimate the sales potential of major new developments. For some products there will be merit in this approach, but for others the sheer cost of test-marketing across Europe will be prohibitive.

Moreover, the consequences of such test market evidence need to be carefully considered. For example, would it really be logical to change a product because it failed in the UK and was successful in France? Or would such evidence mean that it should be withdrawn from the UK and continue as a French national launch? What would be the point of pan-European testing in both countries if the results in one country were to be downgraded? And if the product was changed as a result of the UK evidence, what would this mean for the French results? Such a test market shows great potential for hopeless muddle.

In any event, economies of scale might render such a test market meaningless if a common pan-European need had been identified. Test markets do not usually fail outright but fall short on specific objectives. The results of the preceding test would simply show that there was more potential in France and less in the UK. North American marketers need to clarify carefully the justification for large-scale and expensive test markets across the Community: I am highly doubtful that any useful *actionable* information will ever emerge.

As evidence for this viewpoint, the saga of testing pan-European advertising for the new Philips Whirlpool (U.S.) range of domestic appliances deserves examination.[49] In brief, two advertising campaigns were tested in three European capitals; the winning advertisement in Paris was disliked by the target group in London, and vice versa. The Viennese liked neither. After much deliberation, it was eventually decided that a previous campaign rejected as being too bland would be used; it was innocuous enough to appeal to target groups in each country. So much for the elaborate and expensive test. Incidentally, we can be grateful to Whirlpool and its advertising and research agencies for sharing this experience.

PRODUCT MARKETING DECISIONS FOR EASTERN EUROPE

Because of the political upheaval from 1985 onward, product marketing in Eastern European countries will have some unique aspects in the 1990s:

1. Products that have traditionally dominated national markets will be privatized; one hesitates to call them "brands" in the Western sense.
2. Political uncertainty, high inflation, and hard currency difficulties will make product launch risks high during the 1990s.
3. Poor distribution infrastructures will make the cost of product launches greater (Chapter 12 has more detail).
4. Eastern European customers may well find many Western branded goods beyond their means and be more concerned with survival than with what they would regard as luxury items.
5. There has been strong demand for professional services by governments and leading companies as advice is sought on the change to market economies and as industries are restructured. If successful, such services will have no long-term future as a result of their very success.
6. Product quality is epitomized by Western goods for those that can afford them.

Added together, these issues make Eastern European product marketing particularly challenging. The approach of those companies entering these markets will be characterized by the factors discussed below.

Acquisition and Joint Venture

The largest single reported investment deals have been in the Eastern European car and truck industries. Deals on a smaller scale have been announced in the chemical and fast-moving consumer goods industries. A summary of typical deals is shown in Table 9–2. Other investments are being explored in industries such as mining and ores. It will be evident that, outside the car industry, the capital sums committed to early in 1992 were relatively small compared with the resources of the companies involved. Moreover, whole swaths of Eastern European industry, from clothing to machine tools, remain untouched.

There are three principal reasons for acquisition and joint venture activity by North American companies as an alternative to launching new products:

1. To obtain access to vast potential markets in Eastern Europe quickly.
2. To employ the cheap but well-educated labor of Eastern Europe for goods that might be exported back to the West.
3. To develop the vast natural resources of some Eastern European countries in global markets (e.g., oil and diamonds).

Detailed analysis of these areas is beyond the scope of this book. Our objective is rather to show that Eastern European product marketing in the 1990s will need to consider acquisitions and joint ventures as the speediest method of entry despite the Western marketing preoccupation with advertising and promotions.

Investment to Improve Productivity, Infrastructure, and the Environment

Investing in Eastern Europe is not straightforward. Productivity is low, and there are real problems over the absence of a modern industrial infrastructure and decent environmental conditions, all taken for granted in the West.[50] For example, the Schwinn-Csepel bicycle joint venture in Hungary had two years of investment (1989–1991) but still had lower productivity than its Western European counterparts.[51]

Similarly, the West German chemical giant BASF had to totally upgrade its newly acquired polyurethane facility in East Germany. More-

TABLE 9–2
Selected Acquisitions and Joint Ventures in Eastern Europe, 1990–1991

West	East	Activity	Type of Deal	Total Possible Value (US$ millions)
		Cars and Trucks		
Volkswagen Germany	Skoda Cz/Sl*	Car assembly	31% share rising to 70%	5,900
Fiat Italy	Yelabuga USSR	Car and gear boxes	Joint venture	4,680
Fiat Italy	FSM Poland	Cars	51%	1,400
GM United States	Opel Hungary	Car engines	100%	220
		Engineering		
Ingersoll Rand United States	Russia	Power tools	100%	N/A
Siemens Germany	Skoda Koncern Cz/Sl*	Power generation equipment	67%	170
International Paper United States	Poland	Papermaking	100%	935
		Chemicals		
BASF Germany	East Germany	Basic chemicals	100%	280
Bayer Germany	East Germany	Basic chemicals	100%	273
		Fast-Moving Consumer Goods		
Coca-Cola United States	Poland	Drinks	100%	50
Procter & Gamble United States	Cz/Sl	Detergents	100%	20
Pepsico United States	Wedel Poland	Chocolate	40%	80
RJR Nabisco United States	Russia	Tobacco	52%	N/A

*Cz/Sl denotes Czech and Slovak Federal Republic, commonly called Czechoslovakia.

Source: Aldersgate Consultancy.

over, it had serious problems because the former communist managers were unwilling to cooperate in modernization. When it drew up the first set of accounts, the company discovered that 20 percent of costs were taken up by such items as crèches, schools, a hospital with 30 doctors, an abattoir, and a heated swimming pool.[52]

The company attitudes of managers and workers in Eastern European companies suggest that product quality issues and after-sales service development opportunities, as discussed earlier in this chapter for the West, take on a rather different meaning in some parts of Eastern Europe. Eastern companies set lower standards, partly as a result of the equipment available and partly from the mentality of the monopoly of a managed economy: inferior goods could always be sold.

Long Time Scales

The Western product marketing payback period in fast-moving consumer goods and some electronics of around three years is perhaps too short for Eastern Europe. The exceptions to this are likely to be projects involving limited funds to a restricted target group (e.g., foreign currency retail shops in Moscow).

Simple and Low-Key Product Launches

Because of the difficult distribution infrastructure and low wages, major product introductions will need to be simple and inexpensive over the next few years in the East. However, this does not mean lack of interest by customers, just lack of purchasing power: witness how the long queues in Moscow for Lenin's tomb are now rivaled by those for McDonald's. But it does mean that Eurobranding will need to be phased in over a longer time than in the West, and detailed product positioning studies may be irrelevant.

Professional Services Activity

Professional services has been an important area of demand over the last few years. Western lawyers, accountants, educators, and consultants have made a substantial contribution during the early 1990s. In the long term, this will be replaced by national activity.

Difficulty in Repatriating Earnings to the Home Country

There is little point in launching products in Eastern Europe if the profits cannot be sent back to North America. Naturally, it is possible to take a long-term view, but the difficulties may be significant:

- Eastern European currencies are not freely exchangeable with Western ones: the exchange rate is not fixed. Profits earned in zlotys or rubles cannot be easily converted into Western hard currencies.
- Bureaucracy is excessive and bank administration to arrange profit transfers very slow.

Some products, particularly capital goods, are being sold to Eastern Europe only under the protection of Western government guarantees on prices and profits. Others are being sold under bartering arrangements (see Chapter 10). All such schemes will overcome the difficulties in earning adequate profits in the West. But they take time to organize and may limit Western involvement.

NOTES

1. P. Cecchini, *1992: Benefits of the Single Market* (Aldershot, England: Wildwood House, 1988), p. 55.
2. Ibid., p. 58.
3. Ibid., p. 50.
4. Ibid., p. 4.
5. R. Lynch, *European Business Strategies* (London: Kogan Page, 1990), chapter 6.
6. R. Owen and J. Dynes, *The Times Guide to 1992* (London: Times Books, 1990), p. 58.
7. European Commission, *White Paper on Completing the Internal Market* (Brussels: OPOCE, 1985).
8. Cecchini, p. 28.
9. Owen and Dynes, p. 68.
10. M. Chittenden, and J. Lees, "UK Footballers Fear the Brussels Bruiser," *Sunday Times*, May 5, 1991.
11. G. de Jonquieres, "Just One Cornetto . . .," *Financial Times*, October 28, 1991, p. 14.

12. European Commission, *Panorama of EC Industry 1991/92* (Luxembourg: OPOCE, 1991), pp. 73–76.

13. D. Buchan, "Twelve Slip into Unflagging Pace in Frontiers Marathon," *Financial Times*, June 17, 1991.

14. "Laws unto Themselves," *The Economist*, June 22, 1991, p. 98.

15. Department of Trade and Industry, *The Single Market—The Facts* (London: HMSO, August 1990), pp. 44–46.

16. W. Ramsay, "The Challenges and Opportunities for New Product Development in the FMCG Industry," ESOMAR Seminar, Barcelona, 1990.

17. J. Peckham, *Wheel of Marketing* (self-published, 1973), p. 34.

18. P. Kotler, *Marketing Management: Analysis, Planning, Implementation and Control*, 6th ed. (Englewood Cliffs, NJ: Prentice Hall, 1988), p. 446.

19. C. Harris, "Women of Europe Put Whirlpool in a Spin," *Financial Times*, March 1, 1990, p. 24.

20. "Whirlpool in Europe: But Will It Wash?" *The Economist*, July 13, 1991, p. 84.

21. Peckham, p. 34.

22. D. K. Clifford, "Managing the Product Life Cycle," *McKinsey Quarterly*, Spring, 1965.

23. H. B. Thorelli, and S. C. Burnett, "The Nature of Product Life Cycles for Industrial Goods Businesses," *Journal of Marketing*, Fall 1981, p. 97.

24. C. Lorenz, "Competition Intensifies in the Fast Track," *Financial Times*, June 28, 1991, p. 14.

25. Lorenz.

26. G. Oliver, *Marketing Today*, 3rd ed. (London: Prentice-Hall, 1990), p. 242.

27. "Living Dangerously in the Fast Lane," *Financial Times*, September 18, 1991, p. 21.

28. V. Terpstra and R. Sarathy, *International Marketing*, 5th ed. (Orlando, FL: Dryden Press, 1991), p. 253.

29. de Jonquieres, p. 14.

30. Lynch, chapter 4.

31. Harris.

32. "Why Cesar Disposed of Mr Dog," *Financial Times*, October 1990.

33. Lynch, pp. 67–68.

34. A. Baxter, "Electrolux Prepares to Clean Up across Europe," *Financial Times*, September 27, 1991, p. 28.

35. A. Wolfe, "The Single European Market: National or Eurobrands?" *International Journal of Advertising* 10, no. 1 (1990), p. 199.

36. A. C. Nielsen, "International Food and Drug Store Trends 1988," *Annual Marketing Review*, (1988) p. 34.
37. J. L. Lambin and T. B. Hiller, "Volvo Trucks Europe." In J. A. Quelch (ed.), *The Marketing Challenge of 1992* (Reading, MA: Addison Wesley, 1990), p. 349ff.
38. "World Industrial Review: Focus on Suppliers," *Financial Times*, January 8, 1990, p. 4.
39. S. Holberton, "An Idea Whose Time Has Not Only Come but Will Prevail," *Financial Times*, March 20, 1991, p. 10.
40. M. Cusumano and A. Takeishi, "Supplier Relations and Management: A Survey of Japanese, Japanese-Transplant and US Auto Plants," *Strategic Management Journal* 12 (1991), pp. 563–88.
41. A. de Mayer and K. Ferdows, "Removing the Barriers to Manufacturing: Report on the 1990 European Manufacturing Futures Survey," INSEAD, December 1990.
42. Ramsay, pp. 12–13.
43. Oliver, chapter 13.
44. Terpstra and Sarathy, chapter 9.
45. A. Hill, "EUREKA's Match-Making Prowess Silences Sceptics," *Financial Times*, July 22, 1991.
46. G. de Jonquieres, "Unilever Adopts Clean Sheet Approach," *Financial Times*, October 21, 1991, p. 13.
47. Cusumano and Takeishi, p. 577.
48. J. Wyles, "Fiat Strategies Take on a Japanese Flavour," *Financial Times*, June 1, 1990.
49. Harris.
50. "Eastern Europe: Business Supplement," *The Economist*, September 21, 1991.
51. "A Bicycle Made for Two," *The Economist*, June 8, 1991.
52. "The Money Pit," *The Economist*, June 22, 1991.

10

| European pricing decisions

Because of the complexity of European pricing decisions, it is useful to take the process in stages. As in Chapter 9, we begin by examining the basic influence of EC policy issues, such as law and tax, on pricing decisions. For companies manufacturing in North America, marketing to Europe involves exporting: single European pricing decisions therefore need to address the export price implications. Because all companies marketing to or across Europe will be affected by currency fluctuation until 1997, we shall consider its pricing implications.

If North American producers can develop the differentiated benefits explored in Chapter 9, they may be able to charge a premium price. But not every product will meet its marketing objectives this way: some may seek to compete on lower prices based on lower costs. In European price setting, therefore, there is a need to examine both competitive pricing and cost issues. Finally, the chapter tackles the special issues that arise in Eastern Europe.

The subjects covered in this chapter are the following:

- European pricing: the influence of the EC.
- European credit and export pricing considerations.
- European pricing and currency issues.
- Single Europe pricing decisions.
- Eastern European pricing decisions.

Although there is no magic formula for determining European prices, it is useful to set out the flow of the logic; this is shown in Figure 10-1 for the EC and EEA. Special Eastern European pricing considerations are not shown.

FIGURE 10–1
Single Europe Pricing Decisions

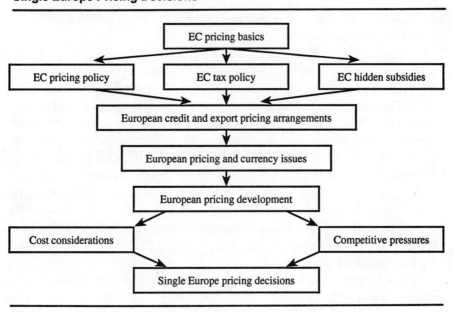

EUROPEAN PRICING: THE INFLUENCE OF THE EC

To pursue its objective of creating one market, the EC has inevitably become involved in policies that affect pricing and taxation. In addition, its influence extends into public purchasing and state aid, which can subsidize exports within the EC. We shall examine these matters in turn.

EC Pricing Policy

As we saw in Chapter 2, the EC has free competition within its borders as one of its fundamental principles. Articles 85 and 86 of the Treaty of Rome prohibit practices that hinder this process. From the work of the European Commission and the European Court of Justice, it is evident that EC pricing policy is regarded as of major importance in promoting free markets.

To achieve the free-market objectives, the EC has not hesitated to prosecute companies engaging in unfair pricing practices. In December

1985, the European Court of Justice fined the Dutch chemical giant AKZO US$11.5 million for trying to squeeze a small UK company out of the European organic peroxides market; AKZO's tactic had been to undercut the UK company's prices.[1]

Similarly, price cartels or other agreements between market suppliers are illegal in the EC. Europe's top 23 chemical companies, including the U.S. companies Dow Chemical and Monsanto, were fined a total of US$70 million in 1989 for instituting a price-fixing agreement in plastics such as PVC. The Commission's inspectors used unannounced simultaneous visits at chemical plants throughout Europe to catch the companies; the German chemical company Hoechst actually locked the inspectors out and threatened them with the police on burglary charges! With their very wide powers, the inspectors were eventually able to produce the evidence showing price- and quota-fixing meetings among the chemical producers in Zurich, Milan, and Paris. Ironically, in this case, the European cartel was so large and unwieldy that it did not even work well for much of the time.[2]

Not only can the EC fine price fixers, but it can allow in more efficient producers from outside the Community to shake up the existing market. U.S. soda ash producers had an antidumping duty lifted by the EC to allow them to enter the Community in 1991. This followed EC fines of US$60 million in the previous year on European soda ash producers for operating an illegal price cartel.[3]

It would be wrong, however, to give the impression that the EC is a model free-market economy. We have already seen the example of agricultural prices, which are entirely fixed by European politicians at their annual negotiations in Brussels. But it is not just farmers who have exemption. The European motor industry was exempted in November 1984; under a *block exemption regulation*, it was allowed to retain its system of exclusive franchise dealerships. The Commission accepted that motor vehicles are complex and need extensive after-care services. However, there were some safeguards on price variations across the EC, and, at the time of writing, there is a new investigation under way.[4]

Other markets that have been wholly or partially excluded from open price competition include defense industries, art dealing, telephone service pricing, and coal and energy pricing. Some of these agreements have a fixed date at which they will either end or need to be renewed; for example, the coal industry subsidies should expire on 31 December 1993. The overall conclusion with regard to industrywide price activity in the

Community is that, in spite of the Treaty of Rome, it does vary by industry. Hence, analysis needs to be undertaken for each European major market in which a company plans to operate.

EC Tax Policy

What has made EC pricing decisions more complicated over the last few years has been the different taxation policies on products and services practiced by EC national governments. In addition, there has been no EC single-market agreement on personal and corporate taxation, so company profit strategies vary widely across the Community. Some North American companies operate complicated tax regimes in Europe to take advantage of these differences.

Recognizing that it is not consistent with a truly common market for companies and individuals to have different tax burdens in different EC countries, the EC struggled for 16 years to bring uniformity to the tax regime. After discussions lasting from 1975 to 1991, the Commission finally decided to abandon its search for the overall harmonization of taxes;[5] it was just too difficult to reach agreement. Specifically, some sovereign governments were unwilling to pass on their important tax-raising powers to Brussels and were able to block progress because any approval required a unanimous vote in the Council of Ministers. We shall return to taxation in Chapter 12.

Nevertheless, the EC had a major success in mid-1991 by achieving the harmonization of some *indirect taxes*, principally excise duties on tobacco products, alcohol, and petroleum. These were due to be implemented on 1 January 1993 but some variation remained.[6] But the other major indirect tax, VAT, will *not* be harmonized. There was agreement that the normal minimum level of VAT would be 15 percent throughout the Community, but so many exceptions have been allowed that VAT will still need to be checked country by country on all products. In practice, European prices may still vary across the EC for the same basic product into the foreseeable future for this reason alone.

There has also been an understanding on how VAT should be applied to goods moved from one EC country to another; these products had previously been exempt. The full details have now been implemented.[7] Since 1 January 1993, goods from one EC country are entitled to enter another without any documentary formalities—a major step in achieving a single customs union and potentially a significant reduction in the costs of intra-EC exporting. But there are significant extra costs associated with *collecting* VAT on goods across Europe; therefore, there is some extra administrative burden.[7] In practice, there is still a need to establish the procedures country by country.

EC Hidden Subsidies

Nothing is ever simple in the Community. Some countries assist their own industries by paying what amounts to hidden subsidies, particularly to state-owned companies. Such funds may be disguised as cheap loans, write-offs of losses, grant aid, guarantees, or even the purchase of additional shares (if you purchase additional shares in a company, you effectively give them money). Those countries with large nationalized industry sectors are the main subsidizers: Greece, Italy, Spain, Portugal, and France.[8] The net effect is that such subsidies may enable state-run companies to compete at lower costs than other EC companies; this could in turn allow state-run companies to charge lower prices than private companies. North American companies need to understand that any problems they experience here are not because of bias against non-EC companies; UK and German companies may be equally affected.

The European Commission has begun a stricter regime to investigate all state-owned companies with a turnover in excess of US$314 million. The companies will have to supply extensive details of all financial dealings.[9] The EC competition commissioner, Sir Leon Brittan, has estimated that around US$18.7 billion of state funds have been paid out to public sector companies over the period 1986–91 without the Commission being notified.

Unless subsidies change, there will be some EC markets in which it will be difficult for nonstate companies to compete. For example, there have been some problems competing in Italy with the Italian steel companies because of the subsidies given by the Italian government. However, it has been argued by the Italian state that its subsidies have primarily been used to support regional investment programs for the poorest region of Southern Italy, the *Mezzogiorno*; this is permitted under EC rules. Furthermore, it has said that such funds are needed for strategic reasons, where private industry would be unwilling to take the risks and make the investment. Hence, there are arguments on both sides that need to be respected in this matter.

The problem is not only the subsidy but the long time it takes for private competitors to obtain redress: if the issue is taken to the European Court, the precourt stage alone takes nearly a year. Informal contacts by EC officials have sometimes helped. Although not strictly an example of pricing, EC quiet diplomacy over a dispute on barriers to trade may serve to illustrate the point: EC officials were able to speed up the German Bundespost's acceptance of UK-made fax machines and satellite receiver equipment which, it had been claimed, did not meet German standards.[10] Time costs are a real problem in marketing but may be overcome by informal investigation of the correct procedures.

EUROPEAN CREDIT AND EXPORT PRICING CONSIDERATIONS

The European legal and tax framework will apply to all North American companies operating in the EC and will impose a varying cost burden, depending on where they are located. In addition to these costs, there are others that apply when a North American company has a manufacturing base in one country and exports to other EC countries. These additional costs might include:

- Additional freight charges because of the distances involved.
- Insurance while the product is in transit.
- Bank costs for currency conversion, payment, and documentation.
- Forwarding-agent costs to arrange and monitor goods delivery over EC country borders.

Most of these costs are charged based on a percentage of the value of the original item. Because of this approach, small cost differences quickly become larger as each further element in the distribution chain adds its new percentage to the previous cost figure. The Cecchini report argued that these extra costs of exporting were more than offset by advantages such as economies of scale. Although this may be valid, marketers will want to calculate the extent of the export burden.

As an example, Table 10–1 shows the cost breakdown that suppliers from three countries—France, the UK, and the United States—would have for a target French retail price of F20.60; note that only the U.S. supplier outside the EC pays a tariff. In the example, the home French manufacturer can afford to have 10 percent higher costs than the EC producer from the UK and still achieve the same retail price. The manufacturer from the United States needs to have even lower costs.

The example in Table 10–1 is artificial in that it takes no account of the possible price premium for product differentiation or the higher costs of providing service over longer distances. However, it does show what needs to be done: It is the responsibility of North American marketing to make the calculations and then turn to colleagues in finance, production, and distribution to discuss potential areas of action to improve profitability. The areas might include:

- Pricing below full cost if the plant in the United States or Canada has spare capacity.
- Lowering distribution costs by seeking new methods of distribution.
- Instituting product changes that reduce costs either by stripping

TABLE 10–1
The Penalty of Exporting

Competitive Price Target: F20.60 in the French home market

	French Home Manufacturer	UK Intra-EC Manufacturer	U.S. Extra-EC Manufacturer
Manufacturer's FOB price	9.60	8.65	7.60
Ocean freight and insurance, bank costs, forwarding agent's costs	—	0.95	1.20
Landed or CIF value	—	9.60	8.80
Tariff @ 9%	—	—	0.80
CIF value plus tariff	—	9.60	9.60
12% VAT	1.15	1.15	1.15
Distributor cost	10.75	10.75	10.75
Distributor markup @ 15%	1.61	1.61	1.61
Retailer cost	12.36	12.36	12.36
40% retail margin	8.24	8.24	8.24
Consumer price	20.60	20.60	20.60

Note: Export prices can be quoted at various stages in the shipment process. Two typical quoted prices are *FOB price*, which means "free on board" (i.e., the price as the goods pass across the ship's rail), and *CIF price*, which means "cost, insurance, and freight" (i.e., the price for shipping the goods to a named destination).

Source: Goran Grabacic, Inex-Interexport, Belgrade.

peripheral benefits or finding some cheaper method of manufacture.

- Shipping in semifinished form and assembling the final product in the EC country concerned in screwdriver plants (so called because this is the only implement needed in final manufacture).

In practice, a combination of cost cutting, some economies of scale, and some product differentiation, so that the domestic price does not have to be matched exactly, may all be used by North American marketers in the pricing assessment for European markets.

However, there is another factor not mentioned that will need to be carefully assessed in the determination of the final price: European currency.

EUROPEAN PRICING AND CURRENCY ISSUES

In Chapter 3 we looked at the European Monetary System (EMS) and the possibility of a single European currency after 1997. We now need to examine the marketing implications of the fact that there will be no single currency before that date; specifically, we must consider the impact on pricing and profitability.

Up to 1997 at least, EC countries will operate with currencies that vary against each other: the variation for France, Germany, the Netherlands, Denmark, Ireland, Luxembourg, and Belgium is a maximum of 2.25 percent either side of a central, set currency rate against the ECU and every other ERM currency; these are the "narrow-band" currencies. At the time of writing, there is a 6 percent variation either side of the agreed currency rate for Portugal and Spain, the "wide-band" currencies. The UK, Italian, and Greek currencies are outside the system completely, with only limited prospects of joining in the immediate future.

Because all EC currencies are also traded as world currencies, they are influenced by fluctuations in the value of other global currencies, such as the U.S. dollar and the Japanese yen. Depending on how world currencies move, it is theoretically possible for an individual EC currency such as the deutsche or the French franc to move from one extreme of its EMS band to the other before the EC central banks have to intervene and bring the value back within the agreed EMS range. This has major implications for European pricing.

Taking the French franc as an example, a fluctuation might, in theory, occur from +2.25 percent to −2.25 percent, giving 4.5 percent in total. It is therefore possible that a French franc–quoted export price would have changed by 4.5 percent from the time of the EC price quotation to the time an invoice was sent to the EC customer in the country concerned; such changes are not difficult to envisage on long-term contracts, for example, on a three-year design-and-build contract for a new chemical plant. The change in the export price of 4.5 percent would be largely outside the control of the company.

Although in practice such an extreme variation is unlikely, the facts are that the average *monthly* variations in individual EC currencies against each other are 0.7 percent for those in the ERM and 1.9 percent for those outside.[11] On large sums over the year, these amounts might be highly significant in terms of EC trading. And all this within the stabilizing influence of the EMS!

In addition to regular short-term currency fluctuation, there is another way major change could occur: The EC countries could agree to change the composition of the central basket of EC currencies against which the variations are measured. This would amount to a "realignment of currencies" within the EMS. It should be noted that such a major realignment of EC values does occasionally occur; the most recent ones were in 1987 and 1992.[12] North American price contracts caught in the middle of such a move would either suffer or gain depending on the relative shift in the realignment.

More generally, unless steps are taken to offset currency changes in the EMS, profitability may be severely affected. As a rough measure of profit impact, compare the drop in prices of 4.5 percent described above against the average profitabilities, shown in Table 10–2, of top European companies in selected industries in 1987, a year of realignment. Although it is not possible to measure the effects precisely, such a movement might send some companies into loss on their European business or at least reduce profitability dramatically.

It is not just the variation that may cause problems. There is evidence that the sheer uncertainty also has disadvantages for exports.[13] According to Currie and Williamson, the band within which EMS currencies operate can act as barrier to long-term export sales growth, for both the customer and the supplier, for three reasons:

1. Branded products, relying on repeat purchases, cannot be allowed to fluctuate in price constantly in local markets across Europe; the producer has to absorb the cost.

TABLE 10-2
Profitability of Some of Europe's Top Companies: 1987

	Return on Capital*	Sales Margin*
Pharmaceuticals	18.6%	15.7%
Cars, trucks, and spares	15.7%	7.2%
Metals and mining	11.3%	6.8%
Telecommunications equipment	10.1%	5.5%
Iron and steel	4.2%	3.1%

*Before tax and interest charges.

Source: Aldersgate Consultancy.

2. Products and services with heavy start-up costs will be disadvantaged during this period if there is currency uncertainty surrounding the price.

3. Where products need a trial period for customers to assess quality, currency price variations during this period will have discouraging effects.

Ultimately, in all the preceding cases, the supplier is likely to have to bear the currency fluctuation costs. Prices of some global commodities, such as oil, are quoted in U.S. dollars. This will, of course, reduce the currency burden for North American companies, but it will not eliminate the impact on European prices in local currency. North American customers located in the EC may still have a problem with prices.

What, then is to be done by marketing? Specialist advice is, without doubt, essential, but the marketer in discussions throughout the EC should consider the following four matters:

1. *Currency of quotation*: In 1988 only 22 percent of UK exports to Western Europe were quoted in the currency of the importing country.[14] It is possible that other EC countries show similar figures. There is a case for using the ECU for cross-border billing: it has been used by the French glass multinational St. Gobain because the ECU fluctuates less than individual EC currencies and because it is more equitable between EC partner companies.[15]

2. *The precise costs included in the price quoted*: The exact costs included need to be absolutely clear. This applies not only to export price quotations, which might vary depending on whether

transport and insurance costs are included, but also to transactions between company subsidiaries or joint venture partners. These must be written into the detailed contractual arrangements. I recall my relief at having persisted in clarifying the detail of a contract between the UK and Finland: a totally unexpected dispute later arose and was resolved amicably by reference back to the detailed agreement made earlier.

3. *Hedge against currency fluctuation*: Although the detail of this area is highly technical and beyond the scope of the marketing function, it is normal to hedge against currency losses. For example, if a contract price were quoted in deutsche marks, sufficient German currency might be bought in advance to cover the contract. For the purpose of hedging, large companies may have their own treasury departments, and smaller companies may use their banks or other financial advisers.

4. *Consider other means of currency risk reduction*: Other methods can be employed, including:
   a. A renegotiation clause in a long-term contract against currency changes.
   b. Frequent price list reviews for currency changes.
   c. Buying or selling quantities of a currency outside a specific contract; some companies have made (or lost!) more money on this sublist than on the export deal.

Ultimately, the type of currency deal that is undertaken may depend on the bargaining power of the buyer and seller. If the North American selling company is particularly keen to make a sale, it may quote a fixed price or guarantee a currency rate, thus taking a risk that it would not have contemplated in other circumstances.

SINGLE EUROPE PRICING DECISIONS

Basics: The Balance between Costs and Competition

For reasons already outlined in this chapter, European pricing is likely to be more complex than the price decision in North America. The conventional marketing view of price setting (e.g., See Christopher et al.[16]) balances the two ends of the price spectrum:

1. *Costs*: Setting the market price below marginal cost will probably lose the company money. The price discount paid to distributors to gain market access is a cost that needs to be included here.

2. *Competition*: Pitching the market price above that of the competition will result in minimal sales even if there is some product differentiation.

These same principles apply in European price setting: Figure 10–2 shows the price range normally available. The actual price set within the spectrum will depend on marketing objectives, risk acceptance, competitive stance, and such factors as product life cycle and market positioning. In a European context, these issues are extended because:

- *Costs* will be higher as a result of the greater distances and service costs involved. But they will be offset by economies of scale resulting from larger volumes in the larger EC market.

- *Competition* will have to take account of a whole new range of competitors and customers; some competitors may have a lower cost base.

FIGURE 10–2
Pricing Strategy: Basic Issues

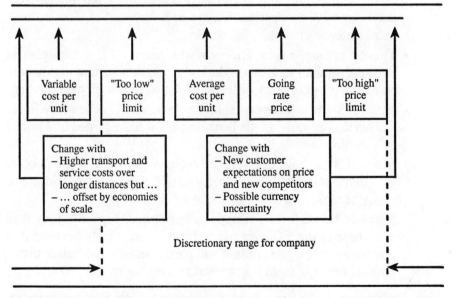

Source: Adapted with permission from M. Christopher, S. Kennedy, M. McDonald, and G. Wills, *Effective Marketing Management* (Bedford, England: Cranfield Press, 1985), p. 112.

Even this oversimplifies what in practice can be much more complex. For example, there may be national price controls or procurement policies that restrict prices (e.g., European pharmaceuticals). There may also be national distribution arrangements that involve excessive margin discounting to obtain distribution (e.g., steel stockholding distributors and major grocery retailers). Such factors vary among EC countries because of the different ways markets have evolved. North American marketers will need to examine these issues on an individual country basis.

Pricing Strategies for Specific National Markets

With the differences in structure, competitors, and customer attitudes that exist among EC countries, the marketing issue that must be resolved is whether prices need to be uniform across the EC. Over recent years, many manufacturers have seen no reason to have common prices:

- Kodak had no plans to line up film prices across the EC in 1990–1991.
- Hoover (part of Maytag, U.S.) vacuum cleaners in Luxembourg were priced at half the cost of those sold in nearby Amsterdam in 1991. The reason appears to have been that retail prices were partly set by *local* distributors, out of the control of Hoover, with local factors as the main influence.
- Timotei Shampoo from Unilever was priced 60 percent higher in Amsterdam than in London during 1990, rather more than would be justified by currency differences. So much for global branding!
- Levi (U.S.) 501s were priced higher in Spain than elsewhere in the EC during the early 1990s because they were regarded and priced as a fashion item.
- Mars (U.S.) candy bars were priced lower in the UK than in other EC countries in 1989, partly because of fierce UK competition and partly because of a lower chocolate solids content.
- Maxwell House instant coffee has been priced higher in Italy than elsewhere in the EC over the last few years, partly because it is positioned as a niche product and partly because the Italian distribution system is more fragmented and higher in cost.

Underlying all the above market pricing considerations are three major factors that have forced companies away from uniform prices:[17]

1. *Competitive stance*: Competition from national products may force a compromise on EC standard pricing.
2. *Product positioning*: Some products, such as fashion items, may be perceived as having different roles in different EC countries. This may affect pricing.
3. *Product life cycle*: There is no reason a product should be in the same phase of its product life cycle in each EC country; differences in income per head across the EC would support this. During the introductory phase, a different pricing strategy may be pursued than in the later, mature phase. This would lead to visible differences in European pricing.

The question that arises is whether there is any reason to align prices across the EC at all. In practice, alignment is undertaken mainly for two reasons:

1. *To build a pan-European brand image*: Jaguar (part of Ford, U.S.) and Mercedes (Germany) cars are at the high-priced end of the spectrum in every European country.
2. *To stop parallel importing* (i.e., illicit importing from a cheap European country to an expensive one): Presumably, in 1991 there was a temptation to traffic in vacuum cleaners between Amsterdam and Luxembourg!

It might be argued that industrial markets are more pan-European and that prices should therefore be more uniform. In practice, however, the situation may be just as complex as for consumer goods. Because the size of the industrial purchase is often larger, the customer must take into account the cost of financing the purchase by leasing, loans, or other means. Not only do currency rates vary among countries, but the cost of raising capital to pay for goods, that is, the *interest rate*, is also different. Thus, the price to the industrial customer may also differ significantly across Europe.

Moreover, for European industrial markets, price itself may be less important in the marketing mix than other areas, such as the product itself, the company's R&D program, and the level of service backup, both in general and specifically in a technical context. Writing about international industrial marketing, Cunningham comments:[18]

It is widely accepted that improvements in the competitive performance of a company, particularly in international markets, are more likely to arise by focusing management attention upon marketing and technological skills than relying upon mere price factors derived from economies of scale.

This view of the relative importance of pricing is consistent with evidence from German industrial companies, where price was rated as less important than commercial and technical abilities for German companies exporting to France, Italy, Sweden, and the UK.[19] The conclusion for European marketers is that price may not be as important a factor in the European marketing mix as European Commission studies commissioned from economists sometimes assume.

Transfer Pricing for Multinational Companies

For multinationals manufacturing products in one country for sale across the EC, there are further pricing issues: What *transfer price* does the manufacturing company charge the selling company? For example, what price does the U.S. company Kraft General Foods' German subsidiary charge its sister UK company for producing decaffeinated Café HAG for the UK market?

- Does it price at its production and distribution costs? If so, then how can the German company's profitability be measured if it makes no profit?
- Does it price at the same level as if the product were bought from UK suppliers? If so, where is the incentive for Kraft GF, UK, to purchase from Germany?
- Does it price at a standard markup on its costs? Then what incentive has Kraft GF, Germany, if it can make a profit on any cost level?

The issue is complex. One large plant for coffee decaffeination in Germany might produce economies of scale and more consistent quality than several smaller factories in different countries, but there can be difficult pricing issues to resolve as a result. Moreover, the assumption that economies of scale should be the prime factor in decision making has been questioned: several commentators (e.g., Stalk and Hout) have argued that *accelerated product development* is becoming more important in the 1990s.[20] To be stuck with a large, inflexible plant capable only of producing yesterday's products when product life cycles have shortened may be the slippery slope to real European marketing problems.

Finally, in pricing for multinationals, consideration will need to be given to the different corporation tax regimes that persist throughout the EC: if profit is taxed higher in some countries than in others, there may be wholly legitimate advantages to generating profits in lower-tax countries. The main difficulty is to identify the tax implications of this aspect of European pricing; expert advice must be sought.

EASTERN EUROPEAN PRICING DECISIONS

In principle, many of the issues that govern Western European pricing also apply to the countries of Eastern Europe. But three added complications tend to overshadow the other issues:

1. Uncertainty from political developments.
2. High rates of inflation.
3. Currency stability and convertibility.

Uncertainty because of Political Developments

According to the OECD, the principal factor behind the collapse in the early 1990s in trade between all the former communist countries was the inability or unwillingness of the former USSR to purchase goods from other Eastern European countries with hard currency.[21] The whole centralized basis of trade between the USSR and its former satellites has fundamentally changed. Bartering arrangements have sprung up between old suppliers and customers, but, essentially, all these countries are now attempting to generate hard-currency sales from the West where possible.

With so much uncertainty, it is not possible to see clearly how the new states, such as Russia and the Ukraine, that have replaced the USSR will develop. At the time of writing, they appear to be in difficulty, with real hardship among many ordinary people through rising prices and unemployment. The situation is similar in other Eastern European countries.

What is clear is that political developments must increase the risks associated with European marketing. This situation is likely to continue for most of the decade. For individual Western companies, marketing projects associated with Eastern Europe should have either a short payback or higher profitability to compensate for the risk; this implies that pricing may have to be pitched higher than would apply for an equivalent project in Western Europe.

High Rates of Inflation

According to OECD data, the political and economic uncertainty in Eastern Europe has been accompanied by high rates of inflation.[22] This has made the business background uncertain, particularly in terms of pricing for goods and services for sale in Eastern European countries. OECD estimates for 1991–1992 price inflation show the lowest inflation rate to be Czechoslovakia's, at 11 percent, and the worst the USSR's, at 2,000 percent, with Romania next, at 200 percent.

Pricing for high-inflation economies essentially means that it is not undertaken in the currency of the country or, if it is, the EC itself or Western national governments guarantee the profitability of the contract.

Currency Stability and Convertibility

The high rates of Eastern European inflation have been coupled with difficulties over currency issues in Eastern Europe. Rubles and Zlotys purchase fewer goods, as their buying power is reduced rapidly by inflation. In addition, they lack convertibility to Western currencies and have no stable international value. In these circumstances, it is difficult to undertake trade at all, let alone price the goods to be traded.

Many North American companies thus insist that trade take place only in hard currencies, such as dollars or deutsche marks. Alternatively, companies are engaged in bartering or countertrade, where goods are exchanged for other goods, with no currency involved at all. Specifically, in the latter case, USSR oil and diamonds were regularly used to pay for much needed Western goods.

Bartering companies usually deal in goods that they would not normally trade, such as oil for a heavy engineering plant. Receiving oil, in which it does not trade, could cause a problem for the heavy engineering company, so an intermediate trading company is often employed to provide the bartering links between the West and the East; an international trader will agree to sell the oil into the international oil spot market on behalf of the engineering company. However, it will make a charge for undertaking this task: typically, costs will be higher by 2–12 percent.[23] Effectively, this raises the cost of the whole deal and needs to be taken into account in European pricing.

To some Eastern European readers, I am well aware, the preceding discussion may appear to be a rather harsh commentary on their new-found freedom and need for Western assistance. The difficulty is that most individual North American companies do not have the resources to bear the evident risks: these risks need to be taken at intergovernmental level. That is why U.S. and Canadian national governments, the EC, and institutions such as the International Monetary Fund have such an important role.

NOTES

1. R. Owen and M. Dynes, *The Times Guide to 1992* (London: Times Books, 1990), p. 131.
2. W. Dawkins, "Victory for the Cartel Busters," *Financial Times*, April 12, 1989, p. 9.
3. C. Cookson, "US Lobs a Cut-Price Spanner into Europe's Cosy Soda Ash Market," *Financial Times*, April 29, 1991.
4. J. Griffiths, "Bad Dreams Return to the Motor Trade," *Financial Times*, May 10, 1991, p. 11.
5. L. Kellaway, "Brussels Aims to Untangle Strands of Taxation Patchwork," *Financial Times*, February 4, 1991. See also M. duBois "EC Official Backs Less Ambitious Policy than Harmonizing Corporate Taxes," *The Wall Street Journal*, June 22, 1992, p. A9C.
6. D. Buchan, "European Dream Begins to Take Real Shape," *Financial Times*, June 26, 1991, p. 2.
7. J. Wilkins, "Taxing Time Ahead for EC Exporters," *Financial Times*, September 25, 1991, p. 14.
8. L. Kellaway, "Britain on the Trail of Aid to State Companies," *Financial Times*, November 19, 1990.
9. A. Hill, "Brussels Tightens Grip on State Aid to Industry," *Financial Times*, July 25, 1991, p. 2.
10. "Laws unto Themselves," *The Economist*, June 22, 1991, p. 98.
11. M. Emerson, and R. Huhne, *The ECU Report* (London: Pan Books, 1991), p. 23.
12. D. Currie, and P. Williamson, "Will ERM Entry Make British Companies More Competitive?" *Business Strategy Review*, Autumn 1990, p. 3.
13. Ibid., p. 5.
14. Ibid., p. 9.
15. V. Terpstra and R. Sarathy, *International Marketing*, 5th ed. (Orlando, FL: Dryden Press, 1991), p. 545.

16. M. Christopher, S. Kennedy, M. McDonald, and G. Wills, *Effective Marketing Management* (Bedford, England: Cranfield Press, 1985), p. 112.

17. G. de Jonquieres, "Counting the Costs of Dual-Pricing in the Run-up to 1992," *Financial Times*, July 9, 1990.

18. M. T. Cunningham, "The British Approach to Europe." In P. Turnbull and J.-P. Valla (eds.), *Strategies for International Marketing* (London: Croom Helm, 1986), p. 165.

19. Turnbull and Valla (eds.), table 3.21.

20. C. Lorenz, "Competition Intensifies in the Fast Track," *Financial Times*, June 28, 1991, p. 14.

21. OECD, "Economic Outlook No. 50," December 1991, p. 53.

22. OECD, "Economic Outlook No. 52," December 1992, p. 123.

23. J. Wills, L. Jacobs, and A. Palia, "Countertrade: The Asia-Pacific Dimension," *International Marketing Review* 3, no. 2 (Summer 1986), pp. 20–27.

11

European promotion decisions

European promotions are used to communicate with customers and persuade them to purchase a company's products or services. Methods include advertising, direct mail, exhibitions, and, most important in some markets, the company's own sales force.

The basic thrust of this chapter is that European promotional options and activities differ so much from country to country that, unlike European product and place decisions, it may be difficult for North American companies to develop a pan-European promotional strategy. For most companies, some European promotional decisions will be at country level and some pan-European; the issues are where to strike the balance and what level of European promotional program will prove cost-effective.

We start by examining the EC and individual-country legislation to provide a realistic background against which to look at the decision-making process. We then consider the EC promotional industry, which spent around US$58 billion in 1989.[1] We shall examine how companies are currently allocating funds and how promotional activities differ among countries. We then examine promotional objectives and the European promotion options available. Finally, we consider the decision-making processes for Western and Eastern Europe.

The subjects covered in this chapter are the following:

- European promotions: basic regulation.
- Current EC advertising and the promotional activity.
- European promotional objectives and the promotional mix.
- Western European promotional decision making.
- Eastern European promotional decision making.

The overall decision-making process for Western Europe is summarized in Figure 11–1.

FIGURE 11–1
European Promotional Decisions

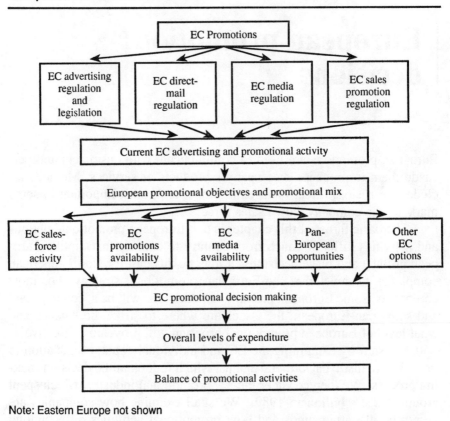

Note: Eastern Europe not shown

EUROPEAN PROMOTIONS: BASIC REGULATIONS

This section is concerned with legislation and other regulatory issues surrounding EC promotions. Because the EC itself is a young institution compared with its member states, individual countries have developed their own legislation, regulation, and other controls on promotions. Some are being standardized across the EC, but others will remain individual to member countries for the rest of the 1990s. Ideally, we need to examine both EC and individual-country issues for each area of promotional activity; in practice, we shall content ourselves with highlighting the main issues and problems.

European Advertising Legislation and Regulation

In Brussels there is an organization representing European advertisers, advertising agencies, and media owners called the European Advertising Tripartite (EAT). This body has had difficulty in dealing with the European Commission because there is no centralized Community policy on advertising.[2]

Each of the European Commission's product sectors, such as agriculture or telecommunications, produces legislation or regulations in its own area; for example, proposals to ban EC tobacco press advertising have come from the health working group, not from any central group representing advertising in the Commission. The driving force behind some of the regulation has often been product-inspired activity concerned with harmonization. The natural process in some cases has been from the product itself to the product's label wording and then possibly to the product's advertisement.

The Commission's lack of a clear view on advertising has been compounded by the many differing approaches of the EC member states. For example, superlative product claims are allowed in the UK, Netherlands, Belgium, and Italy but not in Germany or France (at least not on TV); in the Netherlands and the UK, the use of a superlative has to be backed up by factual evidence.[3] There are already several areas of EC advertising legislation:[4]

- The cross-frontier broadcasting directive, which restricts advertising for tobacco and prescription pharmaceuticals, with guidelines in some other areas.
- Detailed rules on the number and insertion timing of advertising breaks.
- Minimum quota of European material in TV hours broadcast.
- Misleading advertising directive.

In addition to these, the EC is currently examining further advertising regulations in some product areas that would apply in every member state:

- *Tobacco*: This advertising is already banned on TV; a press advertising ban is now likely to follow.[5]
- *Alcohol*: This advertising is heavily restricted across the EC but unlikely to be totally banned, though some would like to see this.[5]

- *Financial services*: Restrictions are being considered; see comment on direct mail later in this section.
- *Pharmaceuticals*: A draft directive has been circulated to member states that would require detailed label information if adopted.[5]
- *Cars*: There is a possibility of restrictions on references to speed and performance.[5]
- *Children*: Some countries already have restrictions in this area of advertising. There appear to be no proposals to harmonize rules in this area.[6]
- *Comparative advertising*: Each EC country has its own rules on advertising comparisons between products; only Germany and Luxembourg ban such comparisons. The Commission has proposed a harmonization of EC rules; if adopted, it will have the effect of liberalizing the rules of some countries.[7]

The European advertising industry would prefer self-regulation to the more restrictive regime of legislation and directives, for reasons based principally in the view that excessive legislation is costly, time-consuming, and unwieldy in an industry that should be dynamic and cost-effective. The Commission broadly takes the view that some regulation is essential but has no strict policy on how far this should extend. North American companies will probably need to check this area on a country-by-country basis.

EC Media Regulation and Development

Press advertising has always been strong throughout the Community and not subject to significant restrictions. However, until the late 1980s, there were either severe limitations or even a complete ban on TV advertising in some EC countries; for example, Germany restricted commercials, and none were allowed on Dutch TV. By 1991 every country in the community had TV advertising. Some countries, such as Italy and France, have seen a proliferation of TV channels over the last 10 years. Others have developed third and fourth channels more slowly. The contrast with North American media availability could not be greater.

An additional dynamic factor in the process has been the introduction of *satellite television*. Because this is essentially supranational, it has been difficult for EC legislators to control its spread and content. In all EC countries, its coverage is totally dependent on homes having either satellite dishes or cables to receive the programs: In both the Netherlands and Ireland over 50 percent of homes are cabled. Germany is investing funds to have 80 percent of homes cabled by 1996.[8] In the UK satellite dishes and cabling will enable 15–20 percent of the population to receive these programs by 1993. None of this has been regulated by the EC (so far!).

In general, the deregulation of television across Western Europe has had a considerable impact, according to Jacobs.[9] Audiences have been attracted from state-run TV to both satellite and terrestrial channels. There were two other media trends in the 1980s:

1. The concentration in ownership of media channels, especially print ownership.
2. The expansion of media owners outside their home countries.

Hence, European media are in the process of transformation in the 1990s. The Commission has not been the initiator of any of these changes; they have all been the result of individual country actions and entrepreneurial initiatives within the EC. They essentially have involved deregulation rather than new controls.

EC Direct-Mail Regulation

Given the real benefits of direct-mail promotion in terms of cost-effective targeting, it is important to note that there are two significant restrictions arising from concerns over confidentiality and personal privacy. One has been implemented, and the other is coming soon:

1. *Financial services*: There is already a directive banning direct-mail life insurance advertisements from being sent from one EC country to another. Direct mail is permitted only within the country of origin in this product category.
2. *Data protection*: At the time of writing, a new directive was still waiting approval by the Council of Ministers. It will severely restrict what data can be stored and make customer targeting more difficult.

EC Sales Promotion Regulation

There is a hodgepodge of national regulations in the area of sales promotion: "money off" vouchers are illegal in Spain but not in Germany; free draws are illegal in the Netherlands but not elsewhere; a "lower price for the next purchase" offer is legal in Belgium but illegal in Denmark and possibly also in Italy.[10] Unless the EC takes the initiative in this area, North American marketers will need to check each EC country individually when mounting promotions, making pan-European sales promotion more difficult.

Conclusions

Pan-European legislation and rules concerning promotional activity have been slow to emerge. The lack of a centralized directorate in this area has not helped, nor has the need to achieve unanimous agreement at the European ministerial level. There is now a hint that some measures will be enacted under the Treaty of Rome, article 100a, which permits majority agreement. If this were to happen, it might speed up the process but also lead to more restrictions in some areas. With the variability in the rules among EC countries, pan-European promotional activity is difficult to plan and implement.

CURRENT EC ADVERTISING AND PROMOTIONAL ACTIVITY

In 1989 around US$58 billion was spent in the EC on advertising, sales promotions, and direct mail.[1] There are some doubts about the accuracy of the data, but it appears that the split between the three sources of activity was roughly as shown in Figure 11–2. EC sales force activity is not included, though it is usually regarded as falling within the overall definition of promotional activity. Total EC advertising and promotional expenditure levels are typical of those of developed countries, but they are still below the levels of the United States and Japan (see Table 11–1).

For individual countries, we have data only for advertising expenditure. Judging by this evidence, the average EC figures in Table 11–1 hide real differences across countries. The individual-country data for advertising only are shown in Table 11–2. It can be seen that the advertising expenditure per head in such countries as Spain and the UK is *double* that of Belgium/Luxembourg and France. This large variation is difficult to explain in terms of the effects of currency translation and different media costs. It is much more likely to be associated with significant differences

FIGURE 11–2
European Advertising and Promotions Expenditures (US$ billions) for 1989

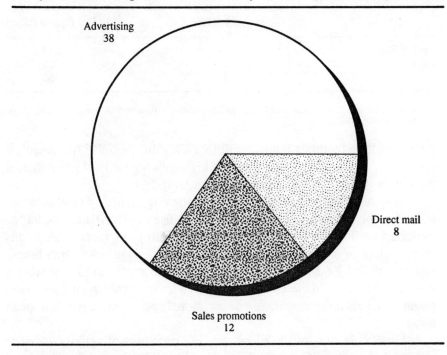

Advertising
38

Direct mail
8

Sales promotions
12

Source: European Commission, *Panorama of EC Industry 1991/92* (Luxembourg: OPOCE, 1991).

among EC countries on the importance of advertising activity in the marketing mix. This variability suggests, therefore, that pan-European advertising may be difficult to justify.

Throughout the EC, advertising expenditure has risen from 0.73 percent of the community's GDP in 1980 to 1.13 percent in 1989; the increase of 55 percent is principally due to extra European competition, according to the European Commission.[11] The growth came about particularly from an increase in TV advertising. Overall, there was a media shift from press to TV advertising during the 1980s, as can be seen from Figure 11–3.

In addition to the recorded shift in TV airtime, it is likely that there has also been considerable growth in *direct mail* across the EC over the period 1980–1989. This is not shown in Figure 11–3. Further significant growth is forecast during the 1990s as the quality of the data- and com-

TABLE 11–1
Promotional Expenditure, 1989

	Total (US$ Billions)	Per Capita (US$)
United States	79	317
Japan	27	222
EC	58	153

Source: Aldersgate Consultancy, from European Commission, *Panorama of EC Industry 1991/92* (Luxembourg: OPOCE, 1991).

puter-handling facilities improves further over this period.[12] At present, it appears that expenditure on direct mail is much higher in North America than in the EC, but the Community is growing fast.

In spite of the growth in TV airtime, there remained in 1989 substantial differences among EC countries on the use of advertising media, as indicated in Table 11–3. In practice, pan-European media campaigns take account of these variations; for example, Kellogg's All-Bran breakfast cereal and Kodak film use color magazine media in Germany to a greater extent than in the UK. Such differences may well mean that media planning needs to be undertaken on a national rather than a pan-European basis.

Finally, in our review of current EC promotional activity, what is unrecorded in any EC material is expenditure on *European sales force*

TABLE 11–2
Advertising Expenditure, 1989

	As Percent of GDP	Total (US$ Billions)
Spain	1.69	5.5
UK	1.50	12.3
Italy	1.32	9.8
Netherlands	1.10	2.5
Denmark	1.09	0.9
Germany	0.96	9.7
Ireland	0.91	0.3
France	0.78	7.3
Greece	0.76	0.3
Belgium/Luxembourg	0.68	1.0
Portugal	0.67	0.3

Source: Aldersgate Consultancy, from European Commission, *Panorama of EC Industry 1991/92* (Luxembourg: OPOCE, 1991).

FIGURE 11–3
EC Advertising Media (% Share by Medium)

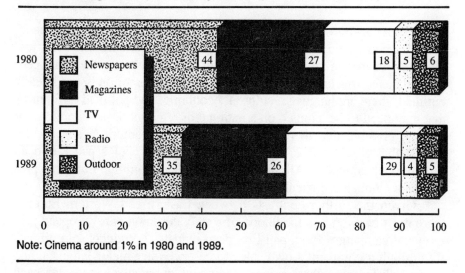

Note: Cinema around 1% in 1980 and 1989.

Source: European Commission, *Panorama of EC Industry 1991/92* (Luxembourg: OPOCE, 1991).

operations, whether by company direct sales forces or through agents and distributors. The significant increase in trade across the EC over the last 10 years must have been achieved at least partially by direct selling. Although the Commission has not recorded expenditure in this area, marketing cannot ignore its great importance in generating the optimal promotions mix for Europe.

TABLE 11–3
European Advertising by Main Media, 1989

	Total Spending (US$ Millions)	Percent Share within Country					
		News-paper	Maga-zine	TV	Radio	Cinema	Posters
Germany	9,190	43.1	31.6	14.6	5.3	1.3	4.1
UK	7,842	30.3	22.3	39.8	2.5	0.6	4.5
France	6,408	18.2	32.5	27.8	7.5	0.9	13.0
Spain	5,464	36.4	16.5	30.1	11.1	0.8	5.1
Italy	4,576	17.0	25.7	51.4	1.6	0.2	4.1

Source: Havas Annual Report 1990.

EUROPEAN PROMOTIONAL OBJECTIVES AND THE PROMOTIONAL MIX

Even for a pan-European customer target group leading to product benefits and pricing on a unified basis across Europe, there are sure to be real problems in managing European promotional activity on the same centralized basis. In addition to the media and sales promotion issues already outlined, there are language, cultural, economic, and political differences that may need to be handled on a national or regional basis. Moreover, it is quite possible that there will be national competitors in a particular market that would further downgrade the relevance of a pan-European promotional campaign. All this makes a detailed, common European promotional campaign difficult across Western Europe.

Given the further contrasts between Eastern and Western Europe, there must be even less likelihood of a truly common pan-European promotional campaign. Even pan-European industrial products sold primarily through a company's own sales force encounter major language and cultural differences that require significant practical changes for each country.[13] A key task for North American companies, therefore, is how to identify and manage the *diversity* of European promotional campaigns. What might be expected to be the same? What will inevitably need to be handled at the national level? The starting point is European promotional objectives. We shall look at these first and then consider the different elements of the promotional mix, exploring these questions for each element.

European Promotional Objectives

We should be now have a clear idea of who our customers are (Chapter 4) and of our long-term and entry marketing strategies (Chapters 6, 7, and 8). From this process, we can answer the following questions:

- Which customers really influence the buying decision?
- How do customers make buying decisions?
- What benefits do they seek?

As with other marketing, it may be necessary to influence more than one set of customers: for consumer products, this includes grocery retailers as well as the individual shopper; for industrial goods, engineers, purchasing managers, and financial staff may all be involved in appraising a complex purchasing decision. For all such groups, we need to set European promotional objectives, for example:

- Introduce new products.
- Stimulate brand awareness.
- Obtain sales enquiries.
- Access a difficult trade buyer.

Ideally, all objectives need to be quantified and measurable. Otherwise it will be difficult to make a choice between options and, at a later stage, assess the *cost-effectiveness* of different European promotional activities; this is the essential criterion for selection. In practice, most companies choose a range of activities, and the best continually experiment to improve the promotional mix.[14]

European Sales Force Activity

For many European industrial and consumer markets, European sales force activity, including agents and distributors acting on behalf of the company, are an important element of the marketing mix. This has the great advantages of offering two-way communication, tailoring the sales message to the customer, and, important, actually taking the order after one or more sales meetings. But European salespeople are cost-effective only if the sales made are sufficiently large: an individually tailored sales presentation for every potential purchaser of this book across North America would be hopelessly uneconomic! The key to sales force cost-effectiveness lies in a balance between the size of the individual sales order and the cost of the selling effort to achieve this. The latter certainly includes the salaries and related costs (usually the largest single element) and possibly technical and other backup costs.

Hence, across Europe, a high-wage economy such as that of Germany may need a different evaluation compared with lower-wage economies such as those of Greece and Portugal. Naturally, what will usually matter for highly technical products and services is the quality of the sales presentation rather than the number in the sales force, but it may be cost-effective to employ more salespeople in some European countries than others. Indeed, in the low-wage economies of Eastern Europe, salespeople may in the early years be particularly useful where more sophisticated promotional methods, such as computerized mail shots, would be unworkable.

Given the significant language and cultural differences across Europe, it is highly likely that European sales teams will be at least partially nationally or regionally based. This may apply even for sophisticated European products. For example, computer companies such as IBM (U.S.) and telecommunications equipment companies such as Northern Telecom (Canada) all employ nationals relevant to the country in which they are selling.

In many European markets, personal selling will not involve selling across frontiers but, rather, selling pan-European products into national markets. For the North American marketer, the issue will be to identify the selling task in each European market, resolve the other areas of the marketing mix, and then let the national sales managers in that market (or agents and distributors) undertake the basic selling task. In these circumstances, it follows for each national sales force that:

- Recruitment and selection will be primarily national.
- Training will be mainly in the national market *except* where special expertise is required (e.g., new pharmaceutical products or new financial services). Extra training may also be needed for some Eastern European markets in some advanced-technology areas.
- Motivation and compensation will vary with national cultures and pay levels.

Nevertheless, all these guidelines depend on the customer. For example, if the new pan-European grocery retail consortium (the European Retail Alliance) does take on a European flavor,[15] it will be essential to field a pan-European sales team to bid for business. This team will need to be trained, motivated, and compensated accordingly. In these circumstances, North American marketing executives based in Europe could become more involved not only in setting up the basic product and price support deals, but also in pan-European presentations. In any event, marketers will need to assess the cost-effectiveness of such activity later.

Overall, European marketing and sales force management will be concerned with:

- Establishing the balance between national and pan-European selling activity.

- Defining the numbers and compensation in relation to the potential selling task country by country.
- Providing the sales support and related European promotional activity.
- Evaluating the cost-effectiveness and compare it with other promotional options.

European Advertising

Invariably, European advertising will be developed in conjunction with one or more chosen advertising agencies; selection of the "right" agency is therefore a key marketing task. But this cannot usefully be undertaken until a *prior* question is resolved: Do we choose one agency for all Europe or pick national agencies in the main European countries? The advantages for these two approaches are shown in Table 11–4.

The choice between national and pan-European agencies will be based partly on customers and the buying decision. It will also be important to evaluate economies of scale and the company's need for a truly pan-European or global network. Following the resolution of these issues comes the usual process of agency selection from a shortlist.

Although this is all splendidly rational, some readers will be sufficiently worldly-wise to inquire where the current balance between na-

TABLE 11–4
European Agency Selection: National or Pan-European?

National	Pan-European
• Supports national subsidiary	• Reflects new European reality and trends
• Investment in existing brand best handled nationally	• Economies of scale in new product development and branding
• Closer to marketplace	• Uniformity of treatment across Europe
• Smaller size more conducive to personalized service and greater creativity	• Resources and skills of major European or global agency
• Diversity of ideas	• Easier to manage one agency group

tional and pan-European advertising activity rests; European evidence is limited. The summary by Whitelock and Chung of empirical advertising practice across international markets concluded that it may be easier to propose standardization across national boundaries than to achieve it.[16] Their research suggested that, even where it is possible to internationalize the message, adaptation of the *copy and slogan* may be essential for local success. In addition, headquarters participation is often higher in establishing *international objectives and budgets* than in creative strategy and media choice. Although the work considered markets beyond Europe, it does suggest that pan-European advertising may need careful local adaptation to be effective. So much for pan-European campaigns!

Consistent with this conclusion, Whitelock and Kalpaxoglou undertook an exploratory study among four multinationals in Greece in 1990 to see whether the single European market would facilitate the use of standardized campaigns; the results showed that three of the four major European/U.S. companies had no policy of standardization of their TV advertising campaigns for Europe.[17] However, the authors point out that this may have been the result of short-term considerations and the need to maintain the previous investment in local brands. With the development of new European brands, there may be an increased need for a new, standardized approach.

Nevertheless, other products may be able to produce greater European consistency in market positioning and advertising. Over the period 1986–1990, United Distillers (UD) repositioned its whisky brands in Europe, North America, and elsewhere around the world.[18] From a large, confused portfolio of whisky brands, a core range was selected, positioned, packaged, and priced for the world and European markets. Brands involved in the work included Johnnie Walker, White Horse, and Haig scotch whiskies.

Following the basic exercise, new advertising campaigns for each UD brand were then launched on the principle of "think globally, act locally" (i.e., a consistent main message tailored with advertising to suit various national markets). To back this approach, a marketing "factbook" was produced for each brand, setting out the basic positioning, core brand values, and pack and label guidelines.

The UD approach may represent a good model for North American marketers to follow in the single Europe. But it must be acknowledged that it is easier with international products such as whisky and cosmetics than with others that have stronger roots in culture, language, and country tastes.

European Sponsorship

Sponsorship involves a manufacturer or brand gaining publicity by supporting an outside event or activity—anything from a charity gala to the Olympic Games. By definition, the chosen event will have only limited connection with the brand, so it cannot usually be used to initiate a new brand. However, particularly in the context of increased pan-European media coverage of some events, sponsorship has become increasingly important in *supporting* European branding. For example, it was used extensively by United Distillers to underpin its brand-building efforts cited above: Johnnie Walker whisky sponsored the 1989 Ryder Cup between the United States and Europe. Similarly, Mars (U.S.) and Coca-Cola (U.S.) were official sponsors of the 1992 Olympic Games. Sponsorship may therefore be conducted at both a pan-European and a national company level.

Sponsorship has the twin benefits of bridging the European language and culture gaps and, in some cases, achieving broad recognition of a brand name. Japanese and U.S. companies seeking brand recognition in Europe, such as Sony consumer electronics[19] and Kodak film products, have also used this approach with success. However, there may be a high entry fee, and the results need careful quantitative evaluation.

European Sales Promotions

In addition to the difficulty of various promotional schemes across Europe, discussed earlier in this chapter, sales promotions are by nature largely short-term devices.[20] Hence, it may not be cost-effective to mount pan-European sales promotions centrally. It may be better to allow the *initiative* to rest with marketing managers in individual European operating companies or the company's European agents and distributors; this would encourage national commitment to achieving the agreed marketing objectives within a budgeted, sales promotion expenditure level. However, there may be occasions when a pan-European scheme is justified but where the scope is likely to be limited. McDonald's (U.S.) activity in this area across Europe is described in Chapter 15.

European Exhibitions and Seminars

For industrial products and some consumer goods, exhibitions may represent a major European marketing and selling occasion. The benefits arise from the opportunity not only to meet potential customers and present products, but also to examine competitive and supplier activity. Many governments provide help for exporters wishing to attend foreign exhibitions. This may extend to assistance to cover up to 50 percent of the setup costs. In reality, exhibitions can be a key device for promoting goods and services across Europe.

Seminars can work in a similar way but usually need an internationally known speaker to attract an audience. Both seminars and exhibitions may operate at either the national or the European level: in both cases, there is no primary level of responsibility for starting the promotion.

All exhibiting requires careful planning to be cost-effective; everything from stand design and interpreters to leaflets and budgetary control needs detailed analysis and management. (Some exhibitions in Europe are better attended than others, so background checking of historic attendance figures is also essential).

In Eastern Europe, exhibitions have been particularly important as a marketing tool. According to the evidence of the international advertising agency group Saatchi and Saatchi, they took the largest share of promotional expenditure in Czechoslovakia,[21] Hungary,[22] and Poland[23] in 1989. Although other areas of expenditure have probably been growing faster since that time, fairs and exhibitions still form a major means of doing business in those and similar countries. European marketers may want to investigate this area of activity as a basic means of developing opportunities with the new democracies of Eastern Europe.

European Direct Marketing

Direct marketing includes direct mail, telephone selling, and newspaper and magazine coupon response activity. The specific advantage of direct mail in Europe is the opportunity to write a personally addressed letter to a carefully targeted potential customer. Clearly, this depends crucially on the quality of European address lists: if they are poor, they are not cost-effective. In fact, the real growth in direct mail in the EC over 1980–1989 has been 4 percent per annum.[24] This indicates satisfaction with the results obtained and, by implication, with the database.

Direct marketing is well developed in Germany, Denmark, Belgium, France, and the UK. In many EC countries, it is also possible to employ an 800 number so that the response is free to the customer. Some countries now offer this facility across Europe. For example, AT&T operates an 800 service allowing EC customers to telephone free from other European countries to the North American mail advertiser; the company will even supply a foreign-language telephone receptionist (for an extra fee!).

The attractions of direct marketing are not to be underestimated, but there are still problems:

* Language.
* Different VAT rates on goods, even after 1992.
* Regulations on data protection, which are very strict in Germany, with EC proposals to raise all countries to this level.[25]

However, because responses are easily and immediately measurable, European direct marketing has the additional advantage of being potentially cost-effective. Both for industrial and for some consumer goods, it is worth considering for the single Europe

WESTERN EUROPEAN PROMOTIONAL DECISION MAKING

This chapter has argued that European promotional decisions need to be judged by what a promotion will cost and what benefits it will deliver. But there are two other questions not really covered by this statement:

1. What overall level of European promotional expenditure should be set?
2. Within overall levels, what is the balance among different European promotional activities?

Overall Levels of European Promotional Expenditure

European promotional budgets can be set as a *percentage of sales*. This has the advantage of relating the costs to the expected results, and it allows easy, centralized budgetary control. But it is clearly difficult to apply to new products, which, by definition, have no sales. Moreover, such a guideline takes no account of competitive activity, and Peckham showed that for grocery brands such considerations are vital.[26] Competitive activity will be no less in many industrial markets.

Evidence from U.S. and European companies in the PIMS database[27] suggests that, where brand share is low, there is little correlation between heavy marketing expenditure as a percentage of sales and product profitability. Where the brand share is high, there is a relationship with such expenditure. However, the difficulty with this connection is that it may be self-fulfilling and therefore inconclusive for European marketing.

Expenditure comparisons with the competition have been used as an alternative method of calculating promotional expenditure. Certainly, to assist in this process, data on competitive advertising expenditure are available for most European markets. However, it may be more difficult to establish information on sales promotion and direct-mail expenditure. Within certain limits, it is possible to estimate competitive sales force costs based on the numbers employed and advertised job vacancies. Overall, the difficulty with such an approach is that there is no guarantee that the competition has the best promotional mix. In addition, no allowance is made for promotional *creativity* that will give a smaller budget stronger European impact.

Ideally, *promotional testing* of a new promotional package might be contemplated, where a specific promotional objective is tested against identified promotional activity in a trial European market. In practice, this may be rather unwieldy and subject to too many outside variables to make the test results meaningful.

Nevertheless, market testing touches on the key difficulty in establishing budgets: basic unfamiliarity with new European markets and what will prove cost-effective. This suggests that a solution may be to examine *both* percentage of sales and competitive spending evidence. For new European introductions, unless there is some unique benefit, these may be used as a guide to European promotional budget setting. As experience and knowledge in a particular market are accumulated, the budget may be varied accordingly.

Balance between European Promotional Activities

Within the overall promotional budget, there is the additional decision of how funds are to be allocated among different forms of promotional activity, for example, should proportionally more be spent on advertising or on exhibitions? As we have seen, the evidence suggests that the balance will vary by industry and by country. However, some general patterns can be discerned through the EC promotions mist on a pan-European basis in terms of the balance of promotions for various industries; these are shown in Table 11–5 and may provide an initial guide for North American marketers.

EASTERN EUROPEAN PROMOTIONAL DECISION MAKING

In principle, establishing the promotional mix in the East is not so very different from the case of Western Europe. In practice, outside the exhibition activity already discussed, promotions revolve largely around media: TV, press, and posters. There is very little below-the-line activity (i.e., sales promotions and direct marketing). This never featured in the propaganda armory of the old state-run economies.

Advertising in Eastern Europe needs to be treated on a country-by-country basis. Consider the following examples:

TABLE 11–5
Approximate EC Promotional Expenditure by Industry, 1989

	Advertising	Direct Mail	Other, Including Sales Promotions	Total Sales (US$ billions)
Fast-moving consumer goods	12.5	0.4	5.0	17.9
Financial	4.5	2.1	2.5	9.1
Durables/cars	6.5	0.8	1.0	8.3
Retail/mail order	4.5	2.8	0.5	7.8
Travel/leisure	4.0	0.8	1.0	5.8
Media	4.5	0.4	0.5	5.4
Industry/government/ other	1.5	1.2	1.0	3.7
Total	38.0	8.5	11.5	58.0

Note: The table excludes personal selling expenditure.

Source: Aldersgate Consultancy, from European Commission, *Panorama of EC Industry 1991/92* (Luxembourg: OPOCE, 1991).

- *Poland* has a number of regional and national newspapers plus state and private TV. Some additional companies are being privatized. Virtually 100 percent of the population has access to a television set, 63 percent a color TV. Some 10 percent have access to satellite TV.[28]
- *Hungary* has two national TV channels, both of which take advertising. It also has a range of national and regional newspapers, but the quality of reproduction is not up to Western European standards. In 1990 there were between 500,000 and 1 million households with access to satellite TV.[29]
- *Russia* has several national TV channels, all of which take commercial advertising. There is a vast range of publications, some of which take advertising; again the quality of reproduction is lower than Western levels. See Ignatius on Russian media and Browning on Eastern European problems.[30,31]

In addition to the above concerns, there are three special aspects of Eastern European promotional activity, including promotions, which we will now consider.

Purchase of Existing Brands

Several Western companies have been able to purchase existing brands. They are likely to have dominant market shares because they were previously state monopolies. For example, Procter & Gamble (U.S.) has bought Rakona detergents in Czechoslovakia; its new purchase has a virtual monopoly in Bohemia and Moravia.[32] It needs to support this brand, probably beyond levels that can be justified by any budget formula over the early years, because dominant brand shares are valuable. However, there is only limited media availability, and this will restrict its actions.

Similarly, Sara Lee (U.S.) has bought a share in the Compack Hungarian trading group and added its Douwe Egberts coffee brand name to packets of Hungarian Omnia coffee.[33] The company needs to promote the brand name, but Hungarian TV is expensive and press reproduction poor, so its promotional options are limited. In addition, the expertise of Western advertising agencies has been employed to a very limited extent in Hungary.[34]

Few Promotional Controls

Some new Eastern European markets appear to have few promotional controls. For example, advertising hoardings sprang up in Prague during 1991 in historic areas that would have been subject to severe controls in some Western countries.[35] Subliminal advertising, banned in the West, has also apparently been used on Czech TV. Account must be taken of these issues in planning promotional activity.

Early European Opportunities

The new Eastern European markets are providing some unique opportunities that need to be explored while they are still available. This implies that a slow approach to the justification of promotional budgets may miss important opportunities.

For example, the U.S.-UK company News International and the West German publisher Burda rapidly launched in 1991 a new color tabloid in East Germany called *Super! Zeitung*.[36] The paper was revolutionary for the East, featuring bare-breasted women on page 1 and a money competition on page 3, as well as a daily feature under the title "Orgasmus Report 91." It also had hard-hitting news stories. The paper was launched quickly with strong promotional activity and a low price compared with its chief rival *Bild*. It made major circulation gains but folded in 1992; the existing well-established papers simply changed their editorial content to offer the same. All this indicates the need to seize early opportunities and devise a strong promotional package that cannot be matched by competitors.

NOTES

1. European Commission, *Panorama of EC Industry 1991/92* (Luxembourg: OPOCE, 1991), pp. 27–42, 27–51.
2. A. Hill and A. Rawsthorne, "Persuaders Gear Up for Challenge to EC Regulators," *Financial Times*, June 20, 1991, p. 18.
3. R. Bennett, *Selling to Europe* (London: Kogan Page, 1991), p. 59.
4. *International Journal of Advertising* 10 (London: Cassell Educational, 1991), pp. 79–87.

5. G. Mead, "Advertising Campaigns for Itself," *Financial Times*, December 2, 1991, p. 2.

6. G. Mead, "Not in Front of the Children," *Financial Times*, December 19, 1991, p. 11.

7. A. Rawsthorne, "Removing Constraints on Knocking Copy," *Financial Times*, August 1, 1991. See also K. Wells, "Global Ad Campaigns Finally Pay Dividends," *The Wall Street Journal*, August 27, 1992.

8. European Commission, pp. 27–45.

9. B. Jacobs, "Trends in Media Buying and Selling in Europe and the Effect on the Advertising Agency Business," *International Journal of Advertising* 10 (1991), p. 283.

10. Bennett, p. 78.

11. European Commission, pp. 27–42, 43,

12. European Commission, pp. 27–52.

13. P. Turnbull and J.-P. Valla, *Strategies for International Marketing* (London: Croom Helm, 1986), p. 273.

14. M. McDonald, *Marketing Plans: How to Prepare and Use Them* (Portsmouth, NH: Heinemann, 1990), p. 140.

15. J. Thornhill, "Retailers Broaden Their Outlook," *Financial Times*, December 17, 1990, p. 3.

16. J. Whitelock and D. Chung, "Cross-Cultural Advertising: An Empirical Study," *International Journal of Advertising* 8 (1989), pp. 291–310.

17. J. Whitelock and E. Kalpaxoglou, "Standardised Advertising for the Single European Market?" Marketing Education Group Conference, Cardiff, 1991, p. 1330.

18. P. Rawsthorne, "United Distillers: From Whisky Galore to Whisky *Grand Cru*," *Financial Times*, June 14, 1990, p. 19.

19. G. Mead, "Starting Price for TV Sponsorship Set," *Financial Times*, February 27, 1992, p. 6.

20. J. Peckham, *Wheel of Marketing* (1973), p. 26.

21. Saatchi and Saatchi, *Doing Business in Czechoslovakia* (London: CBI and Kogan Page, 1991), p. 222.

22. Saatchi and Saatchi, *Doing Business in Hungary* (London: CBI and Kogan Page, 1991), p. 205.

23. Saatchi and Saatchi, *Doing Business in Poland* (London: CBI and Kogan Page, 1991), p. 205.

24. European Commission, pp. 27–49.

25. A. Rawsthorne, "Pan-European in Theory," *Financial Times*, November 29, 1990.

26. Peckham, p. 50.
27. G. Johnson and K. Scholes, *Exploring Corporate Strategy*, 2nd ed. (London: Prentice-Hall, 1988), p. 192.
28. C. Bobinski, "Catching Up with Information," *Financial Times*, May 2, 1991 (supplement), p. 15.
29. J. Dempsey, "Reformer Fights the Politicians," *Financial Times*, September 17, 1990 (supplement), p. 7.
30. A. Ignatius, "Life-Style Pitch Works in Russia Despite Poverty," *The Wall Street Journal*, August 21, 1992, p. B1.
31. E. S. Browning, "Eastern Europe Poses Obstacles for Ads," *The Wall Street Journal*, July 30, 1992, p. B6.
32. A. Genillard, "Soft Soap and Hard Sell in Czechoslovakia," *Financial Times*, July 25, 1991.
33. G. de Jonquieres, "Homegrown Purchases on the Multinationals' Shopping List," *Financial Times*, August 8, 1991.
34. C. Fulop, "The Changing Structure of Hungarian Retailing: Prospects for Foreign Retailers," *Journal of Marketing Management* 7 (1991), p. 395.
35. A. Grenillard, "Freedom Brings Free for All," *Financial Times*, September 5, 1991, p. 10.
36. R. Snoddy, "Murdoch Boosts Eastern Exposure," *Financial Times*, November 12, 1991, p. 30.

Note: The most comprehensive survey of international advertising expenditure statistics, including the EC, the United States, and Japan, is to be found in M. Waterson "International Advertising Expenditure Statistics" International Journal of Advertising, 1992, vol. 11, no. 1, pp. 14–67, Cassell Educational, London, 1992.

12

| European place decisions

With the new customers and national borders of the single Europe, marketers face more complex decisions on place than in domestic North American markets. New export agents and distributors, new retail outlets, new warehousing and stockholding, and even new factory locations may all be required.

For Eastern Europe, the channels of distribution are undergoing profound change. The whole process was highly centralized until the 1990s. The new liberalization has put the system under great strain and, in some cases, causes its partial collapse. Fundamental distribution decisions may be needed.

In Western European distribution decision making, it is essential to have some knowledge of the background EC issues concerning transport, planning, and tax matters. It is also important to have some understanding of existing European distribution structures. Having explored these issues, decision makers need to focus on two main areas: the choice of the distribution channel and the logistics of moving goods along the channel.

The subjects covered in this chapter are the following:

- EC place decisions: basic background issues.
- EC distribution structures.
- EC place decisions: channels and logistics.
- Eastern European place decisions.

The basic decision-making process for the EC and EEA is shown in Figure 12–1.

EC PLACE DECISIONS: BASIC BACKGROUND ISSUES

Delivering the product or service across Europe is a vital aspect of European marketing. Product availability is often an important part of cus-

FIGURE 12–1
European Place Decisions

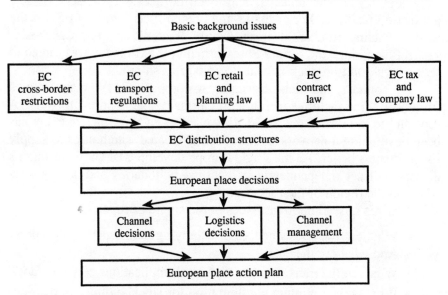

Note: Eastern European decision-making process not shown.

tomer satisfaction, and other elements of the marketing mix, such as advertising, may be wasted if the customer cannot find the product. But most means of increasing distribution impose extra costs on the company. There are direct cost increases in both transport and stockholding and also indirect costs in terms of additional European warehousing and even plant location.[1] On a more modest scale, export agents and distributors also charge higher costs for providing enhanced services.

In the European place decision, most North American companies seek to balance two sets of interests that do not necessarily coincide and may even be in conflict:

1. The *needs of the customer*, such as high-quality service, immediate product availability, a wide range of spare parts, and close attention to individual requirements.

2. The *needs of the organization*, such as minimizing the costs of holding stock around Europe, the costs of distribution to individual customers, and the need to provide extensive service in remote geographical locations.

Although it is important not to exaggerate the differences, it is necessary to establish the correct balance of activity for each market and each company. For some companies, it may even be necessary to acquire new production facilities. For example, the French food company BSN is the world's leading producer of fresh yogurt. When moving into Czechoslovakia, Poland, and the former East Germany, the company was forced to set up local joint production deals to deliver fresh product.[2]

By contrast, the niche German car company BMW manufactures from only three factories in southern Germany and exports all over Europe and to the rest of the world. However, even here, the company has been developing a network of strategically located warehouses to supply its car dealers better. As the single Europe develops, BMW plans that its dealers will act independently of national boundaries and supply anywhere in the region of their location.[3]

But this raises important issues in the single Europe:

- What are the consequences of supplying across national borders? And what are the costs?
- What are the transport, tax, and legal implications of such plans?
- What is the optimum configuration for stockholding and distribution?

We tackle these issues next.

EC Cross-Border Restrictions

The Single Europe Act of 1986 was quite clear: From 31 December 1992, the EC was to be "an area without internal frontiers, in which free movement of goods, persons, services and capital is ensured." Real progress has been made to cut distribution administration and thus costs. For example:

- *Customs controls:* As of 1993, goods are being shipped across EC borders without significant customs controls.
- *Exchange controls:* Foreign exchange transactions are now largely without restriction across the EC. Only Greece, Portugal, and Ireland maintain some controls.

As of 1993, cross-border restrictions have largely disappeared. In this context, European marketing will be chiefly concerned with variations in

VAT rates (see Chapter 10) and differences in product standards (see Chapter 9).

EC Transport Regulations

Standardized hours of driving and measures to enforce these (such as the dreaded "tachograph") have been in operation for some years. As of 1993, cabotage is also allowed across the Community, so that haulers from one EC country have the right to pick up and carry goods within the borders of another country. Prior to this time, they were forced to deliver their goods and then return empty. By having the haulers fill up what would otherwise be empty space, there could be savings of 10–15 percent on transport costs across the EC.[4] North Americans with a knowledge of the US transport industry will recognize the significance of this change.

However, there are problems. Road transport accounts for most intra-EC freight, and the Commission is seriously concerned about the increasing strain on the EC's infrastructure and environment. Traffic congestion and pollution may be tackled by imposing higher taxes on road transport in the future, thus increasing intra-EC road transport costs.[5]

EC Retail and Planning Laws

There is no point in delivering goods to retail shops or warehouses that are not open. Moreover, it makes little sense to try to establish a new warehouse in a location where the local or national government will not allow it to be built. These are just two examples of legal and planning restrictions.

Although North American marketers are not likely to become involved in the details of these issues, they need to be aware that such problems can arise. They fall into three main areas:[6]

1. Compulsory closing hours and days, for example, Sunday closing.
2. Commercial development and planning restrictions, for example, in rural and urban areas.
3. Laws on commercial property ownership, such as leases being subject to certain restrictions in a particular EC country.

It is beyond the scope of this book to go into the details, but marketers should be aware that this whole area is a minefield of national laws. What might have seemed to be a simple distribution idea may turn out to be much more complicated. For example, Italy has strict planning laws, but Greece does not. Greece has widely varying laws on shopping hours, whereas in Germany all-day Sunday and Saturday afternoon closing is fairly consistent across the nation. Unlike the situation in the United States, very few shops are open around the clock. North American marketers will need to check the laws country by country.

EC Contract Law

Whether agreements are made between the company and agents, distributors, retailers, or transport companies, they will entail payment and, therefore, involve contracts. Because civil law codes vary across the Community (see Chapter 2), contract law will not be the same in all EC countries. Bennett[7] recommends that the contract specifies:

- Which EC country or North American law is to apply to the contract.
- The documents required by the buyer prior to payment.
- The currency to be used in the transaction.
- For sales involving credit, the names and addresses of the buyer's and seller's banks handling the transactions and who is responsible for bank charges.

The purpose of spelling out these issues is not to become involved in contract minutiae but to illustrate clearly the detail that is essential in many aspects of this subject. Professional advice may be required.

EC Company and Tax Law Plus Investment Incentives

As mentioned in Chapter 10, the EC has abandoned all hope of harmonizing its company, tax, and investment laws. This may have important implications in terms of where companies invest in the EC. Lower taxation in some EC countries, coupled with EC regional development grants in less-developed parts, has led to complex decisions on the siting of new warehouses and factories—all part of the European marketing logistics mix. Even the simplest decisions may not be what they seem; an example is the decision we looked at in Chapter 10 on locating a factory in Germany and the selling organization in another country for tax and investment reasons.[8] The key point is to approach the problem by making comparisons across EC countries, not only on customers and resources but also on fiscal and tax issues. Clearly, the detail of such arrangements is beyond the scope of this book, but the principle is not. European marketers will need to work with other company functional areas to resolve these matters.

EC DISTRIBUTION STRUCTURES

To make rational decisions on European channels of distribution, it is essential to start by looking at the channels being used now and the changes expected. We shall therefore briefly examine EC distribution infrastructure while recognizing that individual companies may in practice need to seek further detail.

For industrial products, export agents, distributors, and wholesalers will be important channel options. For consumer goods, retailers and direct selling may hold more promise. We shall consider all these areas. Finally in this section, we look at the developing role of specialist EC logistics and distribution companies and their contribution to pan-European place decisions.

EC Distribution Infrastructure

Given the single-market objective, it is perhaps surprising that there is no clear picture of EC freight transport services in the official statistics: sea and air freight services are separated out, but road, rail, and inland waterway EC statistics are usually lumped together and not cross-compared at all.[9,10]

Nevertheless, it is possible to piece together a picture of the major movement of freight within the Community.[11] It appears that road haulage accounts for the bulk of freight traffic, followed by rail and inland waterways; the last is particularly important as the Rhine is a main freight route linking Switzerland, Germany, France, and the Netherlands. Air freight is the least used: it is more expensive but faster on some routes. The major trends over the last few years have been the following:[12]

- *From rail to road*: Road haulage now takes double the tonnage of rail transport.

- *From bulk goods to special cargoes*: Complete handling of shipments from seller to buyer, coupled with containerization and computer tracking of goods, has contributed to this trend.
- *From rail or road transport only to a combination of methods of transport*: For speed and efficiency, road, rail, air, and sea are being used in combination increasingly to cover the distances and provide door-to-door delivery. New forms of packaging and containers have assisted this process.

For the future, the Community of European Railways (CER) has been keen to present rail networks as being capable of major expansion, as well as being more environmentally friendly and fuel-efficient. Grand plans involving the Channel Tunnel, high-speed rail networks across Europe, and additional Alpine tunnels[13] were presented to the Commission by the CER in 1989.

In practice, there are major problems with the compatibility of the various rail networks: even the new German and French high-speed trains cannot operate on each other's tracks.[14] In addition, most of Europe's rail networks experience large losses and receive government subsidies.[15] This is hardly the backdrop for major rail expansion. It is likely that European road transport will remain dominant unless there is positive discrimination against it on environmental grounds.

European Export Agents, Distributors, and Wholesalers

For bulk raw material and other basic goods, the wholesaler is often the most important channel.[16] There is low "added value" from undifferentiated products sold mainly on price. Customers seek high-quality service and short delivery times. For North American marketers involved in these areas, there is little choice but to use wholesalers, probably on a regional basis: pan-European wholesalers are unlikely to supply the service required.

For EC capital goods and industrial goods with greater customer technical and service content, the situation is more complex. The wholesaler or distributor often supplies specialist services such as installation, maintenance, and training; this makes it imperative to find and keep the best distributor in a particular EC country. Conversely, if the distributor can gain significant market share, pressure may be applied to the manufacturer. Two examples are:

1. *Computers*: Strong relationships with dealers and value-added re-sellers have become essential for most high-level sales through-out Europe.[17] As dealing margins have come under pressure, add-ing value through selling computer software or supplying additional services has become essential.[18] Dealers have never been able to dominate the market. Distributor relationships are complex and difficult to maintain on a pan-European basis.

2. *Pharmaceuticals*: In most of the major EC markets, three or fewer wholesalers manage at least 50 percent of the ethical drugs market.[19] By dominating the channel, the wholesalers are in a position to influence heavily pharmaceutical manufacturers. North American drug manufacturers in Europe have small market shares, the largest having only 4 percent. Unless they have patent protection, they are vulnerable. Pan-European buying groups among the wholesalers are also beginning to emerge and perhaps increase the pressure.

In these market circumstances, the European channel dynamics need very careful investigation and resolution. Judging by the examples from com-puters and pharmaceuticals, the channel decisions may have more impact on company profitability than advertising and sales promotions.

European Retailing

In both consumer durables and fast-moving consumer goods, retailing has surpassed wholesaling as the prime means of European distribution.[20] In addition, European retail distribution is highly concentrated through a number of key buying organizations. Table 12–1 shows the concentrated nature of European grocery markets, not only in terms of share taken by the leaders but also on the basis of the small number of key decision points necessary to achieve a sale. Similar concentration has arisen in furniture and consumer durables distribution.

Not only is grocery retailing concentrated within countries, but some leading retailers have also combined into pan-European buying groups, a development which may concentrate buying power even further.[21] How-ever, it is important to keep this type of activity in perspective: many of the largest retailers in France, the UK, the Netherlands, and Germany have *not* joined these groups.

TABLE 12–1
Concentration of European Grocery Buying, 1986

	Percent Turnover of Top 10 Buying Organizations	Number of Key Decision Points
Switzerland	90	14
Sweden	89	9
West Germany*	81	308
Netherlands	79	25
Belgium	66	—
Great Britain	66	12
France	62	145
Italy	35	304
Spain	26	10

*Excludes Aldi.

Source: A. C. Nielsen, as quoted with permission in R. Lynch, *European Business Strategies* (London: Kogan Page, 1990).

In terms of future trends, there is further scope for retail concentration in Germany, France, and southern Europe. Buying groups operating across Europe may also develop (e.g., photographic and video equipment through the Phox chain in France).

Because of new buying groups and the varying nature of retail structures in different markets across Europe, North American marketers must check out distribution channels on both a pan-European and a country-by-country basis throughout target country markets.

Pan-European Logistics and Distribution Companies

European companies involved in supplying third-party warehousing, transport, and distribution—logistics companies—have grown significantly over the last few years. There is a high entry barrier to the establishment of such companies on a pan-European basis: the fixed costs of setting up a reliable, fast service are high.[22] But four trends may lead to growth in this area:

1. Just-in-time requirements mean that some customers want smaller, more flexible quantities of products delivered more frequently.

2. Removal of EC barriers and EC cabotage will make cross-border delivery cheaper during the 1990s.

3. Some manufacturers are seeking to reduce the number of warehouses they use for customers. This means they can cut the number of distributors, but they may want a more complete door-to-door service. Xerox is reported to be reducing world stocks by 30 percent and cutting its European distribution centers from seven to two by this means.[23] Logistics are then used to provide customer service.

4. Some manufacturers and retailers have decided to concentrate on what they regard as core business activities and to pass noncore tasks such as distribution to specialist operators.[23]

All this requires specialist expertise and systems and may directly affect customers and thus European marketing. All the major U.S. carriers are well represented across Europe. However, it should be said that where European sales force activity is still undertaken largely on a *national* basis, these extra savings may be neither possible nor desirable.[24]

EC PLACE DECISIONS: CHANNELS AND LOGISTICS

In Chapter 7 we explored European entry options in broad terms. We now consider the implications of the process as they relate specifically to selecting distribution channels and managing the distribution process cost-effectively. It is convenient to split the issue into three areas:

1. EC channel decisions: options and choice.
2. EC logistics decisions: organization, investment, and management of the chosen channel.
3. EC channel management: ongoing relationships with distributors.

However, we should recognize that these are, to some extent, interrelated.

EC Channel Decisions

Earlier in this chapter, we examined one of the basic issues: the balance between the needs of the customer and the needs of the organization.

There is one other basic consideration: The most significant channel opportunity may arise from developing a new channel of distribution. For example:

- Special "grocery-style" packs of domestic plumbing items have extended distribution and sale of these goods beyond specialist builders merchants to DIY superstores.
- Personal computers sold by mail order, cutting out the local distributor completely, have made significant gains in the PC market.

For European markets, the guiding principle in making the channel decision has to be the costs of making the delivery in relation to the size and nature of the sales order in question. For order that are not large enough to justify calling and delivering directly to the customer, the following procedure applies:

- Plot out the existing channels to customers on a country-by-country basis.
- Establish the leading customers and their needs.
- Identify any dominant customer or intermediary in the channel structure.
- Set out the options available, including any possible links with other channel users.

In practice, it is also important to explore the *nature* of the regular customer contact requirement, that is, a simple sales order call versus a more detailed call involving advice and service. Clearly, where a lengthy call is involved, a qualified local agent or distributor may be essential to provide the level of service. Alternatively, a telephone selling system for regular orders may be set up if there is sufficient demand. However, the latter is difficult to manage without a national office in the European country concerned; it is for this reason that a number of North American companies have set up offices in different European countries, even though sales may be small in the early years.

EC Logistics Decisions

According to Christopher et al., logistics decisions involve five basic elements:[25]

1. *Facility decisions*: Deciding where warehouses and factories are to be located is clearly a long-term issue.
2. *Inventory decisions*: Stockholding has a cost but may be necessary to provide adequate customer service.
3. *Communications decisions*: Information is essential for delivery of the correct goods to the customer. Thus, ordering, processing, and invoicing all form part of the essential information. A system for handling normal customer queries and complaints is also needed.
4. *Utilization decisions*: We have already identified the European trends in pallets and containers that are the essence of this area.
5. *Transport decisions*: The method of transport; the ownership, leasing, or hiring of vehicles; and movement by road, rail, or air are all important factors.

The balance of the issues in logistics decisions will vary with the type of European industry, as well as the European customer. Industry distribution costs for the above areas have been published and may provide a starting point for European expansion.[23]

EC Channel Management

To some extent, the distributor is a customer of the company and therefore needs to be motivated to act in the company's best interests. For example, the distributor may well have an influence on:

- The level of service to customers (e.g., paperwork, handling of returned goods, and quality of telephone answering).
- Availability of stock (e.g., order cycles, stock held, and invoicing).

In these circumstances, therefore, European marketing has an important task in managing the channel. A program of marketing action for North American managers might include:

- Regular communication and visits.
- Training to improve standards.
- Provision of incentives and information about the company.
- Occasional audit procedures involving independent customer contacts.

- Company newsletter to distributors.
- Regional meetings.
- Joint participation in trade fairs and exhibitions.

European Channels and Logistics: Conclusions

If we bear in mind that most companies have an existing logistics structure, European decisions in this area might utilize the following sequence:

1. Where are the new customers located?
   a. What is the volume to these new destinations?
   b. What is the existing structure to service these?
   c. What is the desired speed, frequency, and size of load?
2. What level of service do customers want and are prepared to pay for?
   a. Investigate direct delivery versus warehousing.
   b. Check warehouse locations and size.
   c. Define stock levels and determine how to maintain them.
3. Whose transport services do we use?
   a. Use our own transport or contract out?
   b. What are the options? At what cost? With what reliability and frequency?
4. What organization is required?
   a. How much information handling is needed?
   b. How do we control remote locations?
   c. How do we handle order processing?
   d. How do we handle customer queries and complaints?
   e. How do we give incentives to distributors?

Beyond these considerations, the area of European marketing and logistics is still evolving. The information revolution in terms of telecommunications, fax, and computer will profoundly alter the level of service possible over the next few years. The commencement of the pan-European mobile telephone system and the rapid development of pan-European data telecommunications networks between customer, warehouse, and supplier will transform some areas of logistics over the next 10 years. North America is possibly ahead of some EC countries and certainly ahead of Eastern Europe in this regard.

EASTERN EUROPEAN PLACE DECISIONS

Much of the basic structure for Western European decision making will also apply in principle in the East. We shall therefore use this section to highlight key differences.

Old System: Highly Centralized

The former communist states produced goods in a highly centralized and bureaucratic planning system. For example, in the former USSR, up to nine state bodies were involved in the production and distribution of a loaf of fresh bread to the general public.[26] Little money was invested in the distribution system to bring goods to market; as a result, there is inadequate nationwide storage, transportation, and warehousing. Moreover, computerized control systems do not exist. Essentially, this situation has applied to most Eastern European countries, including Poland, the former Czechoslovakia, and Hungary.[27][29]

New System: Fragmented and Duplicated

The new distribution structure in much of Eastern Europe has been accompanied by the sale of existing state-owned retail shops and the disintegration of what distribution network existed. Hence, PepsiCo (U.S.) reported that in Poland its distribution structure had virtually disappeared, and it had to be rebuilt from scratch.[30] Other companies have found that they need to deliver directly to retail outlets to overcome difficulties.[29] Wholesale distribution structures have largely disappeared, insofar as they ever existed.

   Another consequence of the privatization process has been that retail shops do not specialize, but sell everything. Moreover, the in-store standards of merchandising and display are far below Western levels. This makes the whole issue of entry methods for North American companies more difficult.

Hungarian Experience

Possibly, the Eastern European country with the longest experience of distribution change is Hungary. Fulop has recorded how reforms have come in two bursts: 1968 and the early 1980s.[31] But the 1990s still show many shops without self-service. The state companies and cooperatives still dominate the system.

For example, the largest retailer in Hungary is a cooperative department store chain, Skala. It does retailing, wholesaling, exporting, and importing and has 70 stores. It has recently agreed to have foreign concessionaires in the stores, such as Philips electrical products. Tengelmann, the giant private German retailer, has a 22 percent shareholding in the company. From personal observation in 1992, in-store presentation is way below North American levels.

Other Western companies have simply set up their own chains in Hungary, including Adidas sports goods, Bennetton clothing, Avon cosmetics, and IKEA furniture.

For industrial goods and services, exhibitions and trade fairs have been used to make contacts, as previously outlined. These seem to be followed by direct deliveries; the problem has been payment rather than distribution.

Eastern European Distribution in the Future

Because of their close geographical position and previous trading history, German and Austrian companies have been particularly active in some Eastern European markets, such as Hungary.[31] However, it would be surprising if other countries, such as France and Italy, were unable to make progress through their long history of contacts with Eastern Europe. The problem that all companies will face for the next few years is a distribution system that is unable to meet more than basic requirements. Hence, it may be necessary to build or buy a distribution network and work with a partner in Eastern Europe.

NOTES

1. M. Christopher, S. Kennedy, M. McDonald, and G. Wills. *Effective Marketing Management* (Bedford, England: Cranfield Press, 1985), pp. 96–100.

2. G. de Jonquieres, "Home-Grown Produce on the Multinationals' Shopping List," *Financial Times*, August 8, 1991.

3. J. Griffiths, "BMW—Tailoring Its Competitive Challenge," *Financial Times*, October, 19, 1990, p. 16.

4. "Business in Europe: Survey," *The Economist*, (supplement), June 8, 1991, p. 11.
5. European Commission, *Panorama of EC Industry 1991/92* (Luxembourg: OPOCE, 1991), p. 25-29.
6. Ibid., p. 23-21.
7. R. Bennett, *Selling to Europe*, (London: Kogan Page, 1991), p. 141.
8. L. Kellaway, "Brussels Aims to Untangle Strands of Taxation Patchwork," *Financial Times*, February 4, 1991.
9. European Commission, table 2, p. 23-5.
10. European Commission, *Eurostats: Basic Statistics of the EC*, 27th ed. (Luxembourg: OPOCE, 1990), pp. 285–93.
11. European Commission, *Panorama of EC Industry 1991/92*, section 25.
12. European Commission, *Panorama of EC Industry 1991/92*, pp. 25-2, 25-3.
13. K. Brown, "The Future of Continental Transport Links," *Financial Times*, (supplement), May 9, 1989, p. 37.
14. R. Tomkins, "All-Europe Rail Network Still Lies over Horizon," *Financial Times*, June 3, 1991.
15. European Commission, *Panorama of EC Industry 1991/92*, p. 25.
16. European Commission, *Panorama of EC Industry 1991/92*, pp. 23-4–23-7.
17. "Too Lucrative to Let Go," *Financial Times*, September 17, 1991 (computer software supplement), p. 2.
18. L. Cane and L. Kehoe, "New Order Forces the Pace of Change," *Financial Times*, November, 8, 1991.
19. R. Platford, "Agenda Set by Wholesalers," *Financial Times*, July 23, 1991 (pharmaceuticals supplement), p. 5.
20. European Commission, *Panorama of EC Industry 1991/92*, p. 23-5.
21. J. Thornhill, "Retailers Broaden Their Outlook," *Financial Times*, December 17, 1990, p. 3.
22. A. Hunter, "The Scramble for a Foothold," *Financial Times*, June 22, 1990 (courier and express services supplement), p. 2.
23. M. Terry, "Logistics Firms Don New Clothes for 1992," *Financial Times*, November 6, 1990 (distribution services supplement), p. 2.
24. A. Baxter, "Single Market Spells a Re-think on Logistics," *Financial Times*, January 27, 1992, p. 4.
25. Christopher et al., p. 98.
26. "The Soviet Food Machine," *Education Guardian*, January 14, 1992, p. 3.
27. Saatchi and Saatchi, *Doing Business in Poland* (London: CBI and Kogan Page, 1991), p. 202.

28. Saatchi and Saatchi, *Doing Business in Czechoslovakia* (London: CBI and Kogan Page, 1991), p. 218.
29. Saatchi and Saatchi, *Doing Business in Hungary* (London: CBI and Kogan Page, 1991), p. 203.
30. de Jonquieres.
31. C. Fulop, "The Changing Structure of Hungarian Retailing: Prospects for Foreign Retailers," *Journal of Marketing Management* 7 (1991), pp. 383–96.

13

European human resources and organization decisions

Without doubt, skilled European marketing by North American managers will involve bringing out the best in European managers. It will therefore need to be sensitive to human resources issues within the company; European history is littered with the debris that resulted from language and culture imposing barriers rather than supporting growth. Moreover, North American marketing managers cannot rely on a company's personnel or human resources function to sort out the issues for them; this would be an abdication of their own management responsibility. Initial consideration of these issues must be undertaken early in the strategy process, as well as during the implementation phase.

European marketing strategies and plans will also need an effective organization structure if company objectives are to be met. As the company's involvement in Europe grows, the various national markets being managed may conflict with management objectives in pan-European marketing. Organization structures for marketing may have to be redeveloped to cope with the European dimension.

The EC is in the process of strengthening its involvement in social and working issues, which may affect marketing along with other company functional areas. We therefore start by considering EC social policies in the light of their possible impact on European marketing management.

The basic subjects covered in this chapter are the following:

- EC basics: European social policy.
- European human resources development in marketing.
- European marketing organization.

EC BASICS: EUROPEAN SOCIAL POLICY

European company human resources policies, including those in marketing, must work within the framework set by the agreements of the EC in the area of social policy. Such policies have long been important within the EC, encompassing issues such as employment, labor law, vocational training, social security, safety and health, and collective bargaining between employers and workers.[1] Articles 117–128 of the Treaty of Rome deal specifically with social policy.

Apart from the EC Social Fund, which is designed to help poorer Community areas, and some social representation and discussion in Brussels, the individual EC countries in the past had considerable flexibility on how they pursue and manage their social policies. However, the balance changed at Maastricht in December 1991. A separate protocol on social policy outside the Maastricht Treaty was agreed upon and initialed by all member states except the UK.

Under this arrangement, the 11 countries will make agreements that will go into their own national laws. The European Commission will bring forward draft directives; Community mechanisms such as the Council of Ministers will still be used to ratify them, and the 11 will have the full benefit of EC institutions such as the European Court of Justice.[2] In spite of the UK's dissent, European social policy will be implemented over the next few years.

At this point, some North American readers will ask whether their companies and marketing departments will be affected at all by the Maastricht agreement in this area. For North American companies and organizations marketing solely in the UK, the new social policy developments may have little relevance. However, for those companies involved with Europe, the impact will be quite specific.

North American companies marketing to Western Europe will have to deal with EC countries that have signed the agreement. As soon as they employ workers in EC countries or consider setting up EC subsidiaries or forming EC alliances, they will be involved in issues covered by the protocol. It would therefore be wise for North American companies to monitor carefully all EC social policy developments. Moreover, it is essential that they implement relevant areas when operating in or dealing beyond a buyer-seller relationship with companies in the EC.

As a result of the social policy protocol, some future actions will be decided by EC member states by qualified majority vote, and some will need unanimous agreement. The majority voting procedure greatly speeds up EC decision making in the areas to which it applies; hence, we may expect to see important new European agreements in some social policy areas quite quickly.

The following actions to be agreed upon by qualified majority voting will be taken to "support and complement" government activities in the following areas:

- Working environment, including health and safety.
- Working conditions.
- Information and consultation of workers.
- Equality between women and men.

It was also agreed by the 11 member states that a unanimous vote would be required in other areas, such as termination of contracts of employment, social security, and social protection.[3]

From a strictly North American marketing viewpoint, the new social policy may require initiatives in two areas as policies become clearer:

1. Communication and discussion of European marketing plans with work force colleagues.
2. Organization and reporting policies in the European marketing and sales function that are consistent with EC directives, such as those on working conditions.

Clearly, marketing may also be affected by a plethora of such EC social policies—for example, those on recruitment and training—but these are less likely to require a marketing lead.

EUROPEAN HUMAN RESOURCES DEVELOPMENT IN MARKETING

Probably more important than EC social policy are the language and cultural barriers that exist across the Community and that will continue to make it difficult for North American marketing managers and EC colleagues to work effectively together. This applies particularly where it is necessary to set up a multinational team of managers. When Neale and Mindel studied 40 managers from 13 countries working in the UK oil multinational British Petroleum in 1991, they found the following important differences in cultural attitudes that affected working relationships:[4]

- Many Scandinavians expect to be called by their surnames only. Germans do not anticipate being called by their Christian names, even when they know each other well. Many UK managers are on first-name terms with colleagues.
- Whereas shaking hands is a formal politeness on first meeting in the United States and the UK, French subsidiary company managers did this every morning, to the surprise of others.
- French executives judged that their positions in the managerial hierarchy gave them the authority to make decisions, whereas Dutch, Scandinavian, and UK managers anticipated they might be challenged.
- Germans were the most comfortable in formal hierarchies, whereas the Dutch were the most relaxed. UK managers left more to individual initiative and expected more of individuals.
- UK and U.S. managers were proud to work late at the office, as this emphasized their commitment and ambition. Most others regarded working beyond the normal finishing time as a sign of inefficiency that needed training to overcome. (You can easily imagine the tensions that might arise over this!)

Just in case the preceding misunderstandings are thought to be specific to one company, consider a study undertaken by the UK Parliamentary Defence Committee in 1991 of defense collaboration between UK and French companies.[5] Anglo-French misunderstandings seem to have troubled all the projects studied. The French military regarded their UK colleagues as "perfidious partners," whereas the latter thought the French would march moodily out of projects unless they had control. The British saw the French as "feather-bedded" with unlimited budgets, whereas the French believed the British were too relaxed about their reliance on U.S. military know-how. And so on.

For U.S. and Canadian marketing managers that have worked in an international business environment, these descriptions will be recognized as representing expectations and social pressures that need to be tackled. What is to be done about these cultural attitudes? How are marketing managers to work together across Europe? Solutions are clearly necessary and will emerge only after careful thought and training. Two further studies provide clues.

The Economist Intelligence Unit surveyed international managers to establish what they regarded as the key characteristics of an international manager.[6] Hard functional skills such as marketing were considered much less important than *human resources* skills relevant to an international environment, such as adaptability, coping with unfamiliar situations, sensitivity to other cultures, ability to work in teams, and global outlook. Some of these skills can be improved with training, and some need to be sought in the recruiting of potential managers.

These findings are consistent with the work of Bartlett and Ghoshal, who concluded that the global company could not dominate from the center if it wished to remain successful: links across the various subsidiaries that allowed knowledge and information to flow were required.[7] In turn, such an organization will work only if the culture and atmosphere encourage the free exchange of ideas and the mutual support across different national perspectives rather than Franco-British rivalry. More specifically, Taylor has written on the implications of cultural differences among European managers.[8]

One of Europe's most experienced multinationals is the Dutch-UK company Unilever. It has been working for many years to develop a spirit of cooperation across the organization.[9] This involves *more* than creating formal organization structures. The company recruits managers who can work in teams and who value cooperation and consensus. Unilever also uses multinational shared management experiences to develop these areas and break down cultural barriers. For example, it actively encourages managers to have Unilever work experience outside its UK and Dutch subsidiaries.

The whole process takes years to develop. The lesson for North American marketing management is that cultures usually change slowly and the evolution toward a single Europe still has to be reflected in some company management attitudes. European marketing training and recruitment, along with work outside the home country, will help in slowly breaking down language and cultural barriers. Rothwell has written in this context of the training and development of international managers.[10] Lublin has also written of training in this area.[11]

EUROPEAN MARKETING ORGANIZATION

We now need to consider the organization structure for implementing European marketing. Marketing needs to fulfill three main roles:

1. To contribute to the company's *overall* (i.e., beyond marketing) objectives by its understanding of European customer needs.

2. To turn *company* objectives into practicable *marketing* objectives, strategies, and plans for European marketing in the four P's.
3. To implement agreed-upon marketing plans and contribute to the company's European development.

Basic European Marketing Organizational Structure

The organizational arrangements to achieve the three areas outlined above will vary widely among companies. For example, when a European market is changing fast because of competitive pressures, economic change, or real demand, the structure required needs to be more flexibile and free-wheeling than in a stable market, even one in which the competition is still fierce.

With the need to undertake marketing activity on the European marketing mix, one basic form of marketing organization is to group products together across Europe and appoint a *product manager* to manage these. If the grouping is by brands rather than products, the individual is called a *brand manager*. Usually, several of these brand or product managers are then grouped together under a *marketing manager*, who will in turn report to the *marketing director*. This form of pan-European organization is shown in Figure 13–1.

We have already seen elsewhere in this book that a pan-European marketing organization is appropriate only for markets where customers are broadly similar across Europe and where national languages and cultures are relatively unimportant in the buying decision. Throughout the book, we have seen several examples of pan-European and regional products and services where such conditions apply. But we should also acknowledge that we have seen other situations where a pan-European product manager would be, at best, irrelevant and, at worst, harmful to the organization. We shall look at other organization structures for Europe later in this chapter.

The Role of the European Product Manager

The European product manager is responsible for creating an annual marketing plan for the product. Such a plan might include objectives for the product, strategies to achieve those objectives, and detailed plans to carry out the strategies. Once these plans have been approved by the marketing

FIGURE 13–1
Pan-European Marketing Organization in Manufacturing

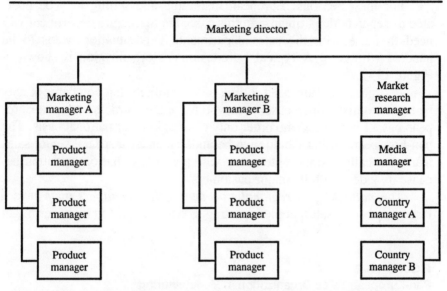

Note: Country managers are used for short-term promotions and sales force liaison.

director (and it is not always easy to obtain this approval!), the product manager will spend the rest of the year implementing the activities agreed on, monitoring the results achieved, and adjusting plans, depending on the effectiveness of the strategies in the marketplace and the competitive activity.

There are also important actions concerning coordination with other functions in the organization. A new product to be introduced cannot appear if *production* has not made it. *Finance* may have pointed out that marketing expenditure is over budget or that the managing director needs to make financial cuts that will affect the marketing budget for the product. Moreover, there may be a need to coordinate across countries.

Marketing and Selling Organizations in Europe

By the very nature of the marketing role just described, there are relatively few managers involved in European marketing as compared with the number involved in European selling. Moreover, the selling organization may need to have a stronger national base in a target European country, even when overall product marketing is ostensibly pan-European.

For these reasons, European marketing and selling may be operated as separate departments. In this case, the marketing department will need to liaise with the sales department. This situation needs to be handled with care. A typical European sales organization is shown in Figure 13–2.

In organizing European selling in a manufacturing company, it may be useful to distinguish customers who place large orders on a pan-European basis from those who order only on a regional or national basis. The pan-European selling would then be undertaken by a special senior sales team, typically a small elite group who are vital to the organization because they deal with its major customers.

The *national and regional European sales managers* may have a large number of salespeople reporting to them, and each manager might

FIGURE 13–2
Pan-European Sales Organization in Manufacturing

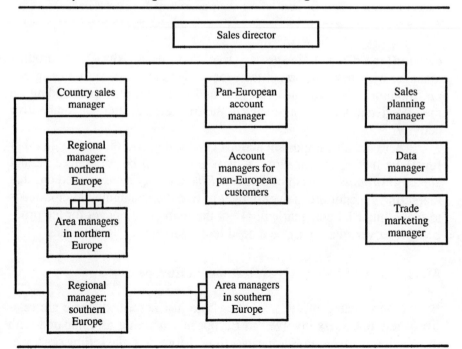

be responsible for a reasonable amount of sales in total but that are made up of many individual accounts in one country or European region. The manager might also have a great deal of autonomy if national EC markets have different customers or competitors.

Over the next 20 years, the pan-European sales function may become stronger as major European customers grow in strength, for example, in some European car and consumer electronics markets. National managers will remain important in some markets but may come to rely on telephone selling and other techniques that are more cost-effective. Such organizational changes will occur in both consumer and industrial selling as a result of the *concentration* of customers in some industries and the *internationalization* of some products, making national customers less important to the overall customer base.

Although European marketing and selling may be organized as different departments, there must be close cooperation between them. Typically, pan-European product managers concentrate on the mass marketing of a product to the final customers, and pan-European sales managers concentrate on selling the product (or service) to a small range of key customers. Clearly, both these tasks are vital, and they can be achieved only by the two groups working closely together.

The links back to the parent company in the United States and Canada are considered in Chapter 14.

Some Other Types of European Marketing Organization

In addition to the product-based structure outlined above, there are many other forms of structure that can be developed to reflect the marketplace. For example, these might include:

European Customer-Based Structures
In industrial marketing, it is quite normal to find a marketing organization responsible for the large, "one-off" products or designs that is completely different from the team responsible for the standardized designs to be sold to many smaller customers. Clearly, the European marketing task is totally different for the two situations.

National Marketing Organization
Where problems of great geographical distance, company history, or major language and cultural differences arise, a largely national structure

may be employed. This means that marketing and sales need to sort out very precisely which marketing decisions are to be taken at the pan-European level and which at the national level.

European Matrix Structures
In a matrix structure, two (or more) sets of individuals have responsibility for making decisions. This structure usually arises where the European "market" can be divided in more than one way, for example, by product or by country:

- *By product:* coffee and confectionery.
- *By country:* France, Germany, the UK, and so on.

Each country market could be equally important in developing the products over time. In addition, there may be some overriding need to coordinate activities, the obvious example being the development of a pan-European brand.

In these circumstances, two sets of organization may need to *coordinate their marketing plans*. Clearly, this may be a slow and tortuous route to achievement of corporate goals, but it may be the only way to satisfy market demand and management requirements in the long term. The Swedish company Electrolux had such an organization in 1989.[12] It was plagued with many problems, principally due to the difficulty that such structures have in assigning responsibility for a marketing task.

Conclusions on European Marketing Organization

European organizations will change their structures gradually. As organizations grow older and larger, they tend to:

- Become more stable.
- Become more formalized in their behavior.
- Become more elaborate in structure.
- Become larger in terms of the size of the units within the structure.
- Need proportionately more staff to administer the elaborate systems.

Some of these developments pose real dangers for European marketing because the resulting organization may not be able to respond rapidly enough to what is happening in the marketplace. The obvious example is the difficulty that some of the global computer companies—such as the dominant U.S. company, IBM—have had in responding to the fast changes in computer markets around the world.[13] And IBM is a company that has been as *customer-oriented* as any; clearly, this is not enough.

As for *European new-product marketing*, there is a case to be made for separating out this vital part of the marketing management process into its own organization. This is the way to ensure that new products:

- Receive high priority.
- Have real targets not hidden by ongoing products.
- Obtain top-management attention.
- Have their own budgets and thus measurable resources.

Some problems may result from splitting off a European new-product development function. Those involved in this area may feel cut off from ongoing European business, and there may be problems over ideas to be handed over by the new-products group to the ongoing marketing group. It is often better if the new-products team can introduce a product into the marketplace in a European launch or series of national product launches: "ownership" of a European project is likely to lead to stronger commitment to its success. I write from my own experience working in the European part of a U.S. multinational, but there is some research evidence to support this perception.

It is essential for all European marketing organizations to recognize that the necessary European integrative mechanisms will change depending on the company's cultural background, the desirability of reaching rapid decisions, and the type of market. Blackwell et al.[14] have identified five forms of control for Europe, in order of increasing centralization:

1. Informal cooperation.
2. Coordinating mechanisms.
3. Central coordination.
4. Central direction (but not day-to-day control).
5. Central control.

The real difficulties of implementing any new pan-European structure are illustrated by the problems of Europe's largest packaging company, CMB, between 1989 and 1991. The company was formed with a pan-European objective by the merger of the leading UK and French packaging companies in 1989. After two years of friction between the group's UK and French senior managers, the managing director left in late 1991.[15] North American marketers underestimate the difficulties in this area at their own peril.

NOTES

1. H. Arbuthnott and G. Edwards, *A Common Man's Guide to the Common Market*, 2nd ed. (London: Macmillan, 1989), chapter 11.

2. D. Gardner, "Astonishing Compromise Threatens to Create a Brussels Benefit for the Legal Fraternity," *Financial Times*, December 12, 1991, p. 2.

3. "Separate Protocol on the Quality of Life," *Financial Times*, 1991, December 12, 1991, p. 7.

4. R. Neale and R. Mindel, "Rigging Up Multi-Cultural Teamworking," *Personnel Management* 24, no. 1 (January 1992), p. 36.

5. UK Defence Committee First Report, *Anglo-French Defence Cooperation* (London: HMSO, December 1991).

6. L. Wood, "Search for Worldly-Wise Company Executives," *Financial Times*, April 9, 1991 (management training supplement), p. 4.

7. C. Bartlett and S. Ghoshal, "Managing across Borders: New Strategic Requirements," *Sloan Management Review*, Summer 1987.

8. S. Taylor, "Cultural Differences and the Euromanager," *Personnel Management* 23, no. 4 (April 1991) p. 57.

9. G. Golzen, "Local Rivalry Wrecks Globalisation," *Sunday Times*, June 17, 1990, section 6.

10. S. Rothwell, "Development of the International Manager," *Personnel Management* 24, no. 1 (January 1992), p. 33.

11. J. S. Lublin, "Companies Use Cross-Cultural Training to Help Their Employees Adjust Abroad," *The Wall Street Journal*, August 4, 1992, p. B5.

12. C. Lorenz, "An Impossible Organization but the Only One that Works," *Financial Times*, June 21, 1989, p. 14.

13. A. Cane, "A Rough Ride into the Unknown," *Financial Times*, June 5, 1991.

14. N. Blackwell, J. Bizet, P. Child, and D. Hensley, 'Shaping a Pan-European Organisation," *McKinsey Quarterly*, no. 2 (1991).

15. S. Thornhill and W. Dawkins, "A Troubled Marriage," *Financial Times*, September 13, 1991.

14

Marketing planning and control for Europe

After detailed analysis of the main European marketing areas, we are finally in a position to draw these together into the complete marketing plan. But such work means nothing unless it is accompanied by monitoring and control systems to ensure that the objectives are achieved. We look at both planning and control in this chapter.

EUROPEAN MARKETING PLANNING

Unless set within the context of the company's overall *corporate* plan, European marketing plans mean very little. The starting point has to be the organization, its corporate objectives, and its planning time frame. Marketing, like other functions in the business, must work within these parameters.[1]

Beyond this, the European marketing planning process follows the subject areas outlined in Figure 1–2. What was perhaps less understandable—and deserves to be clarified now—is the organization's *reasons* for tackling European marketing. The motivation behind the process will provide clues on the areas that need to be explored. Moreover, it will provide the basis for the company's commitment to Europe, which is essential if the planning process is to lead to successful action.

It is quite possible that the European marketing process will not succeed unless the company is prepared to invest top-quality resources. It may fail for the following reasons:

1. European planning is more complex than planning for national activities: cultures, languages, social issues, and competitors are more diverse.

2. European markets are still evolving at a significant pace: there will be new opportunities and problems.
3. Areas that are largely taken for granted in national plans need to be freshly appraised, for example, economies and legal and tax issues.

Beyond these matters, European marketing must decide to what extent it needs to institute some *formal* planning system for Europe, that is, a clear planning format with areas for individual initiative within this structure. Given the managerial and cultural differences within Europe, the evidence from Chapter 13 suggests that such a format is desirable, at least in the formative years. The alternative, informal approach holds considerable potential for confusion and misunderstanding. Beyond these considerations, European marketing planning is likely to follow existing procedures.[2]

EUROPEAN MONITORING AND CONTROL SYSTEMS

With the greater complexity of operations across Europe, there is potential for a marketing function either to lose control or, perhaps more likely, never really to be in control of its marketing activities throughout the marketing period. Suitable monitoring and control systems need to be set up to track what is happening across the company's European markets. They may vary from the elaborate to the simple, depending on:

- The size of the company.
- The degree of autonomy given to European operations.
- The frequency of reporting on performance to the center.
- The formality and nature of information supplied to European headquarters.

Careful thought needs to be given to the type and nature of this information: not only does it affect the center's knowledge of what is happening, but it is also likely to influence the *management* of the European marketing operation. The direct European evidence for this has yet to be established, but some indirect evidence is available from a study by Doyle et al. in 1987.[3] The researchers examined how a sample of U.S. and Japanese companies operated subsidiaries in the UK. They found that both groups of subsidiaries had their performance closely monitored by headquarters at home:

> The types of controls were, however, different. The Americans relied on much more detailed and *formal* controls . . . the Japanese did not favour the detailed standardised planning systems which Western multinationals tend to use, instead they relied on continuous *informal monitoring*. All the subsidiaries indicated that reporting was a 'daily' or 'constant' process with the telephone as the main mode of communication with Japan. Headquarters were invariably viewed as extremely well informed of activities, problems and progress.

This research is consistent with that undertaken more recently by Williams et al. on why some Japanese companies are more effective in reducing costs and increasing productivity than Western companies: Japanese marketing and production information relies less on traditional management accounting data and much more on action-oriented, practical cost projections.[4]

If this means the abandonment by European marketing of some traditional management account reporting and control, then so much the better. The type to consider dropping is that covering nonactionable, historical variances against standard costs set years earlier by an obscure allocation of overheads. European marketers may also wish to note that management accounting has a more limited managerial role in assisting marketing and production executives in Japanese companies, as compared, for example, to the UK.[4]

Managers setting up European marketing information systems need to think very carefully what data they want and what effect this data will have on working relationships across Europe. They may well find it desirable to move toward the Japanese approach of encouraging "loose yet tight" controls.

MOTIVATION AND EUROPEAN PLANNING

Planning and control are major elements of the European marketing management task. They are continuing, interactive activities designed to deliver the corporate objectives. Being part of management, they have a human dimension.

Motivating managers in Europe to devise, monitor, and control marketing plans will be a vital part of the North American manager's task.

Consider how you would feel as a European manager if once a year you diligently prepared plans over many months. Your European management board then trooped over to the United States to present the plans. Approval was given from a U.S. headquarters that seemed remote and largely uninterested. Occasionally, a senior U.S. manager turned up in the European country to shake a few hands, drop a few pearls of wisdom, and review progress in a friendly but superficial fashion. As a European manager, you might find all this scarcely motivating.

Although this might seem exaggerated, North American companies working in Europe may wish to consider carefully:

• How they are perceived by their European colleagues.

• How they will control European performance.

• How they will motivate European managers to achieve U.S. or Canadian corporate objectives.

Beyond these matters, North American senior managers will naturally want to evaluate the performance of their European managers. Moreover, there is little point in this process unless it is coupled with reward for good performance. In Europe, reward systems are still largely nationally based for historic, structural, and cultural reasons.[5] The detail of this area is beyond the scope of this book, but it will need careful consideration if European marketing is to be ultimately successful.

NOTES

1. V. Terpstra and R. Sarathy, *International Marketing* (Orlando, FL: The Dryden Press, 1991), chapter 17.

2. G. Day, *Strategic Market-Planning* (St. Paul, MN: West Publishing, 1984), chapter 8.

3. P. Doyle, J. Saunders, and L. Wright, "A Comparative Study of U.S. and Japanese Companies in the British Market," July 1987.

4. K. Williams, C. Haslam, and J. Williams, with M. Abe, T. Aida, and I. Mitsui, *Management Accounting: The Western Problematic against the Japanese Application*, University of East London occasional paper, 1991.

5. C. Randlesome, *Business Cultures in Europe* (Oxford: Heinemann Professional, 1990).

15

Future European developments and their potential for North American companies

> To renew America, we must meet challenges abroad as well as at home. There is no clear division today between what is foreign and what is domestic—the world economy, the world environment, the world AIDS crisis, the world arms race affect us all. (President Bill Clinton, inaugural address, 20 January 1993)

Our focus here is on future European developments. Europe is still the largest trading partner of the United States, though this is not true of Canada. But if Canada, Mexico, and the United States are linked through the North American Free Trade Area (NAFTA) treaty, then all three North American economies will effectively have some dependence on trade with Europe. North American companies will therefore want to examine carefully the new Europe for its marketing potential. Taking this as a starting point, we shall examine the following topics in this final chapter:

- Marketing implications of the new Western Europe.
- Marketing scope for Eastern European developments.
- A "United States of Europe"?
- Can a North American marketing mix be imported into the new Europe?
- European competition against North American rivals in global markets.
- North American company success in European marketing.

Finally, we will look at the broader issues involved in Europe's challenging future.

MARKETING IMPLICATIONS OF THE
NEW WESTERN EUROPE

Although we have examined the main areas elsewhere in this book, we will identify five specific areas here and investigate their marketing implications further.

World Trade Wars

At the time of writing, the United States and Europe are locking horns in the early stages of a trade war. The French government is adamant that it will fight to preserve EC agriculture subsidies. The United States has introduced heavy tariffs on imported steel and some other products. Both sides seek to protect vocal national sectional interests to the possible detriment of the majority.

The GATT talks are stalled. It is unclear how matters will develop. But there are real economic gains to be made by both sides and other countries around the world if the disagreements can be resolved. It can only be hoped that wiser counsels and true national self-interest will eventually prevail.

Strains in the Exchange Rate Mechanism

After Black Wednesday in September 1992, the UK and Italy joined Greece outside the ERM. Subsequently, other currencies within the mechanism have come under continued pressure as interest rates in Germany have remained high.[1] Without doubt, the ERM is a halfway house toward a single European currency. It follows that there will be real uncertainties right up to possible convergence and a single currency in 1997 or 1999 unless radical changes are made. For North American marketing, this underlines the continuing need to hedge against currency fluctuations (see Chapter 10).

There is also the issue of whether the ERM will survive global bank speculation. The key to resolving this issue is first a reduction and then a continuation in low German interest rates. This is in turn related to achieving a favorable economic outcome from German reunification.

German Reunification

The investment required to bring East Germany up to Western standards has put real strain on the German economy. Because of Germany's pivotal role in EC growth (see Chapter 2), this action has caused an economic slowdown among other EC members, especially those still remaining inside the ERM.[2]

While the German Bundesbank continues to act as Europe's banker, it also adopts a strictly national viewpoint in its control of interest rates; it is legally charged to do this by the German constitution. However, this means that Germany's progress will continue to be slow and cautious.[3] The German economy is unlikely to grow until 1994 at the earliest. The possible benefits from the single European market, which depend partly on German leadership, will be delayed.

Economic Growth in Western Europe

Lower levels of growth are likely to persist for several years in the EC.[4] It might be argued that this would make Europe less attractive as an investment area for North American companies, but this would be rather a crude interpretation of the situation. The likelihood of a lack of growth does not imply that there are no opportunities for North American companies, simply that there are fewer of them. Such prospects need to be examined on an individual-market basis. Moreover, U.S. and Canadian companies will want to build for the year 2000, and the fundamentals are still sound in Western Europe.

Maastricht Treaty

Because it will provide political stability and a clearer sense of direction to the EC, European growth will be assisted by ratification and then implementation of the Maastricht Treaty. Countries have so far stumbled toward this goal, with the UK and Denmark bringing up the rear. The real issue is not so much whether it will be signed but whether and to what extent the "one-Europe" ideal will reemerge.[5] It has been undermined by politicians taking a strictly nationalist view, by structural weaknesses in the ERM, and by the economic slowdown in European economies.

Even before the September 1992 currency problems, the president of the European Commission, Jacques Delors, had said in the previous June, "Europe is still a fragile construction, not immune to setback. You never know from where the next crisis will come."[6] For the reasons outlined above, the single Europe is unlikely to deliver the economic growth that will oil the wheels of integration. The clear implication for North American marketers is that "single Europe" products and goals will be achieved more slowly than once envisaged. Pan-European marketing and branding may suffer as a result. North American companies at the forefront of these moves will, however, want to take a longer-term view. For example, General Mills (U.S.) has joined with Nestlé (Switzerland) to attack the European breakfast cereal market;[7] its time horizon is the year 2000.

MARKETING SCOPE FOR EASTERN EUROPEAN DEVELOPMENTS

Many North American companies have invested in the East, particularly moving into Russia itself, as if it is the last great opportunity.[8,9]

In 1991, according to analysts at U.S. and European banks,[10] Eastern Europe was expected to be the engine of growth for all of Europe in the 1990s. They predicted that Eastern European growth would start slowly in 1993 and then accelerate to 8 percent per year toward the end of the decade. This rapid growth in the East would then fuel growth in Western Europe. There was, of course, nothing to stop such expansion triggering North American opportunities as well.

The reasons behind these predictions of rapid growth were the development of privatization, the coming of new entrepreneurs, and the beginnings of small-business growth in Eastern Europe. Hungary was named as the best bet, Poland had much promise but also real problems, and Czechoslovakia would follow further behind.[11] Romania and Bulgaria had higher risks associated with them because of structural problems in their economies.

With the benefit of hindsight, we can see that matters have moved more slowly in central Europe. Hungary, Poland, and the Czech Republic are suffering from a slowdown in Western economies. Russia and the Ukraine are moving toward hyperinflation, principally because their politicians have refused to learn the lessons from Western experience.[12]

So where does this leave the marketing opportunity in Eastern Europe for North American companies? And the risks? On balance, the openings are still there via:

- Privatization.
- Emerging competition.
- Reform.
- New media opportunities.
- The sale of national Eastern European brand names.

But the potential costs are also high:

- Currency instability.
- High price inflation.
- Legal ownership issues.
- Repatriation of earnings to the home country.
- Structural problems.

Ultimately, there are two types of strategy for Eastern Europe, depending on the time scale:

1. Short term: Use the marketing strategies described in Chapter 7. The risk here should be containable.
2. Longer term: Seek to take a significant share of markets. Here the key will be to do so without overexposing the company to local market fluctuations and even complete collapse. Undoubtedly, this should have higher rewards, but the risks may also be greater. The Conoco (U.S.) oil deal with Russia in 1992 is an example of the long payoff that may be expected.[13]

A "UNITED STATES OF EUROPE"?

Because of the profound marketing implications, we need to consider whether Europe will ever become a federal nation like the United States or Canada. Our starting point is to examine the similarities between North America and Europe. For reasons of space, I have chosen to concentrate on the United States. Canada is covered in the original research in this area.[14]

With all the discussion about the single Europe, North Americans might have the impression that, over time, a federal Europe will emerge with a constitution and political structure not unlike that of the United States; the European Community already has a common flag and a European anthem. If Europe were really to come together, this would make marketing much simpler: common laws, pan-European TV channels, a common currency and prices, and a real identification of its population with "one Europe" nationhood. But what is the likelihood of this happening?

Table 15–1 compares and contrasts the EC and the United States. It is based on research carried out for the "Cost of Non-Europe" project[14] but updated for the 1990s. Although it is not really possible to do the subject justice in a few words, the data provide some indicators.

In general terms, the European Community is different from the United States in its lack of a common language and the absence of federal institutions endowed with major tax-gathering powers and a central planning role. Even if Europeans desired to move closer to a federal system, it would take a generation to make the structural changes. Hence, for the

TABLE 15–1
Similarities and Differences between the United States and the EC

European Similarities	European Differences
• Fierce tax protection between nations and Brussels, similar to interstate tax system	• Weak federal structure and Parliament
• Cultural and religious diversity primarily based on Christian ethic	• Small central EC spending
• Mixed economy with a strong belief in competition	• 10 different languages
• Right to work anywhere in the EC	• Many more state-owned institutions
• Professional accreditation subject to local controls	• Three different legal systems
• Similar values of freedom, democracy, and the rule of law	• National expenditure often much higher proportion of GDP
	• Banks operate across states much more readily in EC
	• No common currency and no federal bank (yet)
	• No major coast-to-coast TV programming or mass-appeal pan-European newspapers
	• Little federal tax gathering

forseeable future, the European Community will not be as cohesive as the United States. This has significant implications for European marketing: there will continue to be more diversity in Europe than in the United States.

In addition, it is probable that the European Community will be enlarged, with many EFTA and some Eastern European states joining by the year 2010; the EC could end up with as many as 25 states. Unless EC decision making is changed radically, it will become slower, or power will still have to rest with individual countries. The issues raised by enlargement of the EC remain largely unresolved at present. Those engaged in European marketing can reasonably assume that many decisions will continue to be taken, at the national or regional level for at least the next 10 years.

With the enlarged trading area of the NAFTA agreement, North Americans may experience some of the same decision-making problems that have occurred in the EC. However, the NAFTA treaty is not designed to bring about political integration; its principal gains are in the area of economic cooperation.[15] Hence, there may be some similarity with the Single Europe Act.

CAN A NORTH AMERICAN MARKETING MIX BE IMPORTED INTO THE NEW EUROPE?

As markets and customer tastes become increasingly global, it might be argued that North American companies should be able to import their existing marketing mix into the new Europe without significant change. There could be some potential cost savings along with the benefits of international branding.

Given the many millions of customers across Europe, it is likely that the North American marketing mix will appeal to at least some of them. The three issues are whether there are:

- Legal reasons for adaptation.
- Trade barrier–related or structural reasons for change.
- Sales advantages from adapting the mix that would more than outweigh the costs.

As far as legal reasons are concerned, we have seen in Chapters 9 to 12 that there are a myriad of regulations, directives, and other guidelines both at the EC and national levels across Europe. Some of the harmonizing legislation has yet to be completed.[16]

Trade barriers and structural difficulties, such as national differences in media availability and environmental laws, mean that specific European markets still impose real obstacles that will require altering the marketing approach.[17] For example, differing national building regulations across Europe will make adaptation essential for North American construction companies.

Beyond these matters, many North American companies, such as Colgate-Palmolive, Gillette, Coca-Cola, and Procter & Gamble, have been able to standardize their branding, product sizes, and packaging. However, a survey by A. C. Nielsen in late 1992 found that, of the many thousands of products available across the EC, there were only 45 "Eurobrands" generally available in at least the four leading countries in an identical format.[18] They were primarily concentrated in two product categories:

- Personal products, such as toothpaste and cosmetics, where North American brands are well represented.
- Alcohol products (e.g., whisky, brandy, and gin), where there are fewer North American brands.

Within a general marketing mix, many U.S. companies have found the need to adapt their specific marketing approach across Europe.

As an example of the adaptation required, we can examine the U.S. fast food company McDonald's. It has had considerable success introducing products such as the Big Mac, Quarter Pounder with cheese, and hot fruit pies across Europe. Indeed, according to the international magazine *The Economist*, the Big Mac has become sufficiently standardized to be used as a common test product in its global price/currency surveys.

Although the Big Mac may be the same across Europe, McDonald's restaurants are not: varying cultures, tastes, and national laws all make for differences. Table 15–2 outlines the results of a 1992 survey on the way in which this North American corporation has had to adjust its marketing mix across Europe. It should be noted that the results concentrate largely on the *tangible* aspects of the mix; Booms and Bittner[19] and others have identified additional aspects of the marketing mix that apply to services such as restaurants—intangible, controllable, and uncontrollable. For example, Table 15–2 mentions the quality of the french fries in Prague.

TABLE 15–2
McDonald's Marketing Mix Survey

Location	Marketing Mix Elements for 10 Days in Late August 1992
Glasgow	Special "funky neon cups" promotion and breakfast menu
London	"Low price for Coke and burger" promotion and breakfast menu
Amsterdam	Coupons for price reductions on local Amsterdam tourist attractions and french fries served with mayonnaise
Vienna	Salad range and vegetarian burger served
Prague	No Diet Coke, limited menu range, and the best french fries in this European sample
Luxembourg	"Chinese Week" menu promotion, with all burgers served in cardboard box
Budapest	No Diet Coke, limited menu range, no medium-size french fries
Berlin	"Chinese Week" menu promotion, with all burgers served in cardboard box

Source: Informal survey by the author late August 1992.

Beyond the Ronald McDonald character, some standard products, and a common layout and menu presentation, there are significant differences among countries in the promotional strategies used by McDonald's restaurants. This is consistent with the comments of a senior company manager, who was quoted as saying that the single Europe was not the main marketing consideration and that the company adapted its marketing mix to local conditions.[20] Other North American companies may need to do the same.

EUROPEAN COMPETITION AGAINST NORTH AMERICAN RIVALS IN GLOBAL MARKETS

The extent to which the single Europe will allow European companies to compete more successfully in global markets is an important issue for North American competitors. We will explore the evidence under four headings:

- Innovation and patents.
- Company size.
- Labor costs and export prices.
- Global market sectors.

Innovation and Patents

In Chapter 7 we identified the importance of innovation in the development of marketing strategy. Patent applications are one measure of activity in this area. We should note that the number of patents says little about the *quality* of the ideas and that Japanese have a reputation for special skill in the *application* of original patents. Table 15–3 sets out the evidence for the main world economies.

On the basis of patents, the evidence suggests that Europe is certainly strong. The overall level of activity was significantly larger than in the United States in the 1985–1988 period. Perhaps the EC does have the edge here.

Company Size

Defining company size by turnover, we can examine the number of companies in each of the major economies appearing in the world's top 500. This is shown in Figure 15–1, where it is seen that the number of EC companies has remained static. The number of U.S. companies has declined while the number of Japanese companies has grown. This may partly be the result of the declining U.S. dollar and the increasing Japanese yen, but it is also likely to reflect real growth in the Japanese economy.

Overall, it seems from this evidence that Japanese rather than Western European companies posed the major threat to U.S. companies in the late 1980s. The single Europe may alter this situation somewhat, but Europeans themselves will be under threat from the Japanese in the 1990s in, for example, the car industry.[21]

TABLE 15–3
Patent Applications, 1985–1988 (as Percent of Total Worldwide)

EC (particularly Germany)	39.1%
United States	25.7%
Japan	23.4%
COMECON	2.1%
Other	9.7%

Source: European Commission, *Panorama of EC Industry 1991/92* (Luxembourg: OPOCE, 1991), p. 93.

FIGURE 15–1
Global Company Size: Number of Companies in Global Top 500

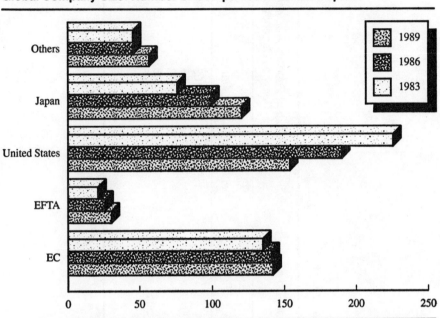

Source: European Commission, *Panorama of EC Industry 1991/92* (Luxembourg: OPOCE, 1991), p. 97.

Labor Costs and Export Prices

According to OECD estimates, it is in the area of labor costs and prices of exports that the United States is well ahead of its rival countries. However, Canada is not so competitive. Table 15–4 shows the main data.

Table 15–4 considers two main factors in assessing competitiveness:

- Changes in relative labor costs.
- Changes through the nominal effective exchange rate.

The table takes into account the strength of the U.S. dollar in late 1992 and the effective devaluations of the pound sterling by 15 percent and the Italian lira by 10 percent in the second half of 1992. The relative depreciation of the Canadian dollar in 1992 is also included.

From the evidence of Table 15–4, the overall conclusion is that the United States is well placed to maintain its position in the world economy.

TABLE 15–4
Country Competitive Positions (1987 = 100)

	Relative Labor Costs in Manufacturing, in a Common Currency				Relative Export Prices of Manufacturers, in a Common Currency			
	Average 1988–1990	1991	1992	1993	Average 1988–1990	1991	1992	1993
Canada	118	126	118	115	105	103	98	97
United States	89	81	77	76	95	93	89	89
Japan	91	88	96	100	99	103	110	112
Germany	98	97	101	105	97	98	101	104
France	91	89	90	91	98	96	95	96
Italy	104	111	107	101	103	109	109	105
UK	105	110	106	95	103	103	101	97

Source: OECD, "Economic Outlook No. 52," December 1992, p. 51.

It may even be able to make modest gains at the expense of Western Europe and Japan. The Europeans will need to raise productivity and stimulate innovation if they are to increase their competitiveness.[22]

Global Market Sectors

Although its overall position looks encouraging, there is little doubt that the United States has been losing ground in particular market sectors of the global economy. It is not possible here to present a thorough analysis of major global markets, but, using data from the European Commission and other sources, some selected sectors can be summarized:[23-25]

- *Pharmaceuticals*: The United States is still well ahead, with companies such as Merck and Johnson & Johnson.
- *Aerospace*: U.S. leadership continues but has declined slightly with the success of the European Airbus.
- *Chemicals*: Europe has four of the top five world companies.
- *Food and beverages*: Coca-Cola, Pepsi-Co, Philip Morris, and Procter & Gamble are strong but compete against the European giants Unilever, Nestlé, and BSN.
- *Oil:* Exxon and Mobil are rivaled by the European companies Royal Dutch Shell and BP.
- *Telecommunications equipment*: France's Alcatel has taken over from AT&T as the world's largest, with Siemens (Germany) also strong.
- *Motor vehicles*: General Motors and Ford are still the largest, but the Japanese are catching up and European companies are investing heavily.

Overall, in terms of specific market sectors, Europe and Japan have made some advances against the United States. But North American companies are still well placed to exploit global sales opportunities in the 1990s. Much of this will depend on the success of the Uruguay Round of the GATT talks: the United States and Canada will lose in some of the above areas if "Fortress North America" takes hold.

NORTH AMERICAN COMPANY SUCCESS IN EUROPEAN MARKETING

Although we have seen that European markets can be quite varied, there seems to be little recognition in some U.S. official government circles that the single European market is actually of importance. If recognition of one's competitors is an important precondition for success, then any U.S. companies sharing this perception are likely to be unsuccessful.

Based on all that has been covered in this book, North American companies are most likely to succeed if they:

- Build on the strengths of their low cost base, the powerful U.S. dollar, and well-trained and motivated work force.
- Work toward the success of the GATT Uruguay Round; U.S. and Canadian companies have more to gain than to lose.
- Seek global opportunities, preferably through innovation and possibly through joint ventures.
- Recognize that Europe still has many hidden barriers to be sought out and circumvented.[26,27]

EUROPE'S CHALLENGING FUTURE

Finally, in the context of opportunities for North American companies, it is important to identify some of the issues representing the European challenge to companies marketing to Europe in the 1990s. It is not possible to determine exactly how they will impact individual businesses, but their influence will certainly be felt.

Consumer Issues

One of the significant European developments of the 1980s was the greater consumer awareness of the issues of health and safety, rights to information, misleading advertising, and the quality of life. In many respects, Europe was catching up with North America. There still has been no great *European* consumer movement but, rather, awareness by individual EC countries, with some more active than others.

Environmental Issues

We have seen in this book that there is a greater knowledge of environmental problems and desire to take action than was previously the case. Indeed, there is now a European commissioner charged with specific responsibilities in this area. Eastern Europe will present even greater challenges than some parts of the West. There will be a cost for North American companies involved in Europe.

Political Uncertainty in Southern and Eastern Europe

Although the research was begun much earlier, this book was begun close to the fighting in Yugoslavia in September 1991. It is being finished as death and destruction lay in a great swath across that former country, with United Nations troops attempting to keep the peace. The futility and brutality of this conflict is there for all to see.

Yet there are still nations and politicians in Eastern Europe who appear to have learned nothing. They seem determined to face each other with dark threats and scores to settle. North American companies involved in European marketing can do little to help, but they need to be aware of the implications for their markets if fighting should result.

European Community Enlargement

One of the great political challenges of the 1990s for Europe will be how to enlarge the Community and still maintain its momentum. The impact on marketing will come through market enlargement as barriers come down. Those North American companies already involved in Europe will be well placed to take advantage of such opportunities.

The Challenge of Europe

The real bonus for North American companies and managers from European marketing is the challenge of the new Europe: new markets, new customers, and new opportunities. The task begun after the Second World War by the whole of the Atlantic Alliance is now to be picked up by the new generation of marketing managers. There is a real future in Europe.

NOTES

1. C. Rapaport, "Europe Looks Ahead to Hard Choices," *Fortune*, December 14, 1992, p. 22.
2. OECD, "Economic Outlook-No. 52," December 1992, p. 74.
3. Ibid., pp. 17–18.
4. Ibid., p. 9.
5. I. Davidson, "Community at a Crossroads," *Financial Times*, January 4, 1993, p. 27.
6. P. Gumbel and M. Nelson, "EC Sidesteps Thorny Issues at Summit," *The Wall Street Journal*, June 29, 1992.
7. C. Knowlton, "Europe Cooks Up a Cereal Bowl," *Fortune*, June 3, 1991, p. 61.
8. A. Ignatius "Lifestyle Pitch Works in Russia despite Poverty," *The Wall Street Journal*, August 21, 1992, p. B1.
9. P. Hofheinz, "Let's Do Business," *Fortune*, September 23, 1991, p. 31.
10. S. Tully, "Now the New New Europe," *Fortune*, December 2, 1991, p. 30.
11. P. Hofheinz, "New Light in Eastern Europe," *Fortune*, July 29, 1991, p. 145.
12. OECD, p. 123.
13. J. Tanner, "Conoco Reaches Oil Agreement with Russia," *The Wall Street Journal*, June 19, 1992, p. A2.
14. J. Pelkmans with M. Vanheukelen, "The Internal Markets of North America." In *European Commission, Cost of Non-Europe*, vol. 1 (Luxembourg: OPOCE, 1988), p. 533.
15. G. Hufbauer and J. Schott, *Assessment of North American Trade Agreement* (Washington, DC: Institute for International Economics, February 17, 1993).
16. Rapaport, pp. 26–27.
17. M. du Bois, "Diversified Producer Still Finds Barriers in the Single Market," *The Wall Street Journal* (Europe), January 12, 1993, p. 1.
18. G. de Jonquieres, "Whither the Cross Border Cornflake?" *Financial Times*, January 4, 1993, p. 8.
19. B. H. Booms and M. Bitner, "Marketing Strategies and Organization Structures for Service Firms." In J. Donnelly and W. George (eds.), *Marketing of Services* (Chicago: American Marketing Association, 1981).
20. N. Buckley, "Only Ronald Strides the Frontiers," *Financial Times*, January 4, 1993, p. 8.

21. C. Rapaport, "Getting Tough with the Japanese," *Fortune*, May 4, 1992, p. 26.
22. P. Hofheinz, "Can Europe Compete?" *Fortune*, December 14, 1992, p. 47.
23. European Commission, *Panorama of EC Industry 1991/92* (Luxembourg: OPOCE, 1991), pp. 95–112.
24. A. Kupfer, "How American Industry Stacks Up," *Fortune*, March 9, 1992, p. 18.
25. R. Lynch, *European Business Strategies* (London: Kogan Page, 1990).
26. A. Hilton, "Mythology, Markets and the Emerging Europe," *Harvard Business Review*, November–December, 1992, p. 50.
27. Lynch, chapter 6.

Appendix I

The Constitution of the European Community

The written constitution of the EC comes from four main original treaties:

1. European Coal and Steel Community, 1952.
2. European Atomic Energy Community (Euratom), 1957.
3. European Economic Community Treaty of Rome, 1957.
4. European Treaties of Maastricht, 1991, which had still to be finally ratified by the UK Parliament and the German court at the time of writing.

A number of other important agreements also form part of the written constitution:

- Merger Treaty, 1965.
- Budgetary Treaty, 1970.
- Amending Treaty (Court of Auditors), 1975.
- Single Europe Act, 1986.

Appendix II

| The ECU

The ECU is a basket of 10 member states' currency, weighted in accordance with the country's economic strength, which serves as a unit of currency in the Community. The following conversion table gives the current amount for ECU in the currencies of all EC countries, as well as the United States and Japan, as of May 1992:

Belgium and Luxembourg franc	40.2592	Irish punt	0.8012
Deutsche mark	1.9589	Greek drachma	265.122
Dutch guilder	2.1935	Spanish peseta	149.319
Pound sterling	0.7806	Portuguese escudo	185.559
Danish krone	7.4988	United States dollar	1.1945
French franc	6.5946	Canadian dollar	1.5104
Italian lira	1778.80	Japanese yen	132.238

Appendix III

Summary of rules on cross-border mergers and acquisitions

BACKGROUND

The legislation introduced in September 1990 needs to be seen against the background of the Treaty of Rome and existing practice throughout the EC.

Articles 85 and 86 of the Treaty of Rome, to which all member governments of the EC are signatories, prohibit companies from "practices which may affect trade between Member States and which have as their object or effect the prevention, restriction or distortion of competition within the common market" (article 85). Moreover,

> Any abuse by one or more undertakings of a dominant position within the common market or in a substantial part of it shall be prohibited as incompatible with the common market in so far as it may affect trade between Member States. (article 86)

In practice, matters up to 1990 were partly decided in the European courts and partly by the activities of individual governments. For example, the UK, through the Office of Fair Trading, and Germany, through the Federal Cartel Office, have been active in policing matters. France is also starting to take a more positive approach within the confines of its own very large state industries. Elsewhere up to 1990, however, the action was more irregular; for example, Italy had no controls, allowing the dominance of a few major companies such as Fiat.

In 1990 a new agreement was signed that allowed the European Commission to take the leading role in the largest proposed deals. Since that time, all EC deals over a certain size (defined below) have been automatically referred to the Commission. There are no exceptions to this.[1]

OBJECTIVE OF THE RULES

The objective is to define, strengthen, and reinforce the Treaty of Rome articles, which still continue in force.

All actions are undertaken by the European Commission, which has acquired explicit authority to control all corporate mergers, acquisitions, and joint deals in the EC. It has the right to review in advance large deals and block them if they threaten competition. However, it is not intended to replace national control over smaller deals and covers only the larger cross-border agreements.

The boundaries between national and EC deals have been defined. In practice, the Commission has occasionally returned its decision-making authority to national governments (e.g., the Redland/Steetley UK decision in 1992).

STRUCTURE OF THE NEW REGULATIONS

The European Commission is looking for "concentrations" as a result of new deals done by companies. Such concentrations cover not only full and partial mergers, but also some joint ventures and direct and indirect acquisitions by one or more companies over another. The key test of whether a concentration exists is to determine whether there is a change in control in the company. Not all concentrations fall within the scope of the European Commission. They are referred to Brussels when there is a "Community dimension"; that is:

- The combined worldwide turnover of the companies involved totals of 5 billion ECU (about U.S.$5 billion) or more, and
- The aggregate EC turnover of each of at least two of the companies is 250 million ECU.

However, companies are exempt from the regulation if each company has more than two-thirds of its EC-wide turnover in one EC country.

HOW THE REGULATIONS OPERATE

A company is required to notify Brussels of any proposed deal within seven days of its announcement or completion, whichever is earlier.

There is a "prenotification" form for a proposed deal. This is lengthy and complex. It has been reported that 20 copies of the completed form, plus 15 copies of all supporting documentation, are required.

For any two markets in which the two merging companies together will have a 10 percent share, comprehensive information is sought on all its characteristics. Companies must supply data broken down by EC country, including details of competition; prices charged for products inside and outside the EC; assessment of imports and exports; barriers to entry for both EC producers and others; and a full history of research and development, costs and development cycles, and distribution and service networks.

Companies disregarding the notification or providing misleading data may be fined 50,000 ECU. Mergers will then automatically be suspended for three weeks, but this could be waived if shown to be very damaging. If the suspension is disregarded, the fine is 10 percent of the aggregate turnover.

Having been notified, the Commission has one month in which to decide whether a deal is covered by the regulation and if there are "serious doubts as to its compatibility with the common market." If no doubts exist, the deal can go ahead. However, a member state can still determine whether its own "legitimate interests" are likely to be affected.

If there are serious problems, the EC will open formal hearings, with a major investigation, searches, and the legal sanction of levying fines. It must reach its conclusions within four months.

CRITERIA FOR ASSESSMENT OF CONCENTRATION

In examining whether there is excessive concentration, the EC will determine whether the deal creates or strengthens a dominant position that would significantly impede effective competition in the marketplace. Market share is the most important standard applied. The regulation assumes a concentration to be compatible with the common market when the combined market share of the companies involved does not exceed 25 percent of the common market or a substantial part of it.

In addition, the Commission may also consider industrial and social policies, though these are not enforceable in law.

The Commission has the power to block deals that do not satisfy its criteria. It can also cause them to be modified before they proceed.

THE FUTURE

There are still some ambiguities in the new law that may eventually need to be tested in the European Court.[2]

The threshold for deals to be considered is likely to be lowered to 2 billion ECU. During a full year, the European Commission has estimated that, on the basis of the current threshold, it will handle between 50 and 200 deals, depending on broader issues such as company interest in pursuing such deals and European economic growth.

NOTES

1. P. Montagnon and P. Riddell, "A Delicate Case of Jurisdictions," *Financial Times*, September 20, 1990.
2. G. de Jonquiere, "Independent Agency Needed to Enforce EC Merger Rules," *Financial Times*, September 14, 1990. See also L. Brittan, "Misplaced Doubts on EC Mergers," *Financial Times*, October 11, 1990 (a reply to some criticisms raised in the above articles).

Background reading: S. J. Berwin and Co. *Competition and Business Regulation in the Single Market* (London: Mercury Books, 1992).

INDEX

A

Aaker, D., 133
Absolute level of exports, 14
Ad hoc research, 94
Advertising
    in Eastern Europe, 86-87, 235
    European, 229-31
After-sales service, 183
AKZO chemicals (Dutch), 200
Alcatel Alsthom, company (France), 112
Ansoff matrix, 114, 124
Anti-European countries, 47
Asch, D., 130

B

Balance of exports, EC, 14
Ban, R. J., 26
Bartering companies, 214
Bartlett, C., 261
BASF company, (Germany), 125
Blackwell, N., 267
Bleeke, J. A., 162
Block exemption regulations, 200
Bowman, C., 130
Branding opportunities, European, 179-82
Brands, 110, 173-74, 236
British Airways (UK), 161
Browning, E. S., 236
Business and political background, 46-70
Buzzell, R., 132-33

C

Canada, U.S. is biggest export destination, 17
Cartels, price, 200
Cash cows of the EC, 137
Cathelat, Bernard, 81
Cavusgil, S. T., 93

Cecchini, Paolo, 55
Cecchini report
    conclusions, 56
    duplication in manufacturing, 72
    and economies of scale, 123
    extra costs of exporting, 203
    research study, 55, 56, 57
    summary of industry investigations, 140
    and trade barriers, 169
    underestimation of savings of, 56
Channels and logistics, 249-52
Christopher, M., 93, 208
Chung, D., 230
Citizen Watch Company (Japan), 139
Clothing brands, 110
Coca-Cola, company (U.S.) offensive war
    regarding, 122
Cockfield, Lord, 55
COMECON, 2-3, 13
Common Agricultural Policy (CAP), 19-22, 48
Community of European Railways (CER), 246
Companies
    market entry, 152
    prosecution by EC, 199-200
    state-owned, 202
Company size, 292
Competition, expenditure comparison with the, 234
Competitive advantage, sustainable, 109-13
Competitors
    beating European, 176-86
    selection, 122
Conoco, company (U.S.), 277
Consumer
    issues, 286
    marketing, 78
Continuous

research, 94
sales service, 185
Contract law, EC, 244
Control
  for Europe, 269-72
  and monitoring systems, 270-71
COREPER (Committee of Permanent
  Representatives), 53
Costs and competition, balance between,
  208-10
Costs, seeking lower, 123
Cote, K., 77
Council of Ministers, 24
Council for Mutual Economic Assistance,
  2-3, 13
Countries, examining relative strengths,
  28-31
Country selection, 156-61
Creativity, promotional, 234
Critical success factors (CSFs), 106, 108-9
Cross-border deals, 154
Cross-border restrictions, EC, 242-43
Cross-border trade, barriers to, 169-70
Cs, four, 5, 106, 114-19
CSFs, mistakes in developing, 106
Cunningham, M. T., 144, 211-12
Currencies
  narrow and wide bands, 205
  realignment of, 206
  stability and convertability, 214-15
Currie, D., 206
Customer issues, Eastern European, 84-87
Customers, geographical markets of, 71-74
Customization versus standardization,
  177-78
Cusumano, M., 185, 189-90
Cutler, T., 56
Cvar, M. R., 139

D

Data comparison, European, 97-98
Data sources for Europe, 100-101
Day, G. S., 106, 130
Decision-making process of EC, 63-64
de Gaulle, Charles, 47
Dell Computers, company (U.S.), 162
Delors, Jacques, 58, 276
Developing market strategy options, 113-19
Diamantopolous, A., 92

Differences of Europeans, 76
Direct mail
  growth, 223-24
  regulations by EC, 221
Direct marketing, European, 232-33
Dirigiste approach, 48
Distribution
  infrastructure of EC, 245-46
  structures of EC, 245-49
Distributors, 246-47
Douglas, S. P., 159
Dow Chemical, 200
Doz, Y., 139
Dynamic entity of Europe, 72

E

Eastern Europe
  acquisition and joint venture, 192
  changing distribution channels, 240
  each state uniquely treated, 146
  fragmented and duplicated new system,
    253
  future distribution, 254
  highly centralized old system, 253
  Hungarian experience, 253-54
  infrastructure problems, 148
  investment in, 192-94
  investments, 43
  levels of exposure, 146-47
  marketing scope for, 276-77
  market strategies for, 144-48
  planning for uncertainty, 145-46
  product launches, 194
  product marketing decisions for, 191-95
  professional services activities, 194
  promotional decision making, 235-37
  risk and reward assessment, 126-27
  strategies, 124-27
  structural investment needed in, 126
  taking profits to home country, 195
  trade statistics revelations, 15
Eastern European
  advertising in, 235
  customer issues, 84-87
  issues, 64-69
  markets, 31-32
  opportunities in, 237
  place decisions, 253-54
  pricing decisions, 213-15

progress, 3-4
EC
  absolute level of exports, 14
  balance of exports, 14
  channel management, 251-52
  common agricultural policy and GATT,
      19-23
  compliance with standards and
      legislation, 170-72
  contract law, 244
  Council of Ministers, 24
  cross-border restrictions, 242-43
  current advertising activities, 222-25
  current research activity, 94-96
  decision-making process, 63-64
  direct mail regulations, 221
  distribution infrastructure, 245-46
  distribution structures, 245-49
  Economic and Social Committee, 64
  enlargement, 287
  finances of the, 50
  hidden subsidies, 202-03
  income and expenditures, 51
  main driving force in Western Europe, 46
  marketing considerations, 207-08
  media regulations and development,
      220-21
  moves to integration, 59-63
  origins and decision-making processes,
      47-53
  place decisions, 240-45
  and pressure groups, 50
  pricing policy, 199-201
  progress on standardization, 173
  prosecution of companies, 199-200
  retail and planning laws, 243-44
  sales promotion regulations, 221-22
  strong in cash cows, 137
  tax and investments, 244-45
  tax policy, 201-2
  trading and legal requirements, 168-74
  transport regulations, 243
  and the UK, 47
  weak in stars (high growth markets), 137
  wealth of, 33
Ecological and environmental concerns,
    42-43
Economic
  and fiscal activities, 60

growth in Western Europe, 275
and Social Committee of EC, 64
Economic and Social Committee, 53
Economies of scale, 72, 123
Economist Intelligence Unit, 260-61
Economy, roller-coaster, 26
EC power, 52-53
European Commission, 52
European Council of Ministers, 52
European Court of Justice, 53
European Parliament, 53
Education
  from a marketing standpoint, 36
  tertiary, 36
EFTA, wealth of, 33
Emerson, M., 24, 56
EMU (European Monetary Union), 23-27
Environmental
  developments, 172
  and ecological concerns, 42-43
  issues, 287
  and technical issues, 40-43
ESOMAR, 94, 98
Europe
  challenging future of, 286-87
  control for, 269-72
  data sources for, 100-101
  defined, 2-5
  differences across Europe, 76-77
  factors drawing together, 77-80
  in global markets, 12-16
  importing marketing, mix 279-281
  niche market across, 134
  North American involvement in, 16-18
  positioning products in, 178-79
  profit opportunities in, 7
  redrawing the map of, 9-10
  service development across, 183-85
  United States of, 10, 277-79
European
  advertising, 229-31
  advertising legislation and regulation,
      219-20
  competition, 281-85
  consumer markets, 81-83
  credit and export pricing, 203-05
  customers and market definition, 71-90
  data comparisons, 97-98
  differences of, 76

direct marketing, 232-33
exhibitions and seminars, 232
industrial markets, 80-81
involvement in global markets, 9
involvement in North America, 9
legal and tax framework, 203
marketing, 5-6
marketing strategy, 105-28
markets and cultures, 12-45
mission and objectives, 7-8
place decision, 240-56
pricing and currency issues, 205-8
product benefit, 174-76
product decisions, 167-97
promotion decisions, 217-39
sales force, 224-25, 227-29
sales promotion, 231
sponsorship, 231
technical development projects, 40-42
European Advertising Tripartite (EAT), 219
European Coal and Steel Community
    (ECSC), 47
European Commission, 24, 94
European Community (EC), 2
European Court of Justice, 53
European Currency Unit (ECU), 23
European customers
    exploring, 74-80
    myth of, 76
European Economic Area (EEA) Treaty,
    58-59
European Economic Community (EEC), 49
European Free Trade Association (EFTA), 2
European law, complexity of, 39
European marketing
    organization, 261-68
    research, 91-104
    strategy guidelines, 132-37
European markets, opportunities in, 18
European Monetary Institute, 24
European Monetary Union (EMU), 23-27
European political union, moves toward, 49
European promotions, basic regulations,
    218-22
European rate mechanism, strains in the, 274
European Society for Opinion and
    Marketing Research, 94
Europe pricing decisions, single, 208-13
Euro-prudent segments, 82

Eurostats, 33, 97
`Exchange Rate Mechanism (EMR), 24
Exhibitions and seminars, European, 232
Expenditure comparisons with the
    competition, 234
Export
    agents, 246-47
    EC, 14
    prices and labor costs, 283-85
    sales growth barriers, 206-07
Export customers, EC's main, 13
Export opportunities, developing, 14
Exports
    by United States to Europe, 16
    of socialist countries, 16
Exxon Corporation, 108

F

Fast-moving consumer goods (FMCG),
    143-44
Federal Reserve Bank (U.S.), 25
Fiat telecommunications (Italy), 112
Finances of the EC, 50
Financial burden, North American, 8
Ford, company (U.S.), 110, 123, 177
France Telecom, 112
Future developments, 273-89
Future of Europe, 286-87

G

Gale, B., 132-33
GATT Uruguay Round, 51
GE, company (U.S.), 9, 147
General Agreement on Trade and Tariffs
    (GATT), 22
General Mills (U.S.), 63, 276
General Motors (U.S.), 110
Geographical markets of customers, 71-74
German
    engineering companies, 112
    reunification, 275
Germany, domination of EC trading, 27
Geroski, P., 56, 76
Ghoshal, S., 261
Glaxo, pharmaceuticals, (UK), 112
Global markets, 9, 12-16, 137-40, 285
Glueck, W. F., 106, 129, 130
Gogel, R., 142
Government company privatization, 125

Grand Metropolitan, company (UK), 9

H

Heinz ketchup, 177
Hill, M. R., 100
Hoechst chemicals (German), 200
Home market, defending the, 121-22
Huhne, C., 24, 56
Human resources, 257-68

I

IBM, company (U.S.), 267
Ignatius, A., 236
Income and expenditures of EC, 51
Industrial marketing, 78
Inflation, high rates of, 214
Innovation and patents, 282
Integration
    EC moves to, 59-63
    political and social, 59-63
Issue-driven strategy areas, 113

J

Jacobs, B., 221
Jacobson, R., 133
Jacobs Suchard company (Switzerland), 9
Japanese companies, global expansion of, 73
Jauch, L., 106, 129, 130
Johnson, G., 132-34
Johnson household products, 77
Johansson, J. K., 160
Johnson & Johnson personal products, 77

K

Kalpaxoglou, E., 230
Kay, J., 74, 139, 141
Keegan, W., 76, 77
Kellogg's breakfast cereals, 77, 142
KLM Airlines (Netherlands), 161
Kotler, P., 76, 175

L

Labor costs and export prices, 283-85
Language proficiencies, high level of, 37
Larreche, J. C., 142
Legal issues, 38-39
Levitt, Theodore, 74, 76
Liander, B., 76

Lintas Hamburg advertising agency, 86
Logistics decisions, 250-52
Lynch, R., 121-22, 124, 152-53, 179

M

Maastricht Treaty, 10, 23, 275-76
McDonald's company (U.S.), 80, 142, 280-81
McGee, J., 141
Madrid Summit of 1989, EC, 23
Management, channel, 251-52
Manufacturing facilities, continuous upgrading, 185
Market
    entrants, 163
    followers and leaders, 134
Market entry
    basic options for, 151-54
    choice among options, 154-56
    companies, 152
    competitive reactions to, 161-63
    concentrating on certain countries, 158-61
    and country selection, 151-66
    main considerations, 163-65
    spreading across Europe, 158
    strategy, 151-56
Marketing
    European, 5-6
    implications for Western Europe, 274-76
    potential, 54-58
    secondary, 92
    of services, 80
    types of, 78
Marketing implications, 62-63
Marketing mix, importing to Europe, 279-81
Marketing organization, 261-68
Marketing research, European, 91-104
Marketing and selling organizations, 263-68
Marketing strategies, 105-08, 129-50
Market planning, 269-72
Markets
    consumer, 98
    and cultures, 12-45
    Eastern European, 31-32
    industrial, 98-99
    pricing strategies for specific national, 210-12
    service, 99

Market sectors, global, 285
Market share, global, 14
Mars, food company (U.S.)
  construction of factory in France, 123
  sacrificed investment, 77
Matrix, Ansoff, 114
Members of the European Parliament
  (MEP), 53
Millar, C., 86, 96
Mindel, R.259
Minitel videotext system, 112
Mission and objectives, 7-8
Monitoring and control systems, 270-71
Monnet, Jean, 47
Monsanto, company (U.S.), 200
Motivation and planning, 271-72
Multinational companies, 172-73, 212-13
Mutual recognition defined, 171
Myth of the European customer, 76

N

Nabisco cookies, 172
National
  governments and their power, 51
  and regional sales managers, 264
Neale, R., 259
Nestlé company (Switzerland), 276
Neuberger, N., 56
Niche market across Europe, 134
Nonaka, J. K., 160
North American
  competition from, 281-85
  European involvement, 9
  financial burden, 8
  involvement in Europe, 16-28
North American companies, guidelines for,
  111, 241-42, 273-89
North American Free Trade Agreement
  (NAFTA), 56, 273
Northern Telecom (Canadian), 7
Nynex, company (U.S.), 163

O

Ohmae, K., 106
Oliver, G., 131
Opportunities
  in Eastern Europe, 237
  new-product, 188-90

Options, developing market strategy
  options, 113-19
Organization for Economic Cooperation and
  Development (OECD), 59
Organizations, marketing and selling, 263-68
Original equipment manufacture (OEM)
  opportunities, 182
Overcapacity and removal of trade barriers,
  124

P

Pan-European
  versus country-by-country approach,
    156-57
  logistics and distribution companies,
    248-49
  marketing segmentation, 80-83
  market research, 96-101
  scale, 134
Patent protection, 173-74
Peckham, J., 175, 234
Pepsi-Cola, company (U.S.), 63, 80, 122,
  125
Percentage of sales, 233-34
Philip Morris (U.S.), 9
Philips NV (Netherlands), 111, 112
Pillsbury, company (UK), 9
Place decisions
  channels and logistics, 249-52
  Eastern Europe, 253-54
Planning and motivation, 271-72
Political
  and defense activities, 60-62
  uncertainties, 213, 287
Porter, M. E., 27-28, 73, 106, 139
Porter's generic strategies concept, 117-18
Power
  EC, 52-53
  national governments and their, 51
Pressures groups regarding the EC, 50
Prices, food, 21
Pricing decisions, 198-216
  the influence of the EC, 199-203
Principle of subsidiary, 61-62
Private-label opportunities, 182
Privatization issues, 126
Procter & Gamble, company (U.S.), 77, 110,
  189, 236
Product benefits, European, 174-76

Product decisions, 167-97
Product development, 186-91, 212
Product life cycle, 135
Product managers, role of, 262-63
Product ranges, concentration of the, 142
Products, developing benefits for existing, 176-86
Profit Impact of Market Strategy (PIMS), 132
Profit opportunities in Europe, 7
Progress, Western and Eastern European, 3-4
Promotional
    controls in Eastern Europe, 237
    decisions, 217-39
    ınix in the East, 235
Promotional activities, 222-25, 234-35
Promotional objectives, 226-29
Promotion expenditures, overall levels of, 233-34
Ps, four, 5
Public relations advisors, 64
Purchasing power, balance of, 33

Q

Quality
    service, 185-86
    threshold, 186
Questionnaire design and responses, 99
Questions asked by managers, 113-14

R

Radion laundry detergent, 110
Ramsey, W., 143, 175, 176
Rates, central or target, 24
RCA, company (France) consumer electronics, 9
Redrawing the map of Europe, 9-10
Reduction of barriers and the Single Europe Act, 135
Reforms, CAP, 22
Reid, S. D., 152
Religion, 38
Research, 94, 98-99, 187-88
Researchers, availability of professional, 100
Retailing, 243-44, 247-49
Ricardo, David, 174
Risks, financial and human, 131-32
Rodger, I., 139
Roller-coaster economy, 26

Rosson, P.J., 152

S

Sales
    force activities in European, 227-29
    percentage of, 233-34
Sara Lee company (U.S.), 236
Sarathy, R., 77
Scholes, H., 132-34
Schumann, Robert, 47
Schwinn, company (U.S.), 126
Segal-Horn, S., 141
Selective technical harmonization, 171
Services
    after-sales, 183
    continuous-sales, 185
    developments across Europe, 183-85
    marketing, 80
    quality, 185-86
Single Europe Act of 1986, 5, 54-58
    additional control allowed by, 53
    exploiting the, 119-21
    and the four fundamental freedoms, 49
    market strategy, 116
    new product development, 186-87
    technical research projects proposed by, 40
Size of company, 292
Socialcultural issues, 34-39
Socialist countries, quality of exports, 16
Social policy, 258-59
Socio-Styles-Systeme, 81
Solchaga, Carlos, 25
Specialization, degree of, 28
Standardization, progress on, 173
Standards and legislation, compliance with EC, 170-72
Strategic alliances, 153
Strategic options, process of developing, 113
Strategies
    for EC and EEA, 119-24
    European marketing, 105-28
Structural problems of Eastern Europe, 32
Subsidiary, principle of, 61-62
Success factors, critical, 106, 108-09
Survey of United Kingdom executives, 7
Sustainable competitive advantage, 106, 109-13
Swedish ASEA company, 139

Swiss Brown Boveri company, 139
SWOT, 130
Synthesewerk Schwarzheide, company
  (Germany), 125

T

Takeishi, A., 185, 189-90
Tariff barriers, reduction in, 22
Taxes, 201-2, 244-45
Technical and environmental issues, 40-43
Telecommunication potential, 42
Terpstra, V., 77, 179
Tertiary education, 36
Testing, promotional, 234
Test-marketing and sales estimating, 190-91
Thatcher, Margaret, 50
Thomas, M. J., 31
Thomson Corporation (Canadian), 7
Thomson SA, company (France), 9, 111
Total quality management (TQM), 185
Trade barriers, and overcapacity, 54, 124,
  169-70
Trademark and patent protection, 173-74
Trade walls, 19
Trade wars, world, 274
Trading and legal requirements, 168-74
Transport regulations, EC, 243
Treaty, Maastricht, 10, 23, 275-76
Treaty of Rome, 47-48, 49, 109-10
Tungsram, lighting company (Hungary), 147
Turnbull, P. W., 152, 164

U

Unilever company (UK and Netherlands), 9,
  110, 189
  Economics and Statistics (E&S)
    department, 102
  standardizing products, 172-73
United Distillers, company (U.S.), 230-31
United States of America, 16, 18
United States of Europe, 10, 277-79

V

Valla, J. P., 164
Vandermerve, S., 82-83
Vehicle manufacturers, commercial, 81

W

Walters, A., 25-26
Ward, J., 77
Wars, world trade, 274
Welesa, Lech, 32
Western European
  economic growth, 275
  investments, 43
  progress, 3-4
  promotional decision-making, 233-35
Western European markets, 27-31, 32-34
Whitelock, J., 92, 230
Wholesalers, 246-47
Williamson, P., 206
Wolfe, A., 181
World Development Report, 1991 140
World trade, 12